THE CONSTITUTIONAL SYSTEM OF THAILAND

This book assesses the numerous attempts to establish a modern system of democratic government in Thailand against the background of Thai politics and culture. The fact that since 1932, when it became a constitu-tional monarchy, Thailand has had 18 constitutions speaks of an unsta-ble political system which has seen rapid and repeated Fluctuations between military rule and elected government. The main focus of this study is a critical discussion of the institutional frameworks which have been established under recent constitutions. Individual chapters deal with elections and parliament, the executive organs of the state, admin-istrative oversight, local government, human rights, and the constitu-tional role of the courts.

Thailand
Note on the cover design

The background is dominated by Thailand's national flag: red (Nation), white (Buddhism) and blue (Monarchy).

Red is depicted as curtains, the nation as a political stage and its con-stant flux. White appears as double edged daggers, stained with red and blue. An aspect of Buddhist doctrine, the 'Law of Karma,' has been effectively deployed in Thai history by the establishment so the masses accept their predicament unquestioningly.

Blue, a story of the two Pyramids. Democracy vs Monarchy:

– on the higher pyramid perches the mighty Garuda, emblem of the King, wielding a Trident. (It is prohibited to replicate the garuda as the emblem used by the monarchy, even in an academic context. The artist has designed her own version, based on Michelangelo's figure in the Sistine Chapel.)
– the lower pyramid is presided over by Pridi Banomyong, the Founding Father of Democracy and the Thai Constitution.

At the heart of the Nation, a thin paper scroll of 'Constitutions' (writ-ten in Thai) rises from Pridi, the most prominent leader in the overthrow of absolute monarchy. This reveals '1932', Thailand's first constitution and its successors. The Thai people have grown accustomed to the fragility of their constitutions – constantly torn up and rewritten after every coup d'état.

On the left of the scroll the Democracy Monument stands in opposi-tion to the half hidden Temple of Dawn, the images representing the continuous tension between new democratic values and traditional religious values.

The Army tank firing at Pridi represents both the military coups which have undermined Thai constitutionalism and the threat of military inter-vention which continues to loom in the background.

Constitutional Systems of the World
General Editors: Peter Leyland and Andrew Harding
Associate Editors: Benjamin L Berger and Alexander Fischer

In the era of globalisation, issues of constitutional law and good governance are being seen increasingly as vital issues in all types of society. Since the end of the Cold War, there have been dramatic developments in democratic and legal reform, and post-conflict societies are also in the throes of reconstructing their governance systems. Even societies already firmly based on constitutional governance and the rule of law have undergone constitutional change and experimentation with new forms of governance; and their constitutional systems are increasingly subjected to comparative analysis and transplantation. Constitutional texts for practically every country in the world are now easily available on the internet. However, texts which enable one to understand the true context, purposes, interpretation and incidents of a constitutional system are much harder to locate, and are often extremely detailed and descriptive. This series seeks to provide scholars and students with accessible introductions to the constitutional systems of the world, supplying both a road map for the novice and, at the same time, a deeper understanding of the key historical, political and legal events which have shaped the constitutional landscape of each country. Each book in this series deals with a single country, or a group of countries with a common constitutional history, and each author is an expert in their field.

Published volumes
The Constitution of the United Kingdom
The Constitution of the United States
The Constitution of Vietnam
The Constitution of South Africa
The Constitution of Germany
The Constitution of Japan
The Constitution of Australia
The Constitution of Finland
The Constitution of the Russian Federation
The Constitution of Austria

Forthcoming titles in this series
The Constitution of France
Sophie Boyron
The Constitution of Ireland
Colm O'Cinneide

Link to series website
http://www.hartpub.co.uk/series/csw

The Constitutional System of Thailand

A Contextual Analysis

Andrew Harding
and
Peter Leyland

·HART·
PUBLISHING
OXFORD AND PORTLAND, OREGON
2011

Hart Publishing

An imprint of Bloomsbury Publishing Plc

Hart Publishing Ltd	Bloomsbury Publishing Plc
Kemp House	50 Bedford Square
Chawley Park	London
Cumnor Hill	WC1B 3DP
Oxford OX2 9PH	UK
UK	

www.hartpub.co.uk
www.bloomsbury.com

Published in North America (US and Canada) by
Hart Publishing
c/o International Specialized Book Services
920 NE 58th Avenue, Suite 300
Portland, OR 97213-3786
USA

www.isbs.com

HART PUBLISHING, the Hart/Stag logo, BLOOMSBURY and the
Diana logo are trademarks of Bloomsbury Publishing Plc

British Library Cataloguing-in-Publication Data
A catalogue record for this book is available from the British Library.

ISBN: 978-1-84113-972-2

Typeset by Hope Services Ltd, Abingdon
Printed and bound in Great Britain by
Lightning Source UK Ltd

To find out more about our authors and books visit www.hartpublishing.co.uk. Here you will
find extracts, author information, details of forthcoming events and the option to sign up for our
newsletters.

Summary Contents

Contents

Table of Cases

CASES BY NAME

Table of Constitutions

Table of Statutes

THAI TRADITIONAL LAW

Table of Treaties and Conventions

Table of Legal Codes, Decrees and Regulations

Preface

On 19 September 2006, during the Thai Prime Minister Thaksin Shinawatra's absence in New York and following mass demonstrations in Bangkok against his Government throughout 2006, the army, in a bloodless coup d'état, moved tanks into central Bangkok and took over the Government. Anger against Thaksin had been particularly acute over the sale of one of Thailand's leading companies, Shin Corp, which was owned by the Shinawatra family, to a Singapore government-linked company for $1.9 billion without the imposition of any capital gains tax. Citing widespread corruption and polarisation of society, the new military junta, led by Royal Army Commander General Sonthi Boonyaratglin and styling itself the 'Council for Democratic Reform', declared the 1997 Constitution of the Kingdom of Thailand abrogated, the Government dismissed, and the National Assembly and the Constitutional Court abolished. There was no resistance to the coup, and indeed polls indicated its widespread, although by no means total, acceptance. The coup was also endorsed by King Bhumipol, who immediately ratified an Interim Constitution (2006) designed to provide for civilian government and the drafting of a new constitution in 2007. A new Legislative Assembly and a civilian/technocrat Government under Prime Minister Surayud Chulanond were speedily installed by the junta, by now renamed the 'Council for National Security' (CNS); martial law was declared, and the process for drafting the new constitution commenced. At the time of writing the 2007 Constitution (effective August 2007) has been in force for more than three years, following a referendum, as was required by the Interim Constitution 2006, in which it was approved by 58 per cent of those voting. The 2007 Constitution has not, however, settled the trajectory of politics, government or the constitutional reform process. In May 2010 the 'Red Shirt' protest movement, which occupied part of central Bangkok for several weeks following a Supreme Court decision stripping Thaksin of half of his assets, was suppressed and dispersed by the army with at least 90 deaths and more than 1,000 serious injuries.

The 19 September 2006 coup was the 17th military coup in Siam/ Thailand since June 1932, when a similar episode overthrew Siam's traditional absolute monarchy and created a constitutional monarchy under the first written constitution. The 2007 Constitution was the 18th written constitution since 1932. The present Government, under Abhisit Vejjajiva, is the 58th since 1932, and Abhisit is the 28th Prime Minister (there have been 37 actual appointments) since 1932. There have been three changes of Government even since the 2006 coup.

Many writers have attempted in recent years to analyse the configuration of Thailand's complex and changing political system. It is not, however, our purpose in this book to pursue this type of analysis. Political parties, political groups and individual politicians are mentioned here only incidentally, and are not the focus of the discussion. Rather, we attempt to discern the nature of Thai constitutionalism as it has developed through the series of tumultuous events summarised in the last two paragraphs, and around which important debates and experiments in reform have been conducted. Our focus will be on the significant areas of constitutional reform which can be discerned in the 1997 and 2007 Constitutions. As Peter Leyland states at the beginning of the first book in this series, on the United Kingdom, a constitution is normally thought of as 'a higher order law [which] will generally be entrenched'.[1] There is, however, clearly a particular difficulty involved in any attempt to explain or analyse the nature of the constitutional system in Thailand. The frequency of constitutional changes is reflected in the facts related above, but these do not even take account of constitutional amendments, some of which have been far-reaching, for example those of 1992–96.[2] The apparent impermanence of any political regime has shipwrecked most attempts to use the written constitution in force at the time as representing the real basis of the constitutional order. In fact the history of Thailand's constitutions presents statistics that, on closer examination, seem even more extraordinary. The 18 constitutions include an astonishing six in the turbulent decade between 1968 and 1978; seven of the 18 have been intended only as temporary or transitional constitutions (usually called 'charter for the administration of the Kingdom' rather than 'constitution') designed to provide for government pending the drafting of a new constitution. Nonetheless, each one of these constitutions, whether interim or permanent (or intended to be

---

[1] P Leyland, *The Constitution of the United Kingdom: A Contextual Analysis* (Oxford, Hart Publishing, 2007) 1.
[2] See ch 2, section VI.

permanent), has expressed itself to be the supreme law, even if that has
turned out to be the case only for a limited period of time. It is of
course no accident that during the period since 1932 there has also been
a strikingly similar number of military coups, since a coup has usually
resulted in at least one new constitution and sometimes two. To consider further the rapid turnover of governments and Prime Ministers,[3]
only five Prime Ministers have held office for more than five years, and
15 of them for less than a year. The present Prime Minister is considered a 'survivor', having been in office for two years at the time of
writing. Constitutional change has thus occurred in parallel with, and is
deeply related to, governmental change.

Having said all this, it is worth keeping in mind what political scientist
Fred Riggs wrote more than 40 years ago; there is still perhaps some
truth in his assessment:

> These constitutional documents cannot be taken seriously as binding state-
> ments of the rules of the political game, as expressions of fundamental law.
> It is apparent that, whenever important shifts in the personnel of the ruling
> clique took place, the previous charter was suspended to permit the promul-
> gation of new rules more compatible with the interests and inclinations of
> the winning group . . . constitutionalism was designed not so much to con-
> strain the rulers as to facilitate their rule.[4]

It is also worth considering the view of Thai historian Thanet
Aphornsuvan, reflecting more recently on the turbulent events of 21st-
century Thailand, and with a slightly different emphasis, that

> Thai constitutions served as histories of political development and conflict,
> and in terms of law, they were the *sum total, not the source*, of the lesser and
> organic laws that existed prior to the promulgation of these constitutions.[5]

On this view we should see the state of constitutionalism reflected in
the constitution only to the extent that its actual implementation to that

[3] Five PMs have held office twice and one three times.

[4] F Riggs, *Thailand: The Modernisation of a Bureaucratic Polity* (Honolulu, East-West
Center Press, 1966) 152–53. Kobkua Suwannathat-Pian goes even further: 'Thai
constitutions may be used as evidence to support [analysis of] an ongoing power
struggle among the various factions of [Thailand's] ruling elite . . .': K Suwannathat-
Pian, *Country and Constitutions: Thailand's Political Development 1932–2000* (London,
Routledge, 2003) at 3.

[5] T Aphornsuvan, 'The Search for Order: Constitutions and Human Rights in
Thai Political History', <http://rspas.anu.edu.au/pah/human_rights/papers/
2001/Thanet.pdf> (2001) at 2 (emphasis added).

point forms the basis of its provisions. This is not of course to say that the written constitution is not a fit subject for analysis, because many of the actual constitutional provisions survive constitutional change episodes. More importantly, most *institutions*, apart from the two houses of the National Assembly and more recently the Constitutional Court, have also tended to continue virtually undisturbed and, although differently configured in each constitution, to have become virtually mandatory features in any constitution.

The approach taken in this book, in line with that taken by others in the series (for example those on France and Vietnam) and despite the drafting of 18 documents called 'the constitution', will therefore be to look at *Thai constitutionalism*, with all its attendant problems, as a continuously emergent concept that does not necessarily hinge fundamentally on the constitution in force at any given time. The emphasis will be on 'constitutionalism' as the outcome of law and political and administrative culture and practice, and on the trajectory of change, rather than (as might be more appropriate for other countries) detailed exposition of particular constitutional provisions. It is the Thai constitutional *system* in its own unique and fascinating *context* (in the true senses of the series title), that constitutes the focus of this study; and by context we mean principally the historical, political, socio-cultural, economic but particularly the legal context. At the same time the series is one designed for the work of constitutional comparison, and our study is informed by the body of general ideas known as 'constitutionalism', in which

> the constitution not only anchors and enforces certain principles, but also represents a clear set of values that determine the validity of legislative and executive action by prescribing the procedure according to which it must be performed or by delimiting its permissible content. The rules may be at one extreme . . . mere conventional norms and at the other, directions or prohibitions set down in a basic constitutional instrument, disregard of which may be pronounced ineffectual by a court of law. Constitutionalism becomes a living reality to the extent that these rules curb arbitrariness of discretion and are in fact observed by the wielders of political power, and to the extent that within the forbidden zones upon which authority may not trespass, there is significant room for the enjoyment of individual liberty.[6]

---

[6] S De Smith, 'Constitutionalism in the Commonwealth Today' (1962) 4 *Malaya Law Review* 205, 206.

Constitutionalism, as a generic concept used and examined in this book, may be further defined in terms of the stated objectives of constitutional reform in Thailand, which are discussed in detail in chapter one. As will be seen in the pages that follow, the fundamental problem of constitutionalism in Thailand has lain not in any failure to fashion plausible constitutional rules or even institutions to enforce them, but in an apparent inability to ensure in practice that the actors consistently stay within the rules designed to define and curb their power. Since the democracy movement of 1973[7] and especially in recent years, the constitutional system has been a site of intense struggle between different political forces, and although we will see that many effective changes have been made, the principles of constitutionalism have in practice had to compete with sometimes overwhelming odds (as occurred in 2006 and 2010, and of course at other times). Following chapter one's analysis of Thailand's constitutional history during the period of constitutional monarchy (1932 to date), the book mainly focuses on the period from 1997, during which concerted but only partially successful attempts have been made to transform the constitutional system from a legitimating device for illegal seizure of power to a means of entrenching constitutionalism.

> To dismiss the Thai constitutions as simply a legitimiser of the culture of political thuggery is to miss completely the true valuable asset of these Charters as in-depth record of the 'democratic' development of Thailand.[8]

It is in the spirit of this observation by a Thai commentator that we undertake this work.

The structure of the book is as follows. In chapter one we proceed to comment on the constitutional and legal history of Thailand in the pre-1932 period, to show how history has conditioned the constitutional system and to explain some of the fundamental problems that have beset Thai constitutionalism and constitutional change in recent years, particularly the constitutional cycle that has bedevilled efforts to establish a stable and effective constitutional system. We then turn to the post-1932 period and introduce the main constitutional players: the monarchy, the military, political parties and the bureaucracy. This chapter analyses the processes and effects of serial constitution-making but deals especially with the Constitutions of 1997 and 2007.

[7] Suwannathat-Pian, above n 4, at 58ff.
[8] *Ibid*, at 30.

Chapter two deals with the legislative branch, analysing the changes in electoral/appointment systems for the lower and upper houses, and the roles of the two houses in the Thai polity in securing popular representation and executive accountability in what is essentially a parliamentary system of government. We consider here also the changing relationship or balancing of powers between the Executive and Parliament, and the appointment and dismissal of governments.

The executive branch of government itself is extensively analysed in chapter three, which examines the State in terms of central executive power and the way in which it is structured. Here we deal with the civil service and the public/private distinction in what we call 'the contracting State'.

Chapter four continues with examination of the executive power, but in the context of the evolving nature of the State in an increasingly multi-layered constitution. Here we look at local government powers. We also deal with the problem of the Muslim south of Thailand as an extreme example of the difficulties of where a centralised state attempts to govern a diverse society.

Chapter five looks at the judicial branch, focusing attention on the crucial role of the Constitutional Court and its interpretations of constitutional review, during its first (1998–2006) and second (2006 to date) iterations. We also look at the National Anti-Corruption Commission as a court-linked, watchdog agency dealing with a problem that is central to Thailand's reforms post-1997.

Chapter six focuses on administrative justice and control over executive powers in administrative law terms, including the Administrative Courts and the Ombudsman, both introduced under the 1997 Constitution.

Chapter seven discusses human rights, examining the constitutional definition, restriction and enforcement of human rights, focusing in particular on another '1997' watchdog agency, the National Human Rights Commission. This chapter also provides case studies relating to human rights violations in the south and the law on *lèse-majesté*, but illuminating several other aspects of the book, namely freedom of speech and regulation of the media.

Chapter eight draws conclusions from the study, and comments on the problems and prospects of evolving constitutional government in Thailand.

We have many people to thank: our PhD students, Surutchada Chullapram and Nuthamon Kongcharoen, for their useful comments and assistance with legal and other details; in Thailand, Judge Vishnu Varanyou, Songkhla Vijaykadga, Sombat Thamrongthanyawong, Pinai Nanakorn, Yordchatr Tasarika, Jingjai Hanchanlash and Henning Glaser for their assistance; David and Jaruwan Engel for their helpful comments and for help with the glossary of Thai terms; and Gordon Anthony, Tom Ginsburg, Ted McDorman, Jeremy Webber, Justin Frosini, Mike Dowdle and our Associate Editors Benjamin Berger and Alex Fischer, for their incisive and insightful comments on individual chapters. Also thanks to Bob McKeever, Stephen Haseler, Chris Dixon, Mark Sidel, Eric Barendt, Duncan McCargo and Anna Razeen for their assistance. We would like to specially acknowledge and congratulate Putachad Leyland for her wonderfully evocative cover design for this book. In addition we have benefited enormously from the generous cooperation of King Prajadhipok's Institute in Bangkok, especially with regard to the KPI Congress VIII, November 2006, on constitutional reform; and from the views, questions and comments of dozens of people in Thailand and at the many seminars, lectures and conference presentations we have delivered all over the world in the last few years. We should in particular like to thank the Centre for Asia-Pacific Initiatives at the University of Victoria for organising the workshop on law and society in Thailand in Victoria in April 2008, and for its support for our research; and last but by no means least, Richard Hart, Rachel Turner, Mel Hamill and Tom Adams at Hart Publishing.

1

Historical Analysis and Contemporary Issues in Thai Constitutionalism

Introduction – Legal and Constitutional History before 1932 – The 1932 Revolution – Constitutional Developments Post-war – The Continuing Struggle for Democratic Constitutionalism – The Drafting of the 1997 and 2007 Constitutions – Why has the Coup/ Constitution Cycle Continued? – Role of the Monarchy and the Military in the Thai Polity – Conclusion

I. INTRODUCTION

THIS CHAPTER SEEKS to provide an historical overview and analysis of Thai constitutionalism. First we look at Thai constitutional history leading up to the 1932 coup against the absolute monarchy, before reflecting on the main developments that followed in its wake. This historical prelude is of fundamental importance to understanding how Thailand's hyper-constitution-making, as set out in the Preface and discussed further in this chapter, can be assessed.

We turn next to consider the significance of the 1997 Constitution which, despite its limited duration, redefined the parameters of the contemporary debate because it not only recognised most aspects of the present institutional architecture but also placed great emphasis on protecting human rights and combating corruption.

The later sections proceed to discuss matters which are not dealt with in an explanatory way in the constitutional texts, namely the military coups and the constitutional role of the military, and the monarchy.

The chapter forms the analytical basis of the remainder of the book by outlining the nature of Thai constitutionalism as it can be understood as the practical outcome of the 18 constitutions and 17 coups of the post-1932 period of constitutional monarchy.

II.   LEGAL AND CONSTITUTIONAL HISTORY BEFORE 1932[1]

In 1767 the inveterate enemies of Siam, the Burmese, inflicted on it a catastrophic military defeat, burning its capital Ayutthaya to the ground. This disaster effectively destroyed the State of Ayutthaya, which had grown from small beginnings to dominance of the central plains of what is now Thailand, swallowing up the Sukothai kingdom in the mid-15th century. Within a year, however, King Taksin had reasserted Siamese power and established a new capital at Bangkok. Taksin later, it is said, became insane and was assassinated by his successor, King Phutthayotfa Chulalok (Rama I), who established the present Chakri dynasty in 1782. King Bhumipol (Rama IX) is the ninth King of this dynasty, but since 1932 Thailand (Siam came to be called 'Thailand' or 'land of the free' in 1939) has operated a political system based on the concept of constitutional monarchy or, as Thai constitutional discourse[2] invariably and officially has it, 'the democratic regime with the King as head of State'.

Before 1932, Siamese notions of public law, as elsewhere in Asia, lay essentially in the interpretation of the concept of monarchy.[3] Since 1932, however, Thailand has always had a written constitution. By the time the Chakri dynasty was established, the Thai concept of monarchy was able to draw on two different traditions of kingship, the Buddhist and the Hindu. The Buddhist tradition derived from King Asoka (304–232 BCE), who was the first secular leader to embrace Buddhism and attempt to Buddhicise the State. Asoka's empire was a vast one, extending over most of South Asia and beyond. He converted to Buddhism in about 250 BCE, and proceeded to establish a model for the relationship between State and religion that became predominant in

[1]   In view of the fact that the expected readership of this book will be mainly non-Buddhist, we have rendered dates in the Western 'BCE/CE' fashion as opposed to the Buddhist 'BE' fashion.

[2]   F Reynolds, 'Dhamma in Dispute: the Interactions of Religion and Law in Thailand' (1994) 28:3 *Law and Society Review* 433.

[3]   M Hooker, 'The South-East Asian Law Texts: Cultural Borrowing and the Concept of Law', ch 4 of *A Concise Legal History of South-East Asia* (Oxford, Clarendon Press, 1978) at 97ff.

the Theravada Buddhist world, and therefore in traditional Siam. This change was far-reaching: the legitimation of kingship came to rest on dutiful actions and the approval of the *sangha* (the Buddhist monkhood), as opposed to descent from a divine source or pure military prowess. Under the Asokan Buddhist theory the King was subject to religious law (*dhammathat*), but also legislated in the form of royal decrees (*rajathat*). In this tradition as developed in the Sukothai and Ayutthaya kingdoms, the King was in effect a meritorious tribal leader who led by example. In the Hindu or Brahmin tradition which was pre-eminent in the Khmer Angkor empire (9th–14th century CE), which also influenced Siam, kingship took on divine status and was closer to the concept of an absolute monarchy. As historian David Wyatt put it:

> The Brahmanical element provided the kingship with the majestic aura of mystery and a legitimate place in the cosmic order, which is easily understandable in physical terms, and buttressed the authority it needed to rule over a varied and widely scattered population. Buddhism, in its modifications of an essentially Brahmanical cosmology, directed the moral authority of the kingship towards ends that were in harmony with the ethical tenets of Buddhism. The Brahmanical concept of the *Devaraja*, the king as god, was modified to make the king the embodiment of the Law, while the reign of Buddhist moral principles ensured that he should be measured against the Law.[4]

It will be seen in this book that Buddhism and monarchy are important aspects of Thai life, forming two of its three pillars represented by the traditional mantra (often called Thailand's civic religion) of 'nation, religion and monarchy',[5] all three of which have great constitutional resonance. Buddhism, according to Somboon Suksamran, is a

> social institution which is important in giving meaning to and being a symbol of national unity. It is a source and medium of the culture and traditions of the Thai nation . . . Buddhism is like a root of our national existence and of the original social, cultural and political identity of the Thai nation.[6]

---

[4] D Wyatt, *The Politics of Reform in Thailand* (New Haven, Yale University Press, 1969) 7–8.

[5] Reynolds, above n 2.

[6] Quoted in P Jackson, *Buddhism, Legitimation and Conflict: the Political Functions of Urban Thai Buddhism* (Singapore, Institute of Southeast Asian Studies, 1989) at 2. As will be seen in ch 4, the identity between Buddhism and the nation has become a problem in respect of the mainly Muslim southern provinces.

An iconic example of traditional Thai kingship is King Ramkamhaeng, who ruled over Sukothai in the 13th century. His well-known inscription indicates something akin to modern constitutional ideas of good governance where it says:

> He has hung a bell in the opening of the gate . . . if any commoner in the land has a grievance King Ramkamhaeng, the ruler of the kingdom, hears the call; he goes and questions him and examines the case, and decides it justly for him. So the people of this city-state of Sukothai praise him.[7]

In more recent times the hierarchical patrimonialism of King Ramkamhaeng's polity has been invoked as the source of a version of modern Thai 'democracy', for example during the period of ascendancy of Field-Marshal Sarit Dhanarajata (Prime Minister, 1957–63).[8]

Traditional law contained the concept of *Rajadharma* (the duty of kings), expressed in the *Tosapitrajadharma* (the Ten Kingly Virtues). In Weberian terms we can characterise the Siamese monarchy as having both a 'traditional' and a 'charismatic' legitimation, in that the King ascended the throne by virtue of heredity and tradition, but was also

> to act rightly towards relations, officials, communities, the whole kingdom, and maintain the righteous order in this world; he is deemed responsible, directly or indirectly, for all the good or bad things.[9]

As a result, a coup against the King was justified if the nation suffered due to the King's actions not being according to *dharma*. Positive law also buttressed royal power. The Palace Law of 1458 laid down complex regulations for officials and severe punishments for their breach; a Law on Offences Against the Government of 1351 also prevented abuse of official powers. The King's Office of Government Inspectors would send

---

[7] P Handley, *The King Never Smiles: a Biography of Thailand's King Bhumipol Adulyadej* (New Haven, Conn, Yale University Press, 2006), 21. The inscription is often cited as evidence of the origins of Thai constitutionalism.

[8] As Suwannathat-Pian expresses this theory, 'the most suitable form of government which would answer the socio-political needs of the country was a system of democracy from above, ie from the top of the societal hierarchy to the masses whereby an enlightened and most capable leader would "willingly sacrifice himself for . . . the common good"': K Suwannathat-Pian, *Country and Constitutions: Thailand's Political Development 1932–2000* (London, Routledge, 2003) at 11.

[9] For Weber's analysis, see R Bendix, *Max Weber: An Intellectual Portrait* (Berkeley, University of California Press, 1977), chs 10,11,12. For discussion of the Siamese monarchy in terms of both rationalism/science and Buddhism, see T Winichakul, *Siam Mapped: A History of the Geo-Body of a Nation* (Honolulu, University of Hawaii Press, 1994), ch 2.

spies to check how provincial governors behaved. What we might nowadays think of as corruption was simply a part of the system of government: officials were expected to raise their own income from those beneath them, since they were accorded no salary as such by the State.

Until the Chakri dynasty there was no clear notion of a single nation in the area of modern Thailand, and the most reformist 19th-century Kings, Mongkut (Rama IV, 1851–68) and his son Chulalongkorn (Rama V, 1868–1910), brought groups of adjacent *mueang* (settlements) together in confederations. Before that time, emerging capitals became loosely-defined political zones. This arrangement amounted to something similar to a feudal system, with local chiefs delivering annual tributes in return for guarantees of defence. There were four main confederations by the 14th century: Lanna, Lanchang, Mueang Nua and Siam. King Chulalongkorn was mainly responsible for defining the modern Thai State by absorbing into his kingdom Lanna, based on Chiang Mai, and other peripheries, such as the Malay/Muslim southern provinces, within defined borders. In fact it has been argued that a European conception of sovereignty and territoriality was forced on Siam by the expansionist pretensions of colonial powers.[10]

The Chakri dynasty was also responsible for legal reform even before the period of modernisation. King Rama I (1782–1806), as a result of a case that was brought before him which involved a woman who had, erroneously in his view, been granted a divorce when she was the guilty party, considered that the streams of justice had become polluted, partly as a result of the destruction of the texts in the sacking of Ayutthaya. He appointed a commission of judges and scholars to record and systematise the entire corpus of traditional Siamese law, and in the process override other legal traditions in outlying areas of the kingdom. This process resulted in a definitive text, the enormous *Law of the Three Seals* of 1805,[11] which comprised the Ayuthhayan *dhammathat* and *rajathat*, a body of law principally concerned with regulating life in an agrarian community. The *Law of the Three Seals* lasted for a century before being overtaken by the reforms of King Chulalongkorn.[12]

---

[10] Winichakul, above n 9, at 81ff.

[11] D Wyatt, *Thailand: A Short History*, 2nd edn (Chiang Mai, Silkworm Books, 2003) 150.

[12] M Vickery, 'The Constitution of Ayutthaya: the Three Seals Code', in A Huxley (ed), *Thai Law: Buddhist Law: Essays on the Legal History of Thailand, Laos and Burma* (Bangkok, White Orchid Press, 1996).

The structure and legitimation of the modern State is configured differently from that of the Siamese State under the early Chakri kings. Anthropologist Andrew Turton, writing in the 1980s, said of Thailand that the

> close identification of bureaucracy, (military led) government, state, nation, monarchy and religion . . . gives the state, and associated institutions, a monopoly of legitimacy rarely found to such a degree.[13]

In Thailand Buddhism represents a national ideology of such significance that each successive regime since the establishment of the Chakri dynasty has found it of great importance to ensure that its political programme was supported by the *sangha* (monkhood), even to the extent that it has if necessary reorganised the *sangha* and suppressed dissent from official interpretations of religion to bring about this result, making quite overt use of legal and administrative controls. King Mongkut had himself been a monk for 20 years before becoming King and had a profound effect on Buddhism through his acts as King, creating the *Thammayut* order as a means of asserting royal control over religion. His outflanking of traditional astrology by appeal to Western science at Waco in 1868, when he successfully predicted an eclipse of the sun, was a crucial moment in which Siam commenced its engagement with modernity, a modernity which King Mongkut justified in Buddhist terms but which led eventually and inevitably, in spite of royal resistance and even international advisers' recommendations, to the adoption of constitutional government.[14]

The accession of King Mongkut in 1851 is reckoned by many to represent a turning point in the history, and particularly the legal history, of Siam, law reform being both symbolically and practically the cornerstone of modernisation. Mongkut explained on taking the throne that he did so as a result of the will of his subjects (that is, not simply by virtue of heredity, thus implicitly disavowing any divine status). He did not engage in extensive law reform, this task ultimately falling to his son and successor King Chulalongkorn, and later completed by

[13] A Turton, 'Limits of Ideological Domination and the Formation of Social Consciousness' in A Turton and S Tanabe (eds), *History and Peasant Consciousness in South East Asia* (Osaka, National Museum of Ethnology, 1984) at 21.

[14] Winichakul, above n 9, at 45–47; A Harding, 'The Eclipse of the Astrologers: King Mongkut, his Successors, and the Reformation of Law in Thailand' in P Nicholson and S Biddulph (eds), *Examining Practice, Interrogating Theory: Comparative Legal Studies in Asia* (Leiden, Martinus Nijhoff, 2008).

Chulalongkorn's sons, King Vajiravudh (Rama VI, 1910–27) and King Prajadhipok (Rama VII, 1927–35). Mongkut, however, laid the ground-work in many ways for the emergence of his country as the progressive, successful, culturally rich, yet also politically unstable and in many ways deeply puzzling one we now know as modern Thailand. It was during Mongkut's reign, in 1855, that the first demeaning or 'unequal' treaty (known as the Bowring Treaty after Sir John Bowring, the Governor of Hong Kong, who negotiated it[15]) was signed. This treaty, described as 'the traditional line of demarcation' between the ancient and modern periods of Siamese/Thai history,[16] gave foreigners in Siam the right to be dealt with according to their own law in consular or later interna-tional courts, setting a precedent for many other similar treaties embody-ing the principle known as 'extraterritoriality', which were all finally revoked between 1920 and 1938, the year before 'Siam' became 'Thailand', three years after the completion of its civil law reforms and six years after the installation of constitutional monarchy and the first written constitution.[17] The treaties expressly required Siam to adopt modern law codes before the treaties would be revoked.

During his reign King Mongkut enhanced religious freedom and mitigated considerably the harshness of some traditional laws, especially regarding women, children and debt slaves. He also authorised the pub-lication of the laws, an act which had recently been treasonable. He was known to be an admirer of the anti-slavery stand of US President Abraham Lincoln. In one case that came before him he annulled a mar-riage into which the female petitioner had been forced against her will – a novel concept. However,

> . . . unlike Western legal theory at the turn of the century, Thai law then did
> not address the individual as the most basic and uniform unit or treat

---

[15]   M Hooker, 'The "Europeanisation" of Siam's Law 1855–1908' in MB Hooker (ed), Laws of South East Asia, vol i (Singapore, Butterworths, 1986) 531; Sir J Bowring, The Kingdom and People of Siam (2 vols) (Kuala Lumpur, Oxford University Press, 1969).

[16]   P Von Mehren and T Sawers, 'Revitalising the Law and Development Movement: a Case Study of Title in Thailand' (1992) 33:1 Harvard International Law Journal 67.

[17]   Hooker, above n 15; F Sayre, 'The Passing of Extraterritoriality in Siam' (1928) 22 American Journal of Comparative Law 70. Extraterritoriality, it should be noted, also applied to the large numbers of Asian foreigners in Siam who were subjects of colonising powers, as well as Westerners, a fact which added considerably to the humiliation keenly felt by the Siamese leadership.

individuals as separate and autonomous beings. Instead Thai law operated
on the principle that individuals were relational beings, inherently unequal,
and in possession of different degrees of rights or privileges.[18]

Mongkut inaugurated a drive towards modernisation, which entailed fundamental reforms that could, according to Siam's rulers, only be achieved
by the replacement of the traditional customary and religious law which
had been codified in the *Law of the Three Seals*. This was achieved by royal
legislation, and by rapid rather than piecemeal development. This transition also involved, in the end, a constitutional paradigm shift that was
equally essential to modernisation. Under traditional jurisprudence the
King was subject to the *dhammathat*, the religious law; he had no real
power to legislate permanent legal change but only to make temporary
provision to protect the people and preserve the *dhammathat*. However,
exceptionally, some decrees were recognised during the Ayutthaya and
Bangkok periods as being uniquely authoritative, and were absorbed into
the *dhammathat* if in conformity with it, just as 'statutes of general application', in addition to law and equity, are absorbed as part and parcel of
the transplanted common law system; they were regarded as in effect
permanent rules.[19] From Mongkut's time the King was no longer merely
the administrator of the *dhammathat* but was a legislator who could make
or unmake any law by the exercise of royal power.[20] The *dhammathat*,
which had in effect for so long been the constitution of Siam, restricting
the King's room for manoeuvre, had finally given way to the *rajathat* – the
decrees of the King – as the pre-eminent source of law in practice. This
development is directly linked to the foundation of the Thai Council of
State, which is discussed in chapter six.

The period of reform was also to become the period of the most
thoroughly absolutist monarchy Siam had known – under King
Chulalongkorn – and involved the progressive domination of peripher-

[18] T Loos, '*Issaraphap*: the Limits of Individual Liberty in Thai Jurisprudence'
(1998) 12:1 *Crossroads: An Interdisciplinary Journal of Southeast Asian Studies* 35, 71.
[19] M Hooker, *A Concise Legal History of South-East Asia* (Oxford, Clarendon Press,
1978) 29.
[20] For a very clear statement of royal absolutism, see King Chulalongkorn's
speech of 1888, as reported in D Engel, *Law and Kingship in Thailand During the Reign
of King Chulalongkorn*, Michigan Papers on South and Southeast Asia No 9 (Ann
Arbor, Mich, University of Michigan Centre for South and Southeast Asian Studies,
1975) at 17–18. See also HH Prince Dhani, 'The Old Siamese Conception of the
Monarchy' (1950) XLII Journal of the Siam Society 160, 172.

ies, in which Siam, using Western techniques of science, warfare, positivist law and colonial government, asserted the new power of the sovereign Siamese State over its own people, its ethnic minorities in peripheral or disputed regions, and in some cases its traditional enemies. As Tamara Loos[21] and Thongchai Winichakul[22] have set out convincingly, Siam avoided direct (although not indirect) colonisation, but it was in its own turn a coloniser, the mark of a true nation in the eyes of Mongkut and Chulalongkorn. This development has determined in many respects the identity, assumptions and orientation of the modern Thai State.

Another consequence of modernisation was the strengthening of Siamese public administration by the extensive reforms of Chulalongkorn from 1892[23]; this involved the articulation of government into many ministries, boards and local authorities. 'Government' is the word here rather than 'governance' in the sense of constitutional development, for which Siam was held by both its rulers and their foreign advisers to be 'unready' rather than merely disinclined. Government had generally conformed to religiously ordained patterns; but as David Engel says, 'if . . . there was some "cosmo-magical principle" underlying the ancient ministry structure, Rama V did not hesitate to disturb the heavens in his reformation of it'.[24] This reformation went as far as the entire transformation, within about two generations (1895–1935), of Siamese law from the traditional pattern as set out in the *Law of the Three Seals* to a modern system of civil law embodying the entire apparatus of a Continental European system: codes, courts, professions, documentation and subjects redefined as citizens. As Andrew Harding has put it:

> Law itself therefore came to depend on changeable legislation, and not on the immutable cosmological law, which according to the legal foundation myth of Theravada Buddhism, were found by Manu written on the walls of the universe in characters the size of elephants. From now on [ie from 1858] the laws would be written in the Government Gazette in characters the size of ants.[25]

---

[21] T Loos, *Subject Siam: Family, Law, and Colonial Modernity in Thailand* (Ithaca and London, Cornell University Press, 2006).

[22] Above n 9.

[23] Engel, above n 20; F Riggs, *Thailand: The Modernization of a Bureaucratic Polity* (Honolulu, East-West Center Press, 1966).

[24] Engel, above n 20, at 26.

[25] Harding, above n 14, 315–16.

What of public law? In 1887 a memorandum signed by 11 princes urged Chulalongkorn to adopt a democratic system of parliamentary government under a constitutional monarchy. The King, while apparently agreeing with the principles that inspired the memorandum, responded that a parliamentary form of government would be difficult to create when so few of his subjects would be able to perform parliamentary duties; administrative reform had to come first, in any case. Both of these arguments left the door of constitutional reform enticingly ajar. A similar position was also held by the foreign advisers who assisted Siam's legal development over four decades from the 1890s to the 1930s. Speaking of constitutional reform, Siam legal adviser, Harvard law professor and US Ambassador, Francis B Sayre, stated in a 1926 memorandum to King Prajadhipok that

> what works well in Great Britain might work disastrously in Siam. Siam should not slavishly copy the system of any Western nation, but should evolve out of her own experience what seems best adapted to her own genius and conditions.[26]

Reformers, in a failed coup attempt in 1912, near the beginning of the reign of King Vajiravudh, intended to create a republic. The King himself was more interested in advancing the idea of nationalism and in inculcating an almost Victorian sense of personal and sexual morality as a mark of '*siwilai*' (civilisation). The foreign advisers, as well as the Chakri kings, at least up to King Prajadhipok, were at any rate clearly of the view that, despite the creation of a free press in Chulalongkorn's later years, an independent bar in the 1920s and the democratic pressures that led to the 1932 coup, public law reform, unlike private law reform, could wait until the population was broadly literate and well educated.

III. THE 1932 REVOLUTION

King Prajadhipok displayed some interest in developing a more democratic form of government, instituting the King's Privy Council in 1927 and considering drafts of a written constitution in 1926 and 1931. His constitutional plans were forestalled by economic and fiscal difficulties stemming from the world depression of 1929–32, by opposition from

[26] Quoted *ibid*, at 329.

within the royal family and ultimately by the coup of June 1932.[27] This coup was led in the name of democratic government by the 'People's Party' – a combination of leftist intellectuals such as constitutional law professor Pridi Banomyong and rightist officers such as Field-Marshal Plaek Phibunsongkram (Phibun). It was not a popular but, rather, an educated-elite uprising, which resulted in the King being compelled to sign a written constitution (the Interim Constitution of June 1932) drafted by Pridi.[28] The coup leaders' statement, issued in the name of the People's Party, stated that the King 'governs without principle. The country's affairs are left to the mercy of fate, as can be seen from the depression of the economy'. However the People's Party had

> no wish to snatch the throne. Hence it invites this [sic] King to retain the position, but he must be under the law of the constitution for governing the country, and cannot do anything independently without the approval of the assembly of the people's representatives.

Thus the objective of parliamentary democracy was clearly espoused by the People's Party.

In an early rapprochement the coup leaders apologised to the King for their disrespect, using humble language appropriate to his position. At the same time he was prevailed upon to remain in the country and not mount a counter-coup, while granting an amnesty to the coup leaders. However, the King in his response inserted the words '*chua krao*' (provisional) at the head of the constitution, thus perhaps inadvertently setting in motion what is now an all too familiar sequence of events around constitutional change (coup, amnesty, interim constitution). The King did not consider that, under the Interim Constitution, the monarchy was given a status appropriate even to a constitutional monarchy such as that of Britain. The people were said to be sovereign, and the King did not even have the power of appointing the Prime Minister or making any order without a counter-signature; moreover, the language of the document smacked to him of communism. The 'final form'[29] of

---

[27] For the general history of the matters discussed in this and the next section, see Wyatt, above n 11, ch 9; Suwannathat-Pian, above n 8, chs 2–5; Chai-anan Samudavanja, 'Political History' in S Xuto (ed), *Government and Politics of Thailand* (Singapore, Oxford University Press, 1987) ch 1.

[28] C Baker and P Phongpaichit (trans and intr), *Pridi by Pridi: Selected Writings on Like, Politics and Economy, by Pridi Banomyong* (Chiang Mai, Silkworm Books, 2000), esp Part II.

[29] The language quoted here is that of the Constitution of December 1932.

the Constitution was 'submitted' to the King by an Assembly of the People's Representatives, comprising 70 members, which had been nominated in the wake of the coup. The King was 'graciously pleased' to fix 10 December 1932 as the date for the 'giving' of the Constitution, which took place 'with great public rejoicing'. This 'permanent' Constitution of December 1932 restored some degree of royal prestige. The Preamble asserted that the King had been asked to grant a Constitution and had graciously bestowed it on his subjects, 'so that the Kingdom of Siam may have the same form of government as that of a civilised country'. The Constitution was clearly inspired by the British version of constitutional monarchy, and envisaged the great functions of State as emanating from the throne:

> The sovereign power emanates from the Siamese nation. The King, who is the Head of the Nation, exercises it in conformity with the provisions of this Constitution . . . [he] exercises legislative power by and with the consent of the Assembly of the People's Representatives . . . the executive power through the State Council . . . [and] judicial power through the Courts duly established by law.[30]

In the meantime the Government was in the hands of a 'Commissariat of the People', or cabinet, led by coup leaders Pridi and Phibun; an elderly jurist, Phraya Manopakorn, was appointed Prime Minister.

Since the 1932 Constitution was Thailand's first attempt at constitutional government, it is worthy of brief analysis. This constitution did not exactly create a parliamentary, constitutional monarchy. The seats in the Assembly were to be half elected and half filled by royal appointment,[31] although all members were to be elected when half of the nation had four years of education or after 10 years, whichever was earlier.[32] This provision was in fact amended in 1942, extending the period by a further 10 years. Given that women over 30 in Britain secured the right to vote only in 1918 and fully equal voting rights only in 1928, it is interesting that from the outset in Thailand equal voting rights were given to women. The Assembly could be convened, prorogued and dissolved by the King, but dissolution applied only to the

---

[30]   Sections 2, 6, 7 and 8.

[31]   This gave the People's Party Government a huge advantage as royal appointments were in general made on its advice. The first general elections were held in November 1933.

[32]   Section 65.

elected membership. The King retained power to make appointments to the Assembly on advice. The Constitution did not, however, expressly provide that the King was obliged to act on the advice of the State Council, and the State Council itself had to comprise only a majority of Assembly members, that is at least 14 out of a maximum State Council membership of 24.[33] The King could also refuse to assent to a bill passed by the Assembly, although his objection could be overridden on reconsideration of the bill by the Assembly.[34] However, the Assembly was empowered to question, and to pass a vote of no confidence in, the State Council or a member thereof. The doctrines of legislative confidence and individual and collective ministerial responsibility clearly applied: the State Council was obliged to resign in the event of a vote of no confidence being passed in the Assembly. The constitutional rights of the Thai people may also be said to derive from Chapter II of the 1932 Constitution, in that sections 12–15 made brief provision for legal equality, religious freedom, liberty of the person and civil liberties. These rights were given to 'all persons' (rather than all Siamese). As became usual, the provisions also set out duties to respect the law, defend the country, and pay taxes.

The machinery established by this brief Constitution of 68 sections is largely based on the Westminster pattern. This might seem strange in view of the fact that Siam, in reforming its legal system, had ultimately rejected the common law as a pattern of reform in favour of an amalgam of mainly French, but also other European, civil law provisions. However, the civil law systems did not offer a tested model of constitutional monarchy comparable with that of Britain.

The revolution was not by any means over. In fact the form of government set out in the 1932 Constitution lasted only for a short time, as the Assembly was dissolved in a royalist counter-attack in April 1933 and the Government ruled by decree, acting under the Martial Law 1914, as provided in the Constitution itself. The cycle of coups was now well under way: another coup in June 1933 restored the Assembly and installed a new Government under Phahon; and another unsuccessful coup, this time by royalist officers, was mounted in October 1933, resulting in a brief civil war in which the People's Party prevailed. Nonetheless, the first parliamentary elections were held in November 1933. Phahon con-

---

[33] Sections 46–47.
[34] Section 39.

tinued as Prime Minister, but in virtual anticipation of later trends the Government was seriously split between its civilian (Pridi) and military (Phibun) factions. The King left for Britain (ostensibly for eye surgery) and demanded greater constitutional powers[35] which were refused. In 1935, as a result of his disillusionment with the Government and further conflict over Pridi's socialist-style economic reform plans, he abdicated the throne, leaving an elderly prince as regent for his nephew, the 10-year-old King Ananda (Rama VIII, 1935–46). Thereafter Phibun asserted greater and greater control as Thai politics veered fashionably to the right, exhibiting some features of the fascist polities of Germany, Italy and Japan (such as a racist anti-Chinese campaign), and indeed siding with Japan's 1942 attack on the European empires in Asia in the Pacific War. Alignment with the Japanese, who appeared to be winning in the early stages of the war, had prevented Thailand from experiencing the outright military occupation experienced by neighbouring countries and allowed its rulers to continue in power.[36]

Despite the momentous events of 1932–46, the December 1932 Constitution remained in force throughout this period, longer, in fact, than any of its 16 successors to date. While it was, by modern Thai standards, a somewhat basic document, it laid down almost all of the fundamental principles that can be found in later constitutions. However, it is important to stress that this Constitution, like most of its successors, did not represent, underpin or create a truly democratic revolution; only partly, and only on its face rather than in fact, was democracy espoused. Nonetheless, initially it appeared to promise a new era of at least progressively democratic and constitutional government.

IV. CONSTITUTIONAL DEVELOPMENTS POST-WAR

With the Japanese defeat came a resurgence of the leftist wing of the People's Party under Pridi, whose brief premiership in 1946 saw the drafting of a new 'permanent' Constitution. The 1946 Constitution was not in fact very different from that of 1932, and did not result from a coup. At this distance it is hard to see why changes were not simply effected by constitutional amendment, but like many of its successors it

---

[35] Principally a veto which could be overridden only by a 75% majority in the Assembly; and the power of granting a pardon.

[36] Wyatt, above n 11, at 247ff.

was intended to and did effect some democratic changes. One of its changes became a more or less permanent feature of Thai constitutionalism: a bicameral and mainly elected legislature: the Senate owes its origin to this Constitution, being in this instance elected by the lower house. A ban was introduced on civil servants and soldiers holding political office.

The mysterious death of the young King Ananda (elder brother of the present King Bhumipol) just a month after he signed the 1946 Constitution into force led to turmoil, and eventually to Pridi being driven first from the premiership and then from Thailand. These events also led to the abrogation of the 1946 Constitution with a coup in November 1947. Just as the 1946 Constitution was associated with Pridi's brief return to power, the 1947 coup, returning Phibun to power, replaced it with another 'interim' Constitution, which was in turn replaced with a 'permanent' Constitution in 1949. We can see here the clearest emergence of a cycle of coup/regime change/constitutional change which was to be repeated many times.

The 1947 Constitution, in operation for two years, took Thailand in a direction largely opposite to that of the 1946 Constitution. It provided for a Supreme State Council composed of five members, appointed by the King and acting as a Regency Council where necessary and to advise the King generally; this revived the Privy Council originally created by King Chulalongkorn in 1874 (Articles 9–20). The King was empowered to appoint the Prime Minister, his decision having to be countersigned by a member of the Supreme State Council rather than the President of the National Assembly (other decisions had to be countersigned by the Prime Minister or a Cabinet Minister). The King was also given emergency powers, another seemingly permanent feature of Thai constitutions first introduced at this time. An appointed Senate of 100 members, the same number as the lower house, replaced the Senate of 1946, which had been elected by the lower house. The King also participated in legislative power by having a full veto over legislation. The political ban on civil servants and soldiers was repealed. A multi-member constituency electoral system also replaced the single-member system which had been in effect since 1932. A strange provision at Article 77 stated that any Cabinet decision rescinding an earlier Cabinet decision required royal approval. This provision seems to indicate for the first time since 1932 a notion of the monarchy as a stabilising institution amid the vagaries of political turmoil and revolving-door governments. This

Constitution went further in re-establishing royal power when it turned out that nearly all the members of the Senate appointed by the King were princes, aristocrats or others close to the King, the Government's recommendations being rejected. The 1947 Constitution also gave the King control over the palace and the royal purse (always an important issue during these early years of constitutional monarchy – it was one of the issues that led to King Prajadhipok's abdication), and government-appointed members of the royal household were nearly all replaced. It was also decided that a new constitution would be drafted following the general elections, which were held in January 1948. The Democrats won a majority for the first time and appointed a royalist Government. However, Phibun was restored to the premiership in April 1948 and remained in office until September 1957.

The Constituent Assembly for the 1949 Constitution, brought into force in May 1949, was dominated by royalists, and as a result the Constitution retained much of the expanded royal power. The Supreme State Council became a nine-member Privy Council appointed by the King himself, albeit with reduced powers, and this is still in operation today.[37] The appointment of the President of the Privy Council required parliamentary approval, but it was the Privy Council rather than Parliament that would name the King's successor. The Senate, again comprising 100 members, was still appointed by the King. The President of the Privy Council, rather than the Prime Minister as previously, would countersign decisions made by the King. The King still had a legislative veto but it could be overridden by a two-thirds vote in Parliament, although the period within which the veto could be exercised was extended from 30 to 120 days. The King also gained the power to call for an amendment to the Constitution by a referendum, thereby avoiding the Legislature and the Executive. Crucially, he retained control over his household and the royal purse. Establishing a principle also applied with the 1997 Draft Constitution, the National Assembly could only approve or reject the draft without qualification – it could not amend it. It should be noted that, although the draft was approved by a large majority of both houses sitting together, a majority of the elected members rejected it. The ban on civil servants and the military holding office was also revived, which did not please the military in general and Phibun in particular.

---

[37] Current provision under the 2007 Constitution is for a maximum of 18 members.

The 1949 Constitution neither pushed Thailand further towards democracy nor provided stability in government. Two violent coup attempts (by a returning Pridi in the Grand Palace Rebellion of February 1949, and by the navy in the 'Manhattan Coup' of June 1951) were overcome by Phibun. Finally, frustrated by the royalist 1949 Constitution and alarmed by the prospect of King Bhumipol returning to Thailand from his education in Switzerland and the US to assume the reins of royal power, Phibun mounted his own coup, the so-called 'Silent Coup' of November 1951, seizing power from the Privy Council, abrogating the 1949 Constitution and appointing himself as regent. As was now becoming usual, the newly-empowered regime set about moulding the constitution instrumentally to its own desires, but this time it preferred actually to revive the 1932 Constitution, with some features of the later constitutions added in by way of amendments. The Privy Council and the multi-member constituencies were retained, half of the legislature being appointed as previously, and the Senate was abolished. The King was with some difficulty prevailed upon to agree to these arrangements, and the amended 1932 Constitution came back into force in March 1952. Hardly surprisingly, the appointed MPs were mainly military appointees as the ban on their holding office did not apply under the revived 1932 Constitution.

Thailand now entered an extended period of military dictatorship which ended only in 1973 with its overthrow by a student rebellion. The constitutions of this period are hardly worth analysing in the same detail as their predecessors, as they were very similar and took Thailand further away from democracy and constitutional government. General Sarit Thanarat overthrew Phibun in a coup in September 1957, repeating the by now familiar cycle. In this case the 'interim' Constitution of 1959 actually lasted for nine years, longer than most of the 'permanent' constitutions in Thai history. It complied completely with Napoleon's famous adage that a good constitution should be short and vague. It had only 20 articles and conferred virtually absolute power on the Prime Minister. Political parties were banned and Parliament was appointed, comprising mainly Sarit's military colleagues. It created a precedent for military rule in its later iterations following a military coup.

General Thanom Kittikachorn succeeded Sarit in 1963 and remained in power, despite regime changes and new constitutions, until 1973. This was the period of the Vietnam War, a conflict that destabilised Thailand and led to repressive measures such as the Anticommunist

Activities Act 1979. The 1959 Interim Constitution (styled 'Charter for the Administration of the Kingdom') was finally replaced in June 1968 in a partial return to the democratic principles of the 1946 Constitution. The 1968 Constitution brought about a return to a bicameral legislature, Parliament being completely elected and the Senate being appointed by the King (again, however, this meant mainly military personnel recommended by the Government). In an interesting departure from the previous constitutions in terms of the separation of powers, MPs were prohibited from being members of the Cabinet. Elections were held in February 1969, which were won by Thanom's supporters. This victory did not prevent Thanom and two of his supporters (they were known as 'The Three Tyrants'), in a remarkable 'self-coup' of November 1971, overthrowing Thanom's own Government and ruling by martial law through a military council, abrogating the 1968 Constitution. In December 1972 Thanom imposed a new Interim Constitution very similar in its essentials to that of Sarit's Charter of 1959. Parliament was chosen by an indirect process in which a body appointed by the King selected 299 of its own members to form a unicameral legislature; and extensive powers were given to the Prime Minister.

V. THE CONTINUING STRUGGLE FOR DEMOCRATIC CONSTITUTIONALISM

Opposition to the repressive rule of the Three Tyrants finally exploded in October 1973 with a mass protest by students and others at the Democracy Monument in Bangkok. This was the first time that Thais had protested *en masse* to demand democratic reform, but the protest resulted in the shooting of demonstrators by the army and in the consequent forcing of the Three Tyrants from office. What followed were debates and decisions that set some precedents for later constitution-making episodes and produced Thailand's most democratic constitution to date, that of 1974. A Constitution Drafting Committee was appointed, comprising lawyers, academics and senior statesmen.[38]

---

[38] For the historical background of the events discussed in this section, see K Suwannathat-Pian, 'The Monarchy and Constitutional Change since 1972' in D McCargo (ed), *Reforming Thai Politics* (Copenhagen, NIAS, 2002) ch 5; Wyatt, above n 11, ch 10.

Not the least of the features of the 1974 Constitution was that it comprised 238 articles, being at least 10 times longer than its immediate predecessor. Like the 1946 Constitution, it was a distinctly parliamentary constitution. Political parties were once again legalised. A hybrid electoral system (single-member and multi-member constituencies) was created, constituencies being province-wide with one MP for a population of 150,000. A province with more than three MPs was to be divided into two or more constituencies, each with at least one but not more than three MPs: this was done in order to prevent populous provinces from dominating the legislature. Parliament appointed the Senate, but the Prime Minster was given the power to countersign the appointments and a simple majority could override the royal veto. Cabinet members had to be MPs.[39] The military were once more prohibited from holding office.

Two years, two elections and four governments later, the 1974 Constitution had not created any real political stability. Indeed political polarisation led to a right-wing backlash which brought the brief experiment with parliamentary democracy to an end with yet another coup in October 1976, this time an extremely violent one in which hundreds of students of Thammasat University were killed by paramilitary groups. The resulting 1976 Constitution essentially reiterated the now familiar provisions of 1959 and 1972, and led to a brief period of civilian dictatorship before another coup, led by General Kriangsak Chomanan, overthrew the Government and resulted in another authoritarian Interim Constitution in 1977 which was, again, practically a reversion to those of 1959, 1972 and 1976. However, since Kriangsak had promised elections under a new 'permanent' constitution, the ensuing 1978 Constitution reverted virtually to those of 1946 and 1974, providing for an elected Parliament and Senate appointed by the Prime Minister. This reflected reduced tensions in Thailand's politics due to the end of the Vietnam War and better relations with Vietnam. In due course those who had fled Bangkok to join the communists in the jungle were invited back and reintegrated in Thai society. Interestingly enough, it was provided that one of the Senate's powers was to block a no-confidence motion passed in Parliament. Constitution-makers were starting to find

---

[39] Thai constitutions have oscillated over this issue, reflecting conflicting ideas of the separation or balancing of powers between the Executive and the Legislature; compare the 1997 and 2007 Constitutions, see section VI below.

alternatives to the military coup as a mechanism for avoiding fragile coalition governments. Political parties were eventually legalised, but the Prime Minister was not required to be an MP.

Kriangsak was subsequently elected as Prime Minister, but was soon replaced by General Prem Tinsulanond who became and remains the longest-serving Prime Minister (1980–88) in Thailand's entire period of constitutional government, apart from Phibun's tenure during the anti-democratic period of the 1950s. This period of comparative stability in government and temporary suspension of the constitutional cycle was clearly very much needed. Despite some democratising measures during this period, Prem himself never ran for office but was appointed by the King. The 1978 Constitution lasted for 13 years, mainly because it offered a compromise between parliamentarism and military rule (jokingly referred to in Thailand as 'premocracy'). This was partly achieved via the constitutional provisions, but partly also through Prem's manipulation of the Constitution.[40] When elections were held in 1986, Prem was chosen once more as Prime Minister, but he was soon ousted as a result of corruption scandals and due to public pressure declined to be appointed as Prime Minister following further elections in 1988.

This rejection of an unelected Prime Minister of a military stripe did not, however, lead to the military being effectively excluded from politics. The next civilian Government under Chatichai Choonhavan (himself in fact a general) was in its turn replaced by a military coup in 1991, which thus reinstated the constitutional cycle which had appeared to be winding down during the 1980s. In the familiar pattern the military under General Suchinda Kraprayoon revoked the 1978 Constitution, and the Interim Constitution of 1991 reverted to something very much like its post-coup predecessors, with the exception that this time political parties were allowed and a civilian Prime Minister, Anand Panyarachun (Prime Minister twice, 1991–92), installed.

Despite the appearance, in these events, of a tediously familiar process, Thai democratic politics, ignited during 1973–76, flared up once again as a result of the military taking power. The military Government commenced the process of drafting a new constitution

---

[40] Military personnel were to be excluded from elections in 1983, but after an attempt to amend the Constitution to remove this restriction had failed, Prem called elections immediately prior to the due date, which meant that the new Government was formed under the transitional provisions in the Constitution, thus outflanking the constitution-makers' clear intentions.

rather than continuing with the Interim Constitution. Indeed the debates about the constitution proved interesting and decisive; here we can see the emergence of democratic assumptions that have coloured constitutional change over the last two decades. The military were in favour of a dominant, government-appointed Senate, the military being able to hold Cabinet office, including that of Prime Minister, and expanded royal powers. This provoked large public protests at Sanam Luang in central Bangkok in November 1991. The King intervened to urge acceptance of these provisions, which he indicated were suitable for the Thai people, and the 1991 Constitution, incorporating the wishes of the military, came into effect in December. Although this Constitution was drafted and approved by a Constitution Drafting Assembly and Parliament appointed by the military, it was nonetheless an extensive document which attempted to balance the Legislature and the Executive powers, allowing Parliament to pass a motion of no-confidence in the Government.

Clear public disapproval of the military turned to outrage when in April 1992, following general elections, General Suchinda himself became Prime Minister at the head of a coalition government and the military responded to protests by killing a number of protesters during the 'Black May' (1992) incident and cracking down viciously on dissent. The protests were led by political activist Chamlong Srimuang, and a period of intense confrontation and violence was ended only when Suchinda and Chamlong were shown on television prostrating themselves before the King and apologising for their actions in polarising the country. The upshot was that the King reappointed senior statesman Anand as Prime Minister in June 1992. Anand and his successor Chuan Leekpai (Prime Minister 1992–96) then supervised a series of constitutional amendments which both altered the 1991 Constitution dramatically and paved the way for its even more radically democratic successor, the 1997 Constitution. These amendments, notably, reduced the powers of the Senate, ensured that the Prime Minister would be an MP, excluded the military from Parliament and government, and provided for a Constitution Drafting Assembly (CDA).[41]

---

[41] D McCargo, 'Introduction: Understanding Political Reform', in McCargo (ed), above n 38, ch 1; P Wasi, 'An Overview of Political Reform Issues', *ibid*, ch 2.

VI. THE DRAFTING OF THE 1997 AND 2007 CONSTITUTIONS

The 1997 Constitution[42] came about in a most unexpected manner, written 'by people who were not in power, and in the face of disagreement on the part of politicians', 'loathing and exasperation concerning the behaviour of politicians' and the events of 1991–92 leading to the setting up of a 58-strong 'Democratic Development Committee' (DDC), which was chaired by eminent physician Dr Prawase Wasi and sat during 1994–95.[43] The DDC, agreed to by then PM Anand Panyarachun (who later chaired the CDA itself), was an initiative of Dr Wasi and law professor Bowornsak Uwanno (who later became chair of the Constitution Drafting Committee (CDC) of the CDA). A movement for political reform was propelled forward during 1994 by legal and political research papers, democracy activism and a hunger strike by former MP Chalard Vorachad. The main claim of this movement was that political reform was essential for the solution of every problem facing Thailand.

The DDC was purely advisory, but made a strong recommendation that the 1991 Constitution be amended to provide for the drafting of a new constitution. It also showed creativity in rethinking some of Thailand's constitutional traditions. For example, it proposed a three-chamber assembly comprising a House of Representatives (300 politicians elected in single-member constituencies), a House of Wisdom (100 intellectuals not being members of any party, elected from a nation-wide constituency) and a House of Advisers (comprising former Prime Ministers, former Speakers of Parliament and other notables, together with vocational representatives selected by the other two Houses). Although this recommendation was not followed by the CDA, one can see the origins here of some of its innovative drafting (see chapter two for discussion of the National Assembly as it in fact emerged from the 1997 process). Inspiration derived from the DDC is reflected in many positions taken by the CDA, for example also on elections, political parties, and the functioning of Parliament and the government, and therefore in both the 1997 Constitution and the constitutional jurisprudence of Thailand as it has emerged over the last 15 years.

---

[42] T Yoshifumi, *Democratisation in Thailand: Grappling with Realities* (Kyoto, Kyoto University Press, 2005), ch 3.

[43] Wasi, above n 41, at 22ff.

It was not expected by the DDC that Parliament or the Government would do anything with these recommendations, but a change of government following the 1995 elections impelled Banharn Silpa-Archa (Prime Minister 1995–96) to set up a Political Reform Committee, which adopted the DDC recommendations. The Constitution was accordingly amended in 1996, and the CDA installed. It functioned 'very painfully and experienced numerous difficulties amidst a lack of understanding, conflicts of interest, and hostile accusations'. Nonetheless,

> as a result of good academic input, good leadership in the CDC and CDA, and broad public participation, the process gradually gained ground and improved in quality.[44]

In due course the CDA completed its remit, and in October 1997 Parliament approved Thailand's most democratic constitution, which came into effect immediately.[45] This Constitution differed enormously from all of its predecessors and came to be known as 'The People's Constitution'. The CDA itself was mainly an elected body: 76 were elected by provincial assemblies, and 23 'experts' were added. In the course of its deliberations the CDA consulted Thai citizens extensively. Several provisions gave more power to ordinary Thai citizens than ever before. For example 50,000 electors could petition Parliament for the passing of a law, and 10,000 could demand impeachment of a political office-holder; a policy of decentralisation of power was adopted; extensive fundamental rights were included in the Constitution. Critically, the 1997 Constitution established a number of new independent agencies, including a Constitutional Court designed to enforce the entire constitutional apparatus; and the Senate was newly configured as a civil-society house rather than a bastion of privilege, endowed with powers to secure the independence of all the independent agencies.

The 1997 Constitution, ultimately unable to prevent a slide into the very polarisation and illegality it was designed to prevent, and despite some faults which seem obvious in hindsight, still represents Thailand's most imaginative, concerted and inclusive effort to settle its constitutional system. It led first to a brief period of political stability (1997–2005) in which its provisions, which required extensive implementation, including

[44] Wasi, *ibid*, at 25.
[45] M Connors, 'Framing the "People's Constitution"' in McCargo (ed), above n 38, ch 4.

the passing of many organic laws and the setting up of many selection committees and 10 new or newly-reformed independent agencies, all against tight deadlines, were smoothly implemented. However, with the election of Prime Minister Thaksin Shinawatra and his Thai Rak Thai Party to power in January 2001, the 1997 Constitution began to unravel. This unravelling occurred in ways that eventually provoked mass protests and a period of great turbulence in Thai politics, which began in 2005 and has continued up to the time of writing. These events will form a further narrative part of several chapters of this book as we dissect the various constitutional developments since 1997. They led in turn to another twist of the constitutional cycle with the coup of September 2006, with which our Preface began, and an Interim Constitution (2006); the drafting of the 2007 Constitution; and the installation of three new governments since it came into effect in August 2007 following its approval by referendum. In spite of the concerted attempts to entrench democratic, constitutional government in the last two decades, the constitutional cycle that began in 1932 seems still to have some rotations left in it.

The drafting of the 2007 Constitution, under the provisions of the Interim Constitution 2006, took the following form. First, the CNS (the military junta, for which see the Preface) appointed 2,000 members to a National Assembly, which nominated 200 of its own members as candidates for membership of a CDA. The CNS then selected 100 of these 200 to actually form the CDA. The CDA, like its predecessor of 1996–97, had a CDC, this time consisting of 35 members (25 members of the CDA plus 10 members selected by the CNS from CDA members and non-members). The resulting draft constitution had to be formally justified by the CDA in terms of how and why it differed from the 1997 Constitution. It was then put to the electorate in a referendum after a period of 30 days, and was indeed approved by a majority of 58 per cent and became operative in August 2007. Interestingly, if it had not been so approved then the CNS was empowered to revise any previous constitution (which we can take as meaning the 1997 Constitution) and present that for the royal assent.

While this procedure combined broad representation with technical skill, many people observed[46] that the process was not at all participatory when compared with the process leading to the 1997 Constitution,

[46] E Kuhonta, 'Constitution at the Heart of Thai Coup', 6 October 2006, <http://www.atimes.com/atimes/Southeast_Asia/HJ06Ae02.html>.

which was so participatory that it was and still is referred to as 'the People's Constitution'. The 2007 Constitution, irrespective of its merits and demerits, is also tainted in the perception of many by the process that led to its adoption under the aegis of a military government that had ousted an elected government.[47] Differences between the Constitutions of 1997 and 2007 will form a major aspect of the discussion in this book. The main areas of difference relate to Parliament, the Senate and the electoral system; the 2007 Constitution also reforms the Constitutional Court and the various selection committees for the independent agencies in order to prevent political interference of the kind seen during Thaksin's premiership. The Legislature proved one of the problematical issues in the 2007 drafting process. One group wanted a 400-seat house equally divided between constituency and party-list seats. Another wanted a house composed entirely of constituency-elected members. The result was a compromise: 320 constituency and 80 party-list seats, with the nuance that the latter was to consist of eight lists of 10 based on eight regions of Thailand, thus maintaining some local connection even for the party-list members.

Although there is much that remains to be said in this book about the 1997 and 2007 Constitutions, our approach in offering a contextual analysis of Thai constitutionalism is to treat the passing of the 1997 Constitution as a truly axial event in Thai constitutionalism and the 2007 Constitution as offering some limited variations on themes introduced in 1997. In this sense Tom Ginsburg's idea of the 1997 Constitution having an 'afterlife'[48] is in our view a highly appropriate way of regarding that Constitution, despite its formal rescinding as a result of the 2006 coup. Like Lewis Carroll's Cheshire Cat, the 1997 Constitution is no longer present but its 'smile' can still be seen quite clearly. Thus we can take the 1997 Constitution and the 2007 Constitution as representing a frame of reference for most of the issues discussed in this book. In very many respects there is no or only minor textual difference between these Constitutions, although as indicated they differ in some major respects which will be discussed in later chapters: notably, the 2007 version alters the selection process for independent watchdog agencies so as to make political interference with the process more

---

[47] See the Preface.

[48] T Ginsburg, 'Constitutional Afterlife: The Continuing Impact of Thailand's Post-political Constitution' (2009) 7(1) *International Journal of Constitutional Law* 83.

difficult; this is achieved by drawing up smaller selection committees which have the final say over appointments as opposed to giving that say to the Senate. There is also a much larger role for the judiciary, both in terms of the jurisdiction of the Constitutional Court and in terms of judicial membership of selection committees. Further, the Prime Minister is allowed to serve for only two terms. Perhaps most controversially, the 2007 Constitution has been regarded as less democratic because a partly-appointed Senate is introduced in place of a fully-elected upper house.

VII. WHY HAS THE COUP/CONSTITUTION CYCLE CONTINUED?

One of the central themes of this book, implicit or explicit in most of its chapters, is an inquiry into why (and also in recent years how) this constitutional cycle has occurred, and with such predictable regularity? Does it indicate that Thailand is somehow stuck in a chain-reaction phenomenon, or does it indicate an intense struggle over democratic and legal/constitutional values which might have a resolution? Is such resolution possible and, if so, how can it be achieved? On the other hand, does the constitutional cycle somehow represent a condition of equilibrium or a balance of forces in which the 'instability' is only apparent but not real?[49] Is there a system of meta-constitutional 'rules' that serves a purpose and provides predictability?

Clearly at this point in the inquiry we can only raise rather than resolve these issues, but some general considerations are obviously relevant and will assist in understanding what follows. The last several pages dealing with Thailand's constitutional history have set out a narrative of alarming, indeed almost unbelievable, complexity that raises more questions than can easily be answered. Why, for example, have military coups almost invariably resulted in the obliteration of the existing constitutional order? Regime changes, which have after all been usually rather short-lived, could be effected simply by constitutional amendment. It seems to be a *leitmotif* or even a guiding principle of constitutional life in

---

[49] A Harding, 'Asian Law, Public Law, Comparative Law Stir-Fry: Theory and Method Considered' in T Groppi, V Piergigli and A Rinella (eds), *Asian Constitutonalism in Transition: A Comparative Perspective* (Mila, Giuffre, 2008) 19ff (discussing 'order and chaos in comparative law').

Thailand that any constitutional change somehow *must* be reflected in a complete, root-and-branch rethink. Or perhaps, despite the frequent changes in constitution, the actual textual changes are more marginal than fundamental. It might of course be considered that one could trace through constitutional changes a certain meta-narrative of consistency or progress towards constitutional government, notwithstanding the superficial appearance of precisely the contrary. More fundamentally, how seriously should we take these constitutions?

One important way of understanding this complexity would be, as suggested above, to look at the emergence of constitutionalism as an idea, rather than consider the particular provisions of short-lived constitutions. However, another partial explanation for it can be put forward. Scrutiny of the interim constitutions will reveal that in each case the coup-makers were provided with legal immunity for the consequences of their actions.[50] Retaining the existing constitutional order (constitutional amendment being clearly out of the question in the circumstances of a coup) would make it impossible to unseat the existing executive and legislative organs legally. It would equally make it impossible for the military junta to govern legally, and would entail personal consequences for the generals in terms of criminal liability for treason, despite the irony of coups usually being presented as highly patriotic events. The courts have also rebuffed attempts to have a coup (and also granting of immunity for mounting a coup) ruled unconstitutional.[51]

An alternative method of dealing with this, as has occurred elsewhere, is to allow for a temporary *deviation* from constitutional rectitude, *provided that* this leads directly back to such rectitude within a short period time. Yet another method would be to draft what is sometimes

---

[50] Eg, the Constitution of the Kingdom of Thailand (Interim) 2006 stated at s 37: 'All acts performed on account of the Acts of the seizure and control of State governing power on 19 September 2006 . . . irrespective of their legislative, executive or judicial force as well as punishments and other official administrative acts and irrespective of whether those acts have been done as a principal, abettor, agent provocateur or commission agent and whether those acts have been done on, before or after the aforesaid date, if those acts are offences under the laws, the persons who commit those acts shall be entirely discharged from such offences and liabilities.' See, further, Constitution of the Kingdom of Thailand 2007, s 309, which validates this immunity provision.

[51] 'The high court held that it was immaterial how a government came into being and that the only real test of its legitimacy was whether in fact it could rule': W Blanchard et al, *Thailand: its People, its Society, its Culture* (New Haven, Conn, HRAF Press, 1958) 202, referring to a decision relating to the 1947 coup.

called a 'Snow White' clause, under which in the event of a coup the constitution is deemed to be only sleeping rather than dead, and must be or will be revived at a later juncture.[52] In Thailand these ideas have not been canvassed but rather the issue has been simply whether to prohibit the military from holding political office. This obviously does not prevent the military from in effect usurping office. It may indeed be that underlying reasons for military coups include the forced exclusion of military officers from politics, and disagreements between the military and the Government over military budgets. It could be argued that in light of the events since 1991, the significance of a coup, even though it cannot effectively be prevented by any legal or political device, has plausibly changed in several respects:

a) First, a military government is no longer as such accepted by the Thai people, and even a military-installed 'technocrat' government like that of 2006–07 does not carry any long-term legitimacy; elections have to be held within a short space of time. Government under an interim constitution cannot be sustained in the way this occurred in the decade 1958–68.

b) Secondly, a coup can achieve legitimacy only by being non-violent and by citing plausible reasons such as extreme polarisation, undermining of constitutional reform, widespread corruption or abuse of power, or an imminent threat to national security or law and order.

c) The coup of 2006 was in fact ultimately *unsuccessful* in that, having been designed to displace the Thaksin Government, it could not prevent Thai Rak Thai's successor, the Thaksin-leaning People Power Party, from gaining power following the December 2007 elections. It was only the defection of several MPs in a no-confidence vote in Parliament in December 2008 that put Thaksin-inspired parties out of power, at least for the time being, and installed the Democrats under Prime Minister Abhisit Vejjajiva. This event will act as a chill factor in future.[53]

---

[52] J Hatchard, P Slinn and M Ndulo, *Comparative Constitutionalism and Good Governance in the Commonwealth: an Eastern and Southern African Perspective* (Cambridge, Cambridge University Press, 2003) 247.

[53] See, fruther, S Sukatipan, 'Thailand: The evolution of legitimacy', in M Alagappa (ed), *Political Legitimacy in South East Asia: The Quest for Moral Authority* (Stanford, Cal, Stanford University Press, 1995).

For these reasons it might be the case that coups will not occur so often in future. Conceivably the coup is already outmoded as a quasi-constitutional device for changing the regime. While the coup remains an ever-present rumour, an ever-predicted possibility, the generals will certainly think more carefully about the implications of their actions in light of the experience of 2006–07. Even the turbulent events of 2008–10, with widespread protest movements affecting economically sensitive areas such as Bangkok's international airport (by 'Yellow Shirt' protesters in 2008) and 20 blocks of its main shopping district (by 'Red Shirt' protesters in 2010), resulted in considerable violence but not a coup. Nonetheless, it is also the case that no person has ever been punished for mounting a successful coup in Thailand, and the worst practical consequence for a coup-promoter has been exile. In our view the coup as a political and constitutional device lies at the root of Thailand's constitutional cycle. That is not to say that coups are necessarily a completely defunct or even a completely delegitimised political weapon; or that new constitutions will not continue to be drafted. However, the question of how to prevent coups remains in our view critical to constitutional and political stability, and the demise of the coup at some juncture might well be a litmus test of such stability having been achieved.

VIII. ROLE OF THE MONARCHY AND THE MILITARY IN THE THAI POLITY

The Constitutions of 1997 and 2007 make curious reading when one considers the fact, which is obvious from the account in this chapter of Thailand's constitutional history, that both the monarchy and the military have played a significant role in the Thai polity – the former throughout its history, and especially since the early 1970s, and the latter ever since the coup of 1932.[54] These two Constitutions, in contrast with many of their predecessors, do not indicate any special role for the military. They also appear on their face to espouse a constitutional monarchy along the European pattern, the King having mainly ceremonial powers, or substantive but somewhat nominal powers such as the power to refuse assent to a bill passed by the Legislature, sending it back for

[54] M Peleggi, *Thailand: The Worldly Kingdom* (Singapore, Talisman, 2007), 91ff; Handley, above n 7; W Stevenson, *The Revolutionary King: The True-life Sequel to 'The King and I'* (London, Robinson, 1999).

reconsideration.[55] In fact, of course, as can be seen from the constitutional historical narrative set out above, both the military and the monarchy are of great importance in understanding Thai constitutionalism.[56] Both clearly have important powers and influence, in practice if not in theory. Neither is always strictly subject to the law. Each has in some circumstances taken the law and the constitution into its own hands.

Kevin Tan proposes an interesting explanation for this apparent disconnect.[57] If we analyse Thai constitutionalism in terms of the separation or balancing of powers in actual practice rather than in the written text, as is entirely consistent with the approach taken in this chapter, we can see that there are not three branches of the State (Executive, Legislature and Judiciary) but five, if we regard both the monarchy and the military as having powers of their own. On this view the monarchy in practice is able to exercise what is (strictly speaking, according to the text) extra-constitutional power, as for example when the King appointed Anand Panyarachun as Prime Minister in 1992, even though Anand did not enjoy a parliamentary majority; the point was that he was a popular choice and, even more importantly, he was the King's choice. Similarly, the King's intervention to ensure that the election of April 2006 was ruled invalid was arguably an exercise of royal influence which did not accord with the spirit at least of the Constitution, under which the Constitutional Court was a separate judicial branch. As for the military, we have discussed above its role in successive coups, constitutions and even constitution-making episodes. In addition to this interventionist political role as part of a strangely anomalous legacy, the Royal Thai Army runs and directly controls a substantial part of free-to-air TV and broadcast radio (regulation and control of the Thai media are discussed further in chapters three and seven). The position it has occupied, and the enjoyment of immunity, indicates that the military is not merely the defence or security branch of the Executive, taking orders from the Prime Minister. Its role goes beyond that in terms both of exercising emergency powers and martial law powers (for which see chapter three), and, limited perhaps in the way we have suggested, the overturning occasionally of the entire constitutional order.

---

[55] Constitution of Thailand (hereafter 'TC') 1997, s 94; TC 2007, s 151.

[56] See Suwannathat-Pian, above n 8, particularly chs 5 and 6.

[57] This idea was proposed by Professor Tan during panel discussion at the King Prajadhipok Congress VIII, 'Constitution Reform: Comparative Perspectives', held in Bangkok, November 2006.

The position of the monarchy is comparable in some respects but very different in others. While the extra-constitutional role of the military remains overt and controversial, the extra-constitutional role of the monarchy is subtle but taken for granted, including, in one sense, by the constitutions themselves, which invariably indicate in the Preamble that the constitution is 'graciously bestowed' by the King. It is also necessary for a coup to be validated by the King signing a royal decree issuing an interim constitution which grants immunity to the military, as occurred in 2006; in this sense these two powers are inextricably mixed. It is the King's consent rather than popular assent which gives a coup such legitimacy as it enjoys. Without that assent the coup would become a revolution.

Another difference is that the power of the monarchy has grown enormously during the reign of the present King Bhumipol (Rama IX, 1946–date), whereas, we have argued, the power of the military has declined in spite of the 2006 coup. Indeed it is now difficult in many respects to distinguish the power of the monarchy from the personal standing of the King. With the abdication of King Prajadhipok in 1935, the regency and then death of King Ananda (Rama VIII, 1935–46), and the personal ascendancy of the Field-Marshal Phibun, the monarchy sank to a low ebb, scarcely able to hang on even to some of its ceremonial powers. Sarit reversed this trend, seeing the advantages of promoting the monarchy as an autochthonic, deeply cultural element of Thai democracy and nationhood. King Bhumipol took the logic of this much further as he gained in maturity, personal prestige and wealth from the early 1970s. He acquired considerable Buddhistic merit as a result of charitable works, astutely orchestrated public presence and carefully judged constitutional interventions, while also being protected from any criticism by the law of *lèse-majesté* (this is discussed in chapter seven).[58] For the last 40 years at least of this ninth reign of the Chakri dynasty, the position of the King has been unquestioned and largely unquestionable. His constitutional powers have not changed, as we have shown, except in minor detail during this period, but his words are always listened to and he is able to make decisions which are not indicated or hinted at the constitutional text. He does not directly interfere in the day-to-day operation of government; largely his time has been spent in ceremonial duties of great symbolic significance in both nationalist and

---

[58] Handley, above n 7.

religious terms, raising money for charitable causes, and running and promoting programs (usually agricultural, environmental or social) in parallel with or in support of those of government.

The respects in which the King merely exercises powers provided explicitly by the constitutional text are indicated where they are relevant in the subsequent chapters. In general these powers conform to standard prescriptions for constitutional monarchy, such as assent to legislation, summoning and proroguing the Legislature, and acting on government advice. However, the King has stood as a symbol of Thai nationhood, having also a significant relationship with religion. In the Thai 'civic religion' of 'nation, monarchy and religion',[59] the King has remained central to all three elements. However, McCargo goes beyond this analysis, identifying what he has termed a 'network monarchy' existing after the early 1970s and which is now under threat; he describes the way in which the King exercises influence over events rather than constitutional power. Under this network monarchy, in the way we have noted:

> the monarch was the ultimate arbiter of political decisions in times of crisis; the monarch was the primary source of national legitimacy; the King acted as a didactic commentator on national issues, helping to set the national agenda, especially through his annual birthday speeches; the monarch intervened actively in political developments, largely by working through proxies such as privy councilors and trusted military figures; and the lead proxy former army commander and Prime Minister Prem Tinsulanond, helped determine the nature of coalition governments, and monitored the process of military and other promotions.[60]

Thaksin's premiership (2001–06) struck at the very foundations of this status quo.[61] It was of course based on the domination of Parliament through the Thai Rak Thai Party, and latterly its successors, but its influence demonstrated potential to extend deeply into all other institutions, including the military and the media, thereby threatening the province of the network monarchy. In part, the passionate defence of the monarchy by the 'Yellow Shirt' faction (called the 'People's Alliance for Democracy') at a moment when the succession is thought to be close at

[59] Reynolds, above n 2.

[60] D McCargo, 'Network Monarchy and Legitimacy Crises in Thailand' *Pacific Review*, December 2005, vol 18, no 4, 499–519 at 501.

[61] W Case, 'Thai Democracy, 2001: Out of Equilibrium' (2001) XLI, No 3, *Asian Survey* 525.

hand can be understood in terms of a new insecurity surrounding Thailand's most revered institution and, in turn, a political and military class that has depended upon it.

IX. CONCLUSION

One thing that can be observed about the roller-coaster of constitutional changes since 1932 is that in essence, and with few exceptions, Thai constitutions, while adhering to the principle of constitutional monarchy, nonetheless correspond to two broad types.

The first type ('administrative charter') is a basic document that contains few provisions and is drafted by a small number of people; allows the military to hold political office; concentrates power in the Prime Minister's hands; emasculates Parliament either by giving an appointed Senate predominance over Parliament, or by providing for a unicameral, appointed legislature and perhaps also banning political parties; and often it also gives more powers to the King and his Privy Council.

The second type ('democratic constitution') is a much more expansive document that is drafted by a large representative or consultative body; provides for an elected Parliament in a bicameral legislature where the Senate is less powerful or is itself at least partly elected; allows political parties to flourish and compete; prohibits the military from holding political office; reduces the powers of the King, formally at least, to those of a typical constitutional monarch; involves some dispersal of power to judicial or other independent agencies as well as Parliament; and to some extent allows for or emphasises fundamental rights and civil liberties.

Seen in this light the constitutional cycle is actually more accurately viewed as an oscillation between these two proto-typical constitutions. If this is correct then we could conclude that, although any final resolution or outcome remains unclear, the democratic constitution cannot now be replaced by the administrative charter except perhaps on a purely temporary basis, as in 2006–07. The issues are now what kind of democratic constitution does or should Thailand have, and what kind of definition of 'democratic' and 'constitution' might be involved. It is to these questions that the balance of this book is primarily devoted.

We have seen in this chapter that Thailand has undergone a remarkable period of constitutional instability, if we consider the short life-spans of the 18 written constitutions. Since 1932 at least[62] it has experienced more constitutions and hence more constitution-making episodes than any other country. This experience has no doubt made Thais both knowledgeable about and willing to debate constitutional issues, but also somewhat cynical about the real importance of these debates. It must also be placed in perspective, however. Paradoxically, during this period, and especially since the early 1960s, Thailand has also experienced enormous, unprecedented economic growth and social change. It is one of East Asia's 'tiger' economies.[63] Policy has often been as consistent as politics, governments and constitutions have been inconsistent. Daily life is not shattered by the frequent reversals of political fortune. The activities of the courts and even some other independent agencies have not usually been greatly affected. The monarchy has proved the sole stable element in, and sometimes a stabilising influence on, a chaotic political scene. Distinct improvement is evidenced in many fields of life, and 'instability' does not normally indicate that chaos generally prevails. We do not, however, take the view that this simply means that the rules governing political life are not to be found in the constitution, or that such a position, contrary to the rule of law, so far as it is actually true,[64] represents the final word on Thai legal and political culture. It seems clear from the perspective of 2011 that the failure to solve the constitutional problems Thailand has had to confront in the last two decades is not something that can be taken lightly. We can now see clearly that constitutional instability is not mere dysfunction according to a strictly constitutionalist, rule-of-law idea of how Thailand ought to function. It threatens the very existence of the Thai polity, and its resolution will ultimately determine the nature of that polity.

This is the paradox of constitutional life in Thailand. While many factors remain surprisingly unaltered over time, the attempts so far to create a system in which democratic elections lead to a single party or stable coalition taking power for at least the duration of a parliament, without a successful no-confidence motion, a military coup or a new constitution, have failed signally. In the ensuing chapters we examine in turn against this context and background the various areas and issues

---

[62] Haiti and Venezuela have had more constitutions but over a longer period.

[63] P Phongpaichit and C Baker, *Thailand's Boom!* (Chiang Mai, Silkworm Books, 1996).

[64] In much of the discussion in this book it will be apparent that the constitutional provisions do in fact apply in practice.

of Thailand's fraught and highly-contested system of constitutional governance.

FURTHER READING

C Baker and P Phongpaichit, *A History of Thailand* (Cambridge, Cambridge University Press, 2005).

S Chamarik, *Kanmu'ang Thai Kap Phatthanakan Ratthathammanun* [Thailand and the Evolution of its Constitutions] 3rd edn (Bangkok, Foundation for the Promotion of the Social Sciences and Humanities, 2006) [in Thai].

M Connors, *Democracy and National Identity in Thailand* (Copenhagen, NIAS Press, 2007).

Democratic Development Committee, *Khosana Krop Khwamkhit Nai Kanpatirup Kanmu'ang Thai* [Conceptual Framework Recommendations for Thai Political Reform] (Bangkok, Thailand Research Fund and Democratic Development Committee, 1995) [in Thai].

D Engel, *Law and Kingship in Thailand During the Reign of King Chulalongkorn*, Michigan Papers on South and Southeast Asia No 9 (Ann Arbor, Mich, University of Michigan Centre for South and Southeast Asian Studies, 1975).

J Funston (ed), *Divided over Thaksin: Thailand's Coup and Problematic Transition* (Singapore, ISEAS, 2009).

J Girling, *Thailand: Society and Politics* (Ithaca, NY, Cornell University Press, 1981).

P Handley, *The King Never Smiles: A Biography of Thailand's King Bhumipol Adulyadej* (New Haven, Conn, Yale University Press, 2006).

A Harding, 'The Eclipse of the Astrologers: King Mongkut, His Successors, and the Reformation of Law in Thailand' in P Nicholson and S Biddulph (eds), *Examining Practice, Interrogating Theory: Comparative Legal Studies in Asia* (Leiden, Martinus Nijhoff, 2008).

B Kachayodhadej (ed), Members of the Constitution Drafting Assembly of Thailand 1996, *Ruam Sara Ratthathammanun Chabap Prachachon* [Substantial Contents of the People's Constitution] (Bangkok, Matichon Press, 1998) [in Thai].

T Loos, *Subject Siam: Family, Law, and Colonial Modernity in Thailand* (Ithaca, NY and London, Cornell University Press, 2006).

D McCargo, *Reforming Thai Politics* (Copenhagen, NIAS, 2002).

—— 'Network Monarchy and Legitimacy Crises in Thailand' *Pacific Review*, December 2005, vol 18, no 4, 499–519.

N Mektrirat, *Kanpatiwat Sayam pho.so. 2475* [Siam's Revolution from 1932]
   5th edn (Bangkok, Samnakphim Fa Dieokan, 2010) [in Thai].

M Peleggi, *Thailand: The Worldly Kingdom* (Singapore, Talisman, 2007).

S   Prichasinlapakun, *Aphiratthathammanun Thai* [Mega-Constitutions]
   (Bangkok, Sathaban Pridi Phanomyong, 2007) [in Thai].

K Suwannathat-Pian, *Kings, Country and Constitutions: Thailand's Political
   Development 1932–2000* (London, Routledge, 2003).

Y Tamada, *Myths and Realities: The Democratization of Thai Politics* (Melbourne,
   Trans-Pacific Press, 2009).

B Uwanno, *Kham Athibai Wicha Kotmai Rratthammanun* [Constitutional
   Law] (Bangkok, Institute of Legal Education, Thai Bar Association,
   2010) [in Thai].

T Winichakul, *Siam Mapped: A History of the Geo-Body of a Nation* (Honolulu,
   University of Hawaii Press, 1994).

D Wyatt, *Thailand: A Short History*, 2nd edn (Chiang Mai, Silkworm
   Books, 2003).

2

The National Assembly, Elections and the Political Process

Introduction – The Making of the Contemporary Legislature – The Electoral System – Thailand's Two Democracies – Electoral Malpractice and Political Culture – Political Parties: Funding and Regulation – The Election Commission of Thailand – The National Assembly: Procedure and Powers – Accountability of the Executive before the Legislature – Bicameralism and the Senate – Conclusion

I. INTRODUCTION

THIS CHAPTER NOT only sketches the evolution of the institutional apparatus of democratic government from the establishment of Thailand's first constitution, it also discusses the special challenges involved in adapting what might be conceived as essentially Western models of democracy in a Thai context. In a formal sense the characteristics of modern democracy, defined in terms of a general right to vote resulting in the election of a legislature from which a form of representative government emerges, have been in evidence sporadically to some extent since the 1930s, but the realisation of a democracy in which the contestation for political power at the ballot box has a clear correlation with the wider distribution of power and wealth among citizens more generally has been much more elusive. In Thailand the routine process of voting has been tainted by the practice of vote-buying, while in Parliament[1] the sustainability of any government has too

---

[1] In Thailand 'Parliament' is generally used to denote the House of Representatives. This is followed in this chapter, in which 'National Assembly' refers to both houses and 'Senate' to the upper house thereof.

often depended on factions with no ideological anchor offering allegiance to the highest bidder. This discussion, which focuses on the very essence of the democratic process, aims to go beyond providing an outline of the creation of the current institutional architecture, seeking to evaluate how recent attempts at constitutional innovation have been directed at addressing such problems by changing the configuration of parliament, by fashioning dedicated oversight bodies, and by setting in place increasingly elaborate regimes of regulation.

II. THE MAKING OF THE
CONTEMPORARY THAI LEGISLATURE

The existence and effectiveness of representative institutions has always been a primary indicator of a democratic system, and in these terms Thailand has appeared to be a leader among Asian democracies, having established electoral franchise and a parliament two decades or so before most others. Indeed, calls for representative government as a check on absolute monarchy, abuse of power and corruption were made by a princely petition to King Chulalongkorn in 1885 and by Buddhist scholar Tienwan in the early years of the last century.[2] The constitutional monarchy established in June 1932 moved rapidly towards a parliamentary system of government. Between 1933 and 1946, Parliaments[3] consisted of an equal number of members elected and appointed by the King; however, this arrangement was expressed (1932 Constitution, section 65) to be a temporary measure, to last until more than half the people had at least a primary education, or at any rate not longer than 10 years after the Constitution came into effect. This 10-year rule was renewed for another 10 years by constitutional amendment in 1942. The first direct elections[4] of MPs took place in November 1937. Most Thais – including women – were able to vote for MPs in single-member constituencies of around 200,000 electors. The latter figure was reduced to

[2] C Samudavanija, 'Political History' in S Xuto (ed), *Government and Politics of Thailand* (Singapore, Oxford University Press, 1987) ch 1 at 27–28.

[3] The Legislature, whether unicameral or bicameral, is usually referred to as the 'National Assembly' in English translations of Thai constitutions. Here 'Parliament' indicates the House of Representatives, and National Assembly indicates the whole Legislature including the Senate. 'MP' indicates a member of the lower house.

[4] Elections were held in December 1933, but MPs were here elected indirectly by provincial representatives.

around 150,000 in 1949, at which figure the average number of electors remained, despite different electoral systems and an increasing population, until the 1997 Constitution, which introduced an entirely new system for organising electorates (see section III below).

The 1946 Constitution introduced several innovations that have become recurrent features of Thai democracy. First, the legislature became bicameral[5] with the selection of members for the Senate, who were endowed with a six-year term, as opposed to the four-year term for MPs; the Senate consisted of 80 members who were selected by Parliament. Secondly, Parliament, consisting of 178 members, became for the first time entirely directly elected. Thirdly, political parties were allowed to form for the first time, and 11 were actually formed. Fourthly, government officials and military officers were not allowed to sit in either house.[6] Interestingly, as an index of the fact that changing constitutions often in practice changed rather little on the ground, it was usual through the 1930s and 1940s for appointed – and even sometimes elected – members to continue in office following the coming into force of a new constitution, members being added in by-elections where necessary to fulfil the constitutional mandate.[7]

The 1974 Constitution, which was introduced in the wake of protracted popular demonstrations against institutionalised repression,[8] represented the next benchmark in the elaboration of Thai notions of democracy, and it involved further innovations. First, in a largely symbolic gesture, the Speaker of Parliament, rather than the President of the Senate, was designated the President of the National Assembly, thus asserting the primacy of the elected over the appointed house.[9] Secondly,

---

[5] The bizarre second iteration of the 1932 Constitution, brought back into force between March 1952 and October 1958, reverted to a unicameral system. As is indicated in ch 1, sections IV and V, the unicameral legislature became a feature of what are there termed the 'administrative charters' (for the administration of the Kingdom) as opposed to the 'democratic constitutions' which provided for a bicameral legislature.

[6] This was reiterated in the later Constitutions of 1974, 1978, 1991, 1997 and 2007.

[7] For example, 100 MPs were elected in January 1948 under the Interim Constitution of 1947; the 1949 Constitution, in force in March 1949, required 21 extra MPs, who were elected in a by-election in June 1949 and remained in office until February 1952.

[8] C Baker and P Phongpaichit, *A History of Thailand* (Cambridge, Cambridge University Press, 2005) 188ff.

[9] This was revived with the 2nd Amendment to the 1978 Constitution, in August 1988.

the single-member constituency was varied so that, while maintaining the ratio of one MP per 150,000 electors, each constituency had either two or three MPs, and a province entitled to more than three MPs was divided into two or more constituencies. Thirdly, the number of political parties hugely increased; it had risen to 30 when registration was first required under the Political Party Act 1955, and then to 57 under the Political Party Act 1974. The representation of these parties in Parliament obviously varied according to electoral fortunes and the electoral system adopted, but in general the larger number of parties tended to result in unstable, coalition governments. This proliferation of parties was due to their having a local rather than national base. As a result of elections held between 1975 and 1988, for example, between nine and 19 parties were represented in Parliament; the four elections in the 1990s each resulted in 11 parties winning seats in Parliament. It was not until after the 2001 election that Thailand had a one-party government (Thai Rak Thai, 'TRT') for the first time in its history, and even then TRT had to merge with two other parties for this to occur.[10]

As a result of the many constitutions discussed in chapter one, the actual size of both houses increased rapidly. The so-called 'semi-democratic' 1978 Constitution provided for the number of Senators to be no more than three-quarters of the number of MPs, and this rule was repeated in the 1991 Constitution, the numbers rising by 1996 to 270 Senators and 393 MPs. The 1997 and 2007 Constitutions, on the other hand, fixed the number of members of each house. Currently, under the 2007 Constitution, Parliament consists of 480 MPs. This is hardly different from the 1997 Constitution, except that the party-list MPs are fewer (there were 100 under the 1997 Constitution) and the party lists themselves are based on eight regionally grouped *changwat* (provinces) as opposed to the whole country. The Senate consists of 150 members, as compared with 200 under the 1997 Constitution. The constitution-makers have traded in the idea of a fixed ratio of electors to MPs in favour of equal and partly proportional representation in a Parliament of a fixed and manageable size.

The 1978 Constitution introduced further innovations. Parliament was empowered to pass a motion of no-confidence in the Executive;

---

[10] Amalgamation of parties is now prohibited during Parliament's 4-year term: TC 2007, s 104.

and the Executive was empowered to dissolve Parliament. Matters were taken somewhat further in the 1991 Constitution, which reduced the power of the Senate vis-à-vis Parliament (Amendment No 3 of June 1992) and required the Prime Minister to be an MP (Amendment No 4 of September 1992).[11] The last two decades have also witnessed extensive constitutional engineering designed to prevent electoral malpractice, a problem which has grown along with the frequency and significance of elections and the number of political parties. The treatment of these crucial issues will be discussed below.

III. THE ELECTORAL SYSTEM

The integrity of the electoral system can be regarded as being at the very core of Thai democratic and constitutional reform. Moreover, wider experience of constitutional practice demonstrates that the protection of individual human rights commonly flows from, and indeed depends upon, a guarantee of the right to vote. Under the 1997 and 2007 Constitutions there has been a strong commitment to democratic process, even though the meaning of 'democratic' has proved to be highly contested during the tumultuous political events taking place from 2005 to date.[12] In formal terms constitutional and related organic laws provide that all Thai nationals over the age of 18 have the right to vote; indeed since 1937 the right to vote (as opposed to being a candidate) has not been circumscribed in any way by gender,[13] property or educational qualifications, and is now in fact stated as a *duty* to vote.[14] Voting is thus a fundamental aspect of contemporary Thai citizenship, and the evidence of turn-out rates indicates that Thai citizens are actually

---

[11] During periods of authoritarian rule, eg under generals Sarit and Thanom in the 1960s, the Executive had been separated from the Legislature.

[12] The political polarisation of Thailand during this period between the so-called 'Red Shirts' and 'Yellow Shirts' (supporters and opponents, respectively, of former PM Thaksin Shinawatra), has resulted in both camps claiming to be truly 'democratic'. In both cases, however, this claim is suspect.

[13] In fact Thailand was one of the first countries to treat male and female citizens equally in this respect. In 1897 a Local Administration Act introduced by Prince Damrong provided for equality of men and women in voting: Subhatra Bhumiprabhas, 'The Feminist Prince', *The Nation*, Bangkok, 27 August 2009.

[14] TC 2007, s 72.

becoming somewhat weary of voting in so many national and local elections, despite the sanctions for failing to vote.[15]

Under the 1997 Constitution, 400 MPs were elected on a single-member constituency basis and 100 chosen from national party lists. The 1997 reversion to single-member constituencies[16] was designed to create a closer link between politicians and the electorate; the prevailing opinion appears to be that this intention was not fulfilled in practice.[17] The 2007 Constitution thus provides for a multi-member majoritarian system, in which 400 members are directly elected for four years by a simple plurality 'first-past-the-post system'. The remaining 80 members are selected by party preference from eight regional lists, proportionally to the number of directly elected members from the party in question (following amendment to ss 93–98 of the Constitution in 2011 the total will increase to 500 members (375 FPP from single member constitutencies and 125 from a nationwide party list)). The ostensible objective of these changes from the 1997 Constitution is to reduce the power of party headquarters and enhance the link between MPs and the people they represent. Regard also has to be given to 'opportunity and approximate proportion between women and men'.[18]

The basis on which constituencies are defined is complex, but the system is now designed to achieve the simple objective of approximately equal representation in multi-member constituencies of two or three members. First, the total number of electors recorded by the national census is divided by the prescribed number of directly-elected members. This produces a ratio of electors to members, which is applied so as to determine the number of MPs for each *changwat*; a *changwat* with less than the ratio gets one MP, and a *changwat* with more will get the number of MPs corresponding with the number of electors according

[15] P Chambers, 'Superfluous, Mischievous or Emancipating? Thailand's Evolving Senate Today' (2009) 28:3 *Journal of Current Southeast Asian Affairs* 3, 17.

[16] This had not applied since the 1974 Constitution introduced multi-member constituencies.

[17] A Harding and P Leyland, 'Constitutional Design in Thailand: the Management of Electoral Process in an Emerging Democracy' (2010) 4 *Journal of Parliamentary and Political Law* 299, at 304–06. See sections V and VI below for further discussion of the operation of the party-system.

[18] TC 2007, s 97. The first female MP was elected in 1949, and the proportion of female MPs has slowly risen to the present (December 2007 election) 12% of constituency MPs and 8.8% of party-list MPs; see <http://thailand.prd.go.th/democracy/view_democracy.php?id=4359>.

to the ratio. As a *changwat* grows in population far beyond the ratio, it is divided up into further constituencies.

The composition of the Senate has also changed between these two Constitutions. Under the 1997 Constitution, 200 Senators were, for the first time, not appointed but elected in multi-member constituencies, which were congruent with the 75 *changwat*, under a majoritarian system; the number of Senators per *changwat* varied according to the population, with the capital Bangkok, for example, having as many as 18 Senators. This was a dramatic innovation which was designed as part of the entire scheme of the 1997 Constitution. Members of any political party were expressly prohibited from standing for the Senate. This was intended not only to offer broader representation than was provided by election to the House of Representatives, but also to create a relatively neutral, non-partisan Upper House. By way of contrast, a parliamentary candidate had to be a member of a political party. Moreover, a senator's six-year term was no longer renewable. Thus the Senate was conceived as politically independent and as a crucial popular or civil-society-based check on the politicians and the parliamentary majority. The Senate was also given powers, essential in the scheme of the 1997 Constitution, to control the membership of all the independent agencies set up or newly reformed by the 1997 Constitution.[19] In practice, however, the independence of the Senate was undermined by Executive influence and by an increasing tendency for the wives or other family members or close associates of locally prominent politicians to stand as, in effect, proxies in senatorial elections, thereby flouting the intention if not the letter of the law.[20] Instead of the 'civil-society house', the Senate came to be known as the 'political-proxy house'.

The 2007 Constitution reverts to a partly-appointed Senate. This has proved controversial, and could be termed either a compromise between competing principles or a failure to build on the experience of the Senate under the previous Constitution. The Senate now has 150 members; 74 senators are appointed for a three-year term and are drawn (14–15 each) from the academic, government, private and professional sectors; 76 are elected to a six-year term by a first-past-the-post system – one for each of the *changwat* plus Bangkok. Those qualified for election to the Senate can

---

[19] See ch 1 for further discussion of this system and its failure in practice.

[20] S Chantornvong, 'The 1997 Constitution and the Politics of Electoral Reform' ch 13 of D McCargo (ed), *Reforming Thai Politics* (Copenhagen, NIAS, 2002), at 207.

also be candidates for selection. The appointed Senators are selected by a Senate Selection Committee consisting of the President of the Constitutional Court, the Chairperson of the Election Commission, the President of the Ombudsmen, the Chairperson of the National Anti-Corruption Commission, the Chairperson of the State Audit Commission, a Judge of the Supreme Court of Justice and a Judge of the Supreme Administrative Court.[21] This committee – noticeably – does not involve any politician, excluding even the Leader of the Opposition who sits on other selection committees.[22] The Committee selects:

> persons who may be beneficial to the performance of powers and duties of the Senate from persons nominated by academic institutions, public sector, private sector, professional organizations and other organizations . . . [and] regard shall be had to knowledge, skills or experience of the nominated persons which will be beneficial to the performance of the Senate, and the composition of the selected persons shall have regard to interdisciplinary knowledge and experience, gender opportunity and equality, close apportionment of the persons nominated by the organizations . . . and opportunity of socially vulnerable groups.[23]

The idea of a non-political Senate is elaborated in the 2007 Constitution further than under the 1997 Constitution. A candidate for selection must be at least 40 years old and may not be, nor have been within the last five years, a member or an office-holder in a political party (as opposed to merely at the time of candidacy under the 1997 Constitution). And as with candidates for parliamentary election, a university degree is essential. Interestingly, in light of the creeping nepotism evident in senatorial elections, an aspiring senator cannot be an ascendant (for example, parent or grandparent), spouse or child of an MP or a holder of political office. In addition, candidates for election (but not selection) must demonstrate a connection with the relevant *changwat*, such as being on the *changwat* house register or having studied for five years in the *changwat*. There is also a two-year ban on former senators holding political office and 'the campaign to be launched by the

---

[21] TC 2007, s 112.

[22] In a strange potential conflict of interest, the Senate is empowered to impeach the very office-holders who, as selection committee members, are empowered to select half of their numbers. Furthermore, the Constitutional Court, whose President sits on the selection committee, would have jurisdiction to decide any disputes concerning the selection process.

[23] TC 2007, s 114.

candidates in the election is limited to the matters related to the performance of duties of the Senate'[24]; in other words, candidates are allowed to explain why they would be effective senators but not to ask voters to support a particular political manifesto. In practice accusations of cronyism have persisted, since, despite the elaborate safeguards detailed above, the ruling elite are perceived as being able to dominate the selection process and appoint members concerned to defend the status quo.[25]

Candidates for election to Parliament are subject to somewhat different rules. They must be at least 25 years old, and *must have been* a member of one political party for 90 days prior to nomination (or 30 days in the case of a dissolution of Parliament). They must also demonstrate a connection with the *changwat*, as for senatorial candidates, or with the relevant group of *changwat* in the case of party-list candidates. Interesting disqualifications[26] include: being disqualified from holding political office, and having been expelled, dismissed or removed from the official service, a State agency or State enterprise on the ground of dishonest performance of duties or corruption; being a drug addict; and being a Buddhist monk, priest or novice.[27]

The requirement for a university degree (bachelor's degree or higher) is controversial, having been introduced in 1997 for all Members of the National Assembly and retained in the constitution-drafting process of 2007. It looks like an anti-democratic measure at odds with the general tenor of recent reforms.[28] Surprisingly, however, it was introduced as a result of, rather than despite, public demand, and affords interesting evidence of how democracy is seen by Thai voters. The rule speaks to a notion of democracy apparently held by most Thais, in which representation in the legislature is a specialist task (rather like being represented in court by a qualified lawyer) which should be performed by the educated

---

[24] TC 2007, s 112.

[25] Eg, it was the Senate which has pressed for stricter enforcement of the repressive *lèse-majesté* law. See 'The Senate Forms Panel to Monitor Enforcement of *Lèse-Majesté*' Prachatai, *South East Press Alliance*, 27 January 2009.

[26] The complete list is in TC 2007, s 102.

[27] For discussion of the legal treatment of Buddhist monks, priests and novices, who are traditionally supposed to be unconcerned with mundane matters, see A Harding, 'Buddhism, Human Rights and Constitutional Reform in Thailand' (2007) 2 *Asian Journal of Comparative Law* 1, and in particular the discussion there of Surakiart's case.

[28] In 2007 there were more than two million students in higher education out of a total population of 64 million.

class who are conceived here as also being more trustworthy than the 'self-made' men or women who predominated in pre-1997 legislatures. This notion seems to have been privileged over the ideal of equal citizenship. It is seriously open to doubt, however, whether the rule is democratic in principle, given that only a small percentage of Thais are able to satisfy the criterion; or effective in practice in terms of improving political morality.[29] It is evidence of the existence in Thailand of the 'two democracies' which we discuss further in section IV below.

IV. THAILAND'S TWO DEMOCRACIES

Notwithstanding the developments discussed above and the entrenchment in some form of the principle of democratic representation in virtually all of the various constitutions since 1932, there are strands of Thai society which have been and remain resistant to full or complete democracy. As Girling observed:

> [T]he Thai middle strata also fear the 'turmoil' a more open society might lead to. And the experience of the democratic years, 1973 to 1976 reinforces this fear. Like the established members of the nineteenth century European middle classes, they believe that the 'masses' are not ready for democracy; they are too ignorant, short-sighted and too easily swayed by emotions to obey its rules and make it work.[30]

A similar point is elaborated by Anek Laothamatas in a frequently-quoted piece which first proposed (we suggest prophetically in view of the political polarisation evident during the period 2005–10) the idea of 'two democracies' in Thailand[31]:

---

[29] See, however, the views of a former Speaker of the House of Representatives, Uthal Pimjaichon, in 'Democratic Path to People-Based Society: Experience, Perspectives and Criticism' in N Rathamarit (ed), *Eyes on Democracy: National and Local Issues* (KPI, Nonthaburi, 2006) at 305.

[30] J Girling, *Thailand: Society and Politics* (Ithaca, NY, Cornell University Press, 1981) 145.

[31] A Laothamatas, 'A Tale of Two Democracies: Conflicting Perceptions of Elections and Democracy in Thailand' in R Taylor (ed), *The Politics of Elections in South East Asia* (New York, Cambridge University Press, 1996). See also J Logerfo, 'Attitudes Toward Democracy Among Rural Northern Thais' (1996) 36 *Asian Survey* 904–23; C Samudavanija and P Chotiya, 'Beyond Transition in Thailand' in L Diamond and M Plattner (eds), *Democracy in East Asia* (Baltimore, Md, Johns Hopkins University Press, 1998).

[V]oting in farming areas is not guided by political principles, policy issues, or what is perceived to be in the national interest, all of which is [regarded as] the only legitimate rationale for citizens casting their ballots in a democratic election. The ideal candidates for rural voters are those who visit them often, address their immediate grievances effectively, and bring numerous public works to their communities. [These candidates are however regarded by the middle classes as] parochial in outlook, boorish in manner, and too uneducated to be competent lawmakers or cabinet members . . . Ideally, patron–client ties might be replaced by a more responsive and effective system of local government. On top of that, voters are [yet] to be convinced that principle-or-policy-oriented voting brings them greater benefits than what they may get from local patrons . . .

In similar vein Logerfo, in a study of rural northern Thai political attitudes, refers to

a larger attitudinal complex that enables locally influential figures, often involved in illegal business activities, to win elections and engage in corruption of all kinds so long as they continue to deliver the goods to their constituencies.[32]

In terms of the contemporary struggle between the Red and Yellow movements, Ferrara identifies the very same interests at work, in the sense that there are those who believe that

Thailand needs the [appointed] Privy Council and the military to save it from the loathsome, back-stabbing politicians its supposedly misguided, child-like population continues to elect. And if the absence of a democratic counter-weight allows unelected, anti-democratic institutions to call the shots on every matter of significance . . . the chronic ineffectiveness of democratically elected governments further strengthens the military and the Privy Council in their self-appointed role as the guarantors of reason, stability and order.[33]

Of course, any such assumptions about the right to govern not only conveniently overlook the serial corruption and abuse of power that were practised during periods of military rule, but also that the PAD (the People's Alliance for Democracy, or 'Yellow Shirt' movement) has been equally prepared to conduct politics in an unscrupulous fashion.

Indeed, as we turn to review the current situation, the two democracies can still clearly be discerned but have taken on disturbing significance

---

[32] See Logerfo, above n 31; and see M Nelson, *Central Authority and Local Democratization in Thailand* (Bangkok, White Lotus Press, 1998) 168.

[33] F Ferrara, *Thailand Unhinged* (Jakarta, Equinox Publishing, 2010) 86.

during the current period of extreme political polarisation of Thailand following the popular demonstrations of 2005 and the military coup of September 2006. The coup ousted from government the allegedly corrupt TRT Party of Thaksin Shinawatra (Prime Minister 2001–06), which had been met with huge and hostile demonstrations in Bangkok during 2005–06. A military-installed technocrat government supervised the drafting of the 2007 Constitution, approved by referendum in August 2007. A return to elected government in January 2008 saw the election of the People Power Party (PPP) under Prime Minister Samak Sundaravej, which was close to Thaksin, and this again prompted huge demonstrations by the PAD, which effectively brought government to a standstill as well as causing considerable economic disruption during most of 2008. Samak was forced to resign following an adverse Constitutional Court ruling in September 2008,[34] but his successor Somchai Wongsawat fared no better, being forced from office in December 2008 when his party was dissolved, again as a result of a ruling of the Constitutional Court.[35] Defections of Thaksin-inclined MPs then enabled the Democratic Party under Prime Minister Abhisit Vejjajiva to take power without an election (December 2008)[36]; but the supporters of the pro-Thaksin parties (the 'Red Shirts'), which are (as of early 2011) in opposition, mounted large demonstrations against the Government orchestrated to cause maximum disruption, and demanded new elections. These protesters were dispersed with violence by the military in May 2010. The Red Shirts rest their case on a clear electoral majority in the general elections of January 2008, subverted by a kind of fraud on the constitution; the Yellow Shirt leaders of the PAD, consistently with Girling's observation above, have stated a policy objective of parliamentary reform representing a 'new politics', under which only 30 per cent of MPs would be elected and 70 per cent chosen from functional constituencies, effectively removing the right of Thai citizens to select their legislators.[37] It seems clear that such a reform would receive little support across Thailand.

[34] See chapter 2, Section IV.

[35] *Ibid*. The decision disbanded Somchai's People Power Party. Somchai is Thaksin's brother-in-law, and his tenure of the premiership provoked large protests by the Yellow Shirts.

[36] Dissolution of a party enables its members to join another party within 60 days (TC 2007, s 106(8)), despite party-hopping rules discussed below.

[37] See 'People's Alliance for Democracy's Narrow Nationalism in Thailand', available at <http://www.timesonline.co.uk/tol/news/world/asia/article4678338.ece>, 5 September 2008.

V. ELECTORAL MALPRACTICE AND POLITICAL CULTURE

As a matter of law in Thailand at the present time, voting remains compulsory for all citizens, and measures may be taken against a person who fails to vote without good reason.[38] The purpose of this measure, introduced in 1997,[39] was to make vote-buying more difficult by increasing the numbers of votes that would need to be bought to make a difference to the result. The enduring problem, however, has been how to ensure fair elections: 'Corruption riddles governance, business and elections, and corruption scandals define the entire political process'[40]; 'At best, Thai electoral politics can qualify as democracy in form only. From the point of view of almost all Thai politicians involvement in politics is the best way to access wealth'.[41] Entry into politics has mainly provided already wealthy individuals with the opportunity to gain election and thereby to obtain further enrichment. In order to secure votes, election candidates in many parts of Thailand would expect to gain the vote of local constituents by offering individual electors a cash payment. The lack of truly representative parties in a society with a traditionally Buddhist social hierarchy poses deeper questions about the degree of genuine political participation. Moreover, the phenomenon of vote-buying is not universally regarded as wrongful conduct but often as a reciprocal return of favours.[42]

Despite there being a secret ballot and explicit attempts to stamp out vote-buying, the practice has been pervasive and taken for granted. One influential commentator observed that

> Vote-buying, a longstanding Thai practice, was actually exacerbated by new legislation passed at the end of the 1970s, intended to clean up elections and restructure political parties. By the 1995 and 1996 elections it had reached epidemic proportions: to stand a serious chance of winning a typical

[38] Organic Act on the Election of Members of the House of Representatives and Senators 2009, s 25. This recent Act replaced the Organic Act on the Election of Members of the House of Representatives and Senators 1998.

[39] *Ibid*; and TC 1997, s 68.

[40] L Thornton, 'Combating Corruption at the Grassroots: the Thailand Experience 1999–2000' (Washington DC, National Democratic Institute for International Affairs, 2000) 7.

[41] S Phatharathananunth, 'Civil Society and Democratisation in Thailand: A Critique of Elite Democracy' in McCargo, above n 20, at 127.

[42] See, eg, Lauthamatas, above, n 31.

up-country seat, a basic investment equivalent to nearly one million US dollars was required.[43]

Political parties themselves present further difficulties. The wider project to entrench democracy is not simply about granting citizens the right to vote. As mentioned at the outset of this chapter, Thailand has lacked an established political tradition in which political parties organise from the grass roots up to the national level on the basis of a consistent set of policies. Political parties have tended to be numerous, and rather than representing clear ideological positions, they are more usually personal followings, or represent purely regional interests and have a regional electoral base. These parties have also tended to be themselves coalitions of factions, any of which might without warning switch party for some advantage. Changes in government due to no-confidence motions and military interventions have made even controlling the office of Prime Minister somewhat unattractive as an object of party organisation (most Prime Ministers have stayed precariously in office for only one or two years and have had little impact on actual policy).[44] It was therefore one of the challenges of the 1997 drafting process to find means of ensuring that party politics would become less fissiparous and more centripetal, and that governments would be more likely to consist of one party, or at least a reasonably firm coalition of parties. Hence restrictions on no-confidence motions were introduced in 1997 and have been retained (see below, section IX). Rules to prevent MPs switching party (see below, section IX) have also tended to create greater solidarity within parliamentary groups, and increase the power of Prime Ministers and party leaders over their parties' MPs.

Ironically, the object of attaining one-party government for a full parliamentary term was achieved in 2001, but at the expense of entrenching a government (Thaksin's TRT), which would doubtless have horrified the constitution-makers of 1997 in every other respect, not least the fact that TRT was set up only weeks before the election and depended heavily on Thaksin's own fortune for party funding. Although created as a coalition of business interests itself and also having a reputation for corruption, TRT nonetheless bucked the trend by operating

[43] D McCargo, 'Introduction: Understanding Political Reform in Thailand' in McCargo, above n 20, at 7.

[44] There have been 28 Prime Ministers since 1932 (several held office more than once). See further, S Bunbongkarn, 'Political Institutions and Processes' in Xuto (ed), above n 2, ch 2, 61.

on a nationwide basis, by making astute use of the media (Thaksin as a media baron was able to control much of it), by appealing to nationalist sentiments and by having a 'National Agenda' comprising an 11-point popular policy manifesto.[45] In other words, this party, conceived as a vehicle for its leader's own advancement, at the same time assumed the convincing guise of a 'modern' national political party.

There remains, however, a persistent conviction amongst Thai constitution-makers that constitutional or legal engineering is required and will be effective to ensure that politicians will be 'good and capable',[46] and that national political parties will both become more viable and be less corrupt and act more in the national interest. While there seems to be broad agreement that in some sense political parties are 'the problem', there seems to be little evidence to support the idea that they can actually be 'improved' by legal engineering. This puzzle seems to be quintessentially the problem of Thai democracy at the beginning of the twenty-first century.

VI. POLITICAL PARTIES: FUNDING AND REGULATION

Tackling the issue of parties from a different perspective, an element of State funding was first established under the 1997 Constitution to provide a catalyst for the development of grass-roots politics and to obviate the need to rely on influential private donors.[47] The Election Commission of Thailand (ECT – see further section VII below) was granted responsibility for administering the funding scheme relating to expenses in subsidising political parties and other activities with respect to the development of political parties. A special committee determines the allocation of this fund, chaired by the Political Party Registrar. The committee secretary is the ECT's Secretary-General. The committee must consist of an Election Commissioner selected by the ECT, a representative of each of the Ministry of Finance and the Bureau of the Budget; three representatives from political parties who are represented in Parliament, plus one representative from political parties without parliamentary representation.

---

[45] P Phongpaichit and C Baker, *Thaksin: the Business of Politics in Thailand* (Chiang Mai, Silkworm Books, 2004) 81.

[46] M Nelson, 'A Proportional Election System for Thailand?', *KPI Politics Update No 2* (KPI, Bangkok, 2007) 12.

[47] Organic Act on Political Parties 2007, ss 55–72.

In practice the rules allowing for State funding have been cynically exploited by political parties, which responded to recognition that their eligibility for this funding would be increased by simply swelling their numbers artificially. Thai Rak Thai, for example, claimed to have a membership of 15 million in 2003, but 2.3 million of TRT's members were also found to be members of other political parties. Instead of 15 million members the real figure was more like 8.5 million.[48]

Other forms of regulation have been attempted. In Thailand, although the principle of freedom of association applies, there is also an attempt to control the behaviour of political parties in line with the provisions of the constitution and electoral law. Under the 2007 Constitution, reflecting a similar provision in the 1997 Constitution,[49]

> A person shall enjoy the liberty to unite and form a political party for the purpose of making the political will of the people and carrying out political activities in fulfilment of such will through the democratic regime of government with the King as Head of the State . . . The internal organisation, management and regulations of a political party shall be consistent with fundamental principles of the democratic regime . . .

In addition, both Constitutions[50] prohibit discrimination (inter alia) on grounds of '*constitutionally* political view'. As these provisions imply, freedom of political association is not absolute, and political parties are regulated by the Organic Law on Political Parties, the latest version of which was enacted in 2007.

The principle of consistency with fundamental principles may be enforced in a number of ways. A prescribed number of members of a political party may refer a party resolution or regulation to the Constitutional Court, which can nullify it. Another provision[51] imposes more specific and drastic penalties, prohibiting any exercise of constitutional rights to overthrow the democratic regime or to acquire the power to rule the country by any means which is not in accordance with the modes provided in the constitution. Where such acts are performed by a political party, any person may request the Prosecutor-General to bring a motion before the Constitutional Court ordering cessation of

---

[48] D McCargo and U Pathmanand, *The Thaksinisation of Thailand* (NIAS, Copenhagen, 2005), at 86.
[49] TC 2007 and TC 1997, ss 65 and 47 respectively.
[50] Section 30 in both cases.
[51] TC 2007, s 63.

the acts, which may also (as with other violations of the law) result in the party being dissolved. A new provision added by the 2007 Constitution adds the further penalty of depriving the president and executive board of the dissolved party of the right to vote for five years, which also entails that they cannot stand for election during that time.[52]

The powers of the Constitutional Court, in particular the powers relating to dissolution of political parties, have proved highly controversial, and have been exercised drastically and with profound effects on Thai politics in recent years. Critically, a decision of the ECT to allow the General Election held on 2 April 2006 to proceed was challenged successfully in the Constitutional Court, which held the election invalid in May 2006.[53] During the election itself, there were many allegations of widespread vote-buying.[54] The ECT failed to uphold objections to the results and the Constitutional Court initially confirmed individual results which had been called into question.[55] Although TRT won the election, following street demonstrations Thaksin announced that he would only serve as a caretaker Prime Minister until a new government was formed; but after taking a short vacation he showed no signs of going. In an unprecedented move the King intervened on 26 April 2006 by addressing the judges of the Constitutional and Administrative Courts directly. He suggested in typically oblique royal language that they should assert their authority under the Constitution to invalidate the election, which had been boycotted by opposition parties.[56] Further investigation of the conduct of the political parties (TRT and the Democratic Party) in the election was expedited by the military government after the September 2006 coup, resulting in the dissolution of TRT, but not the Democratic Party, as a result of a decision by the Constitutional Tribunal under the 2006 Interim Constitution.[57] The TRT Party was unanimously found

[52]   See TC 2007, ss 100(2) and 102(3).
[53]   'Constitution Court Invalidates the April Election and Orders New Election', *The Nation*, Bangkok, 9 May 2006; 'Thai Court Rules Election Invalid', *BBC News*, 8 May 2006.
[54]   These led to the Constitutional Tribunal's decisions of 30 May 2007 dissolving the TRT Party: see below.
[55]   See 'End of the Beginning in Thailand's Crisis', Bangkok Post, Bangkok, 19 May 2006.
[56]   See 'April 2 Election: Charter Court to Examine the Legality of Poll', *The Nation*, Bangkok, 1 May 2006.
[57]   'Summary of the Decision of the Constitutional Tribunal: Thai Rak Thai', The Nation, 6 June 2007.

guilty of all charges, together with three minor parties which were also dissolved. The verdict was based on the fact that a few high-ranking party members were directly involved in bribing several small parties into competing in order to ensure that the minimum 20% turnout requirement was met; the Tribunal dissolved TRT and banned 111 members of its executive committee, including Thaksin himself, from politics for a period of five years. It was also ruled that there was inadequate evidence supporting the charge that the Democrats bribed small parties into exposing some high-profile TRT party members' involvement in election fraud in a series of by-elections in April 2006; and that the Democrat Party did not defame Thaksin or urge voters to cast a 'no' vote in the election. Accordingly this party avoided dissolution. The decision was variously celebrated as a victory for the rule of law and denigrated as representing evidence of double standards.

Another method of controlling political parties was the '90-day rule' which, having been included in the 1997 Constitution,[58] survived the 2007 drafting process in modified form. Under the original rule, a candidate for election to the House of Representatives had to be a member of any and only one political party, for a consecutive period of not less than 90 days, up to the date of applying for candidacy in an election; but under the 2007 Constitution the period drops to 30 days should the lower house be dissolved.[59] The point of this provision is to prevent opportunistic party-hopping prior to an election. Although this can be seen as controlling the behaviour of individual politicians, it also tends to encourage a tendency for parties to hold together (we have noted above the fissiparous nature of Thai political parties). Additional rules prevent party-hopping. Resignation from or termination of membership of one's political party terminates membership of Parliament; where a party is dissolved by the Constitutional Court, a member of it ceases to be an MP unless he or she becomes a member of another

[58] Section 107(4). For a discussion of the unintended impact of this rule see E Kuhonta, 'The Paradox of Thailand's 1997 "People's Constitution": Be Careful What You Wish For' (2008) 48:3 *Asian Survey* 373, at 381, 383.

[59] TC 2007, s 101(3). See Kuhonta, above n 58, at 390, and *World of Parliaments Quarterly Review*, Web Version, Issue No 27, October 2007, available at http://www.ipu.org/english/journal.htm. Reducing the period to 30 days in the event of dissolution would appear to defeat the purpose of the original rule, namely to prevent the formation of new parties at short notice from existing MPs tempted by short-term inducements. The decision to slash the period to 30 days appears to have been a compromise reached as part of the constitutional drafting process.

political party within 60 days[60]; and parties may not amalgamate during a parliamentary four-year term.[61]

Constitutional provisions also require candidates to have a solid connection with the *changwat* in which they stand for election (see section III above). The connection of the candidate with the constituency is indeed a matter fraught with difficulty. The paucity of funding for parties means that parties tend to go in search of wealthy candidates with local influence rather than vice versa; or that wealthy individuals set up their own parties. It is thus local networks of influence that ultimately matter, rather than the courting of individual voters. Indeed it is often reported that members display little interest in their constituencies after being elected,[62] preferring advancement through Thailand's complex factional parliamentary politics.

One possible remedy to several of the problems here outlined is of course to have party-list elections in addition to or instead of constituency elections, as provided in both the 1997 and 2007 Constitutions.[63] The main purpose of this was not simply to consolidate national parties, but to ensure that the best people could be appointed to the Cabinet without the need for a by-election in each case; this would otherwise be needed given that the 1997 Constitution required separation of the Executive from the Legislature after a General Election, so that members of the Government had to resign their parliamentary seats following an election. This proved one of the problematical issues in the 2007 drafting process. One group wanted a 400-seat house equally divided between constituency and party-list seats. Another wanted a house comprised entirely of constituency-elected members. As explained above, the outcome was a compromise.

During 2008, the Constitutional Court's powers over political parties became even more controversial than previously. In 2001, following Thaksin's survival of corruption charges by an 8:7 vote in the Constitutional Court, he expressed the view that a few unelected judges should not be able to dismiss someone elected by 12 million people. In 2008 the Court first ruled against Prime Minister Samak Sundaravej in a matter of conflict of interest which appeared to many quite trivial: he had taken money for appearing in a regular TV cookery programme.

[60] TC 2007, s 106(8).
[61] TC 2007, s 104.
[62] Logerfo, above n 31.
[63] See, further, Nelson, above n 46.

This ruling precipitated his resignation. More drastically, in December 2008 the Court dissolved on grounds of electoral fraud the PPP, the 'successor' party to TRT and closely associated with Thaksin and the 'Red Shirt' cause. As in 2007, a major party was dissolved and its leadership 'red-carded', so that they could not stand for election within five years. The basis of this decision was electoral irregularities in the previous election of January 2008. Such decisions by the Constitutional Court are in fact easily circumvented: in the case of PPP it was well known that they had another party already set up in anticipation of the Court's decision. The 'nuclear' option of dissolution is in fact counter-productive; it manages to be both drastic and ineffective at the same time. It raises the *political* stakes but does not really *in practice* dissolve parties; it fails the test of legitimacy and spawns extra-constitutional political methods.[64] Nonetheless, it did in this case result in a change in government when sufficient Thaksin-supporting MPs changed sides (within the 60-day period allowed by s 106, see section IV above) as to enable the Democrats to take power under Prime Minister Abhisit Vejjajiva in December 2008.

The new regulatory system under the Organic Law on Political Parties of 2007 made further provision for regulating parties, replacing the equivalent legislation of 1998. A revised procedure is set out for applying to form a political party, and the system is overseen by the Registrar of Political Parties. The overarching principles are that there is freedom of association but parties must have regulations which are consistent with the fundamental principles of a democratic regime of government with the King as Head of the State. If elected, members must perform their duties as members of the House of Representatives. Also, any disciplinary regulations must conform with the right of an accused person to be heard. The ECT is now empowered to veto registration of a political party. The law also regulates the similarity of party names. The party's executive committee is under a duty to operate the party according to the Constitution and the law, 'circumspectly, carefully, and honestly, for the benefit of the country and the people, and must promote democracy in the political party'.[65] Interestingly enough, under a new legal measure,[66] which makes concessions to those aggrieved by the punish-

---

[64] Nonetheless, following referral to the Constitutional Court by the ECT for irregularities, a total of 88 parties in existence in 1997 had been dissolved by 2003. Clearly the dissolution option does serve some purposes.

[65] Organic Law on Political Parties 2007, s 17.

[66] *Ibid*, s 17(4).

ment of all members of the TRT Executive Committee in 2007, members of the executive committee shall not be responsible for party actions if they can prove that they were not involved in the action and objected to it at the meeting of the executive committee or within seven days after the meeting. However, the committee also has a duty to ensure that party members and candidates do not break the law. It is forbidden to bribe anyone (or to be bribed) to become a member of a party.[67] In an attempt to encourage genuinely national parties, it is required that a party have members and branches in all provinces.[68] The law contains many provisions regulating the internal procedures of parties, such as meetings, branches, choosing a leader and candidates, financial accountability, donations, State funding and so on. The most important provisions for present purposes relate to the procedure for dissolution of a political party. This is done by the Registrar with the approval of the ECT, and the Registrar is required to send the case with the evidence to the Prosecutor-General who takes the matter to the Constitutional Court. The applicable grounds under section 93 are, in summary form, that the party does an act: to terminate or contradict the democratic regime with the King as Head of State; or contrary to the law or a regulation or decision of the ECT; or harmful to national security.

From the foregoing it will be clear that there is no lack of law to control electoral malpractice, but the critical aspect is of course the manner of implementation of these regulations, which is principally undertaken by the ECT.

VII. THE ELECTION COMMISSION OF THAILAND

A. Role of the ECT

The ECT was first established in 1992. Its constitutional role was defined under both the 1997 and 2007 Constitutions. Under the latter the ECT as presently constituted is described as one of the 'independent organs under the constitution'. It comprises a President and four associate Commissioners, appointed for a non-renewable term of seven years.[69] The Secretary to the Commission is the administrative head. The

---

[67] *Ibid*, s 22.
[68] *Ibid*, s 27.
[69] TC 2007, s 229.

present Commissioners were all appointed under the 2006 Interim Constitution in September 2006. The responsibilities are divided into central administration, election administration, political party regulation and participation.

In terms of the creation of institutional architecture, the introduction of the ECT has been recognised as a stride towards democratic credibility:

> In order to build a system that allows clean elections to take place, an independent election commission was formed: gone were the days when the administration and supervision of local and general elections were undertaken by the powerful minister of the interior.[70]

B. Selection of Commissioners

In order to appoint the ECT under the 1997 Constitution, a broadly representative selection committee of 10 members needed to be set up.[71] Five qualified and suitable names approved by at least three-quarters of the members of this committee were submitted to the Senate. Also, at this preliminary stage the Supreme Court was required to put forward to the Senate another five names of suitably qualified candidates. The Senate then chose five of the 10 nominees by secret ballot.[72] Their election would then be formally confirmed by the King.[73]

The elaborate selection process under the 1997 Constitution failed to prevent controversy over actual appointments. In particular, under Thaksin's premiership (2001–06) there was evidence that the process was manipulated to produce candidates favouring the Government, thereby neutralising the effectiveness of this key watchdog body.[74] The Senate turned out to be the weak link in terms of political influence. The result was that when ECT vacancies arose in 2001, pressure was

---

[70] S Chantornvong, 'The 1997 Constitution and the Politics of Electoral Reform', in McCargo, above n 20, at 204.

[71] TC 1997, s 138.

[72] *Ibid*, s 138(4).

[73] TC 1997, s 138.

[74] J Jansen, 'Thailand Court Rejects Election Commission Nominees in Latest Ouster Bid', *Jurist Legal News and Research*, Bangkok, 31 May 2006. In its quest to get the Commissioners to resign, the Supreme Court judiciary voted 72:4 in a sitting of the entire Court to reject two nominees.

covertly exerted on Senators to ensure the confirmation of nominees acceptable to the Government, even if they were clearly unsuitable.[75]

By way of contrast, the system for making appointments to the ECT under the 2007 Constitution places greater reliance on the judicial branch, but the selection committee is less inclusive as it is confined to senior judges, judges collectively and holders of political office.[76] As the most trusted of Thailand's institutions, the judiciary and the most senior judges in particular have a finger in many constitutional pies, which now exposes them to political influence.[77] In a departure from the 1997 Constitution, if all or any of the nominations are rejected by the Senate, it is not allowed to insert its own candidates but the matter is referred back to the respective selecting body. If the latter votes unanimously to affirm its original selection, the appointment will be sent for formal royal approval – otherwise the selection process will begin again. Thus the Senate is not now able to express its own preferences but merely to confirm the choices of the selecting bodies.[78]

Election Commissioners were intended to enjoy a high level of security of tenure. Once they are appointed a petition for removal can be filed with the President of the National Assembly for referral to the Constitutional Court for determination, provided it is signed by at least 10 per cent of the existing members of the two houses. The grounds for such a petition are restricted to allegations that the candidate fails to meet the appointment criteria, or that there is a fundamental conflict of interest because the Commissioner is already an official in some other capacity, engages in a profession or holds a commercial position.[79] Under the Organic Law of 2007, the Commissioners are required to

---

[75] Phongpaichit and Baker, above n 45, at 175; V Muntarbhorn, 'Human Rights in the Era of "Thailand Inc"' in R Peerenboom, C Petersen and A Chen (eds), *Human Rights in Asia: A Comparative Legal Study of Twelve Asian Jurisdictions* (London, Routledge, 2006) 327.

[76] V Muntarbhorn, 'Deconstructing Thailand's (New) Eighteenth Constitution' (2009) 12:1 *Thailand Law Journal*, , available at <http://www.thailawforum.com/articles/Thailand-Eighteeth-Consititution.html>.

[77] A Harding and P Leyland, 'The Constitutional Courts of Thailand and Indonesia: Two Case Studies from South East Asia' (2008) 3:2 *Journal of Comparative Law* 118, 142.

[78] See P Leyland, 'Courts and Watchdog Bodies: Appointment Processes Reviewed and Compared' in A Harding and T Bureekul, *Constitutional Reform: Comparative Perspectives*, 2nd edn (Bangkok, KPI, 2008) 378.

[79] TC 2007, ss 233, 207.

declare their assets, including those of their spouses and children, and assets held in the name of others.[80]

The Constitutional Court held (as discussed above) that the results of the elections in April 2006 were invalid, partly on the grounds that the scheduling by the ECT was unconstitutional. This was because the length of the electoral campaign was too short, leaving insufficient time for candidates to prepare.[81] Their exposure to censure was well illustrated when three Commissioners, all appointed during Thaksin's premiership under the 1997 Constitution, were successfully prosecuted and sentenced to four years' imprisonment for dereliction of duty. However, they refused to resign and continued to serve for several weeks.[82] On the day following the military coup of 19 September 2006, five new Election Commissioners were confirmed in office. The judicial profile of the reformed Commission is highly significant. Four of the appointees were former judges of high- to middle-ranking seniority, and the fifth Commissioner was a former official from the Attorney-General's office.

C. Powers and duties of the ECT

The ECT is responsible at both national and local levels for determining constituencies, organising the electoral register, running and overseeing the electoral process, and setting out the rules necessary for the running of elections (and now also referenda), including those relating to the conduct of the election campaigns, party funding and expenses, and also rules relating to, and actual determination of, voters' rights, qualification of candidates, and the counting of votes and disputes concerning the electoral process.[83] It also determines cessation of membership of the National Assembly, and has functions relating to the appointment process for half the members of the Senate and in relation to the registration of political parties.

In performing its many functions the ECT is granted extensive administrative, investigative and quasi-judicial powers. Under the two

---

[80] Section 7.

[81] T Henry, 'Thailand Courts to Supervise New Elections after Constitutional Court Voids Results', *Jurist Legal News and Research*, Bangkok, 9 May 2006.

[82] J Jansen, 'Thailand Election Commissioners get Jail Time for Abuse of Power in April Poll', *Jurist Legal News and Research*, 25 July 2006.

[83] TC 2007, s 236; Organic Act on the Election Commission 2009, s 10.

most recent constitutions it has been fashioned to tackle electoral malpractice, and to this end it is equipped with real teeth.[84] The prospect of heavy punishment for contravention of electoral laws was intended to deter potential perpetrators. Where it finds serious wrongdoing the ECT is empowered to issue a 'red card' banning a candidate from engaging in politics for five years (which effectively rules the person out for two parliamentary terms). An equally formidable power is the ECT's capacity to order an election for any member of the House of Representatives or Senate to be re-run where there is proof of malpractice.[85] However, any such decision requires a motion to be put before the Supreme Court, which must decide whether to ratify the motion for it to come into effect. Furthermore, if it observes improper practices the ECT is able to order a person to refrain from any conduct tending to undermine the integrity of an election. It is also granted far-reaching investigatory powers.[86] It is required to initiate an investigation and inquiry for finding facts in a case where an objection has been lodged, or where there is 'convincing evidence' of an impropriety or any violation of election laws. What constitutes convincing evidence is an obvious hurdle to overcome when there are accusations of vote-buying, because cash changes hands in private and witnesses will be reluctant to come forward.[87] In conducting its affairs and investigations the ECT has the power to summon documents and/or persons before it.[88] Since investigation of financial fraud can involve untold technical complexity, the ECT can recruit the assistance of other agencies such as the National Audit Commission, the Anti-Money Laundering Office and the National Anti-Corruption Commission (NACC) in its investigation of electoral malpractice.[89] It is also assisted by an electoral commission for each *changwat*.

---

[84] TC 2007, ss 236–239 and the 2009 Act deal with the ECT's powers.

[85] Elections have occasionally been run as many as five times. Under the Organic Law of 2009, s 113, re-run elections are now held at the expense of the candidate whose actions caused the election to be re-run.

[86] TC 2007, s 236; Organic Act on the Election of Members of the House of Representatives and Senators 2009, ss 49–50.

[87] The requirement for convincing evidence is problematic if the complainant is expected to have it, since the point of any investigation should be to unearth such evidence.

[88] TC 2007, s 236; Organic Act on the Election Commission 2007, s 26.

[89] *Ibid*, ss 11, 53.

Although the ECT has been granted these formidable powers, it has not been easy to exercise them; this is mainly owing to certain procedures which were intended as safeguards. For example, the Commissioners' decision had to be unanimous before a 'red card' or other penalty could be imposed. Assuming that such a decision was made, before it could take effect the ECT was required to notify a special committee made up of the chairpersons of each committee of the Council of State[90] to confirm the legality of the suspension. In the case of evidence of abuse which was discovered after the result of an election had been announced, the ECT was empowered to nullify the outcome of the election in that constituency (or throughout the region or nation) within 30 days of the election and order a re-run.[91] Under the 2007 Constitution the ECT can suspend the candidate's right to vote and therefore also to stand for election. Also, the candidate could be subjected to prosecution under the criminal code.[92]

In addition to providing State funding for political parties (discussed in section VI above), free and fair elections also required regulation of the expenditure that candidates could devote to their campaigns. The 1997 Constitution did not directly deal with the crucial issue of setting financial limits on election spending. Rather, the organic law empowered the ECT to determine the amount of expenditure per candidate and for each party at elections.[93] It also provided that if these limits were violated the ECT had the power to seize cash and/or property belonging to the perpetrator.[94] However, the 2007 Constitution sets out explicitly as one of the ECT's main duties the control of financial contributions to political parties and the auditing of the accounts of political parties.[95] This addition is not surprising given the opposition from individual MPs and Senators to measures designed to tighten up the organic law when it was amended in 2000.[96]

---

[90] See ch 6, section I.

[91] Organic Act on the Election Commission 2007, s 8. Any such decisions were first subject to scrutiny from senior officials of the Council of State.

[92] TC 2007, s 237; see Organic Act on the Election of Members of the House of Representative and Senators 2007, ch 3.

[93] Organic Act on the Election of Members of the House of Representatives and Senators 1998, ss 40–41.

[94] *Ibid*, s 43.

[95] TC 2007, s 236(3).

[96] Chantornvong, above n 20, at 206.

D. Performance of the ECT

A fully independent electoral body was conceived under the 1997 Constitution as an essential weapon against abuse, and the verdict on the ECT's initial performance in the Senate elections of 2000 and the parliamentary elections of 2001 was positive. As an index of the ECT's 'zero tolerance' approach, in the province of Samut Prakan in the Senate elections of 2000, five elections had to be held before a winner was declared. Many politicians were punished by the ordering of new elections.[97] Unfortunately, opinions were revised when it was clear that in many cases the candidates found by the ECT to have cheated were actually finally elected, indicating that ECT intervention was not necessarily in practice a political setback for such candidates.[98]

It has already been observed that the ECT was placed under a duty to oversee the conduct of elections at local and national level. It is worth stressing again that, under the 1997 Constitution, to minimise the potential for vote-buying, Thai citizens were specifically required to vote and an electoral system partly based on party lists had been adopted.[99] As a result, recent elections have witnessed exceptionally high turnouts, and the party-list method has placed more focus on the party than on the personality of candidates. Secondly, we have seen that the ECT began its work by taking decisive action where it found evidence of abuse. In the senatorial elections held in March 2000, 78 candidates were alleged to have cheated. They were issued with 'red cards' and disqualified; five rounds of elections were run before the Senate was complete. However, at the general election which was held the following year there was evidence of more extensive malpractice. McCargo states that

> widespread challenges to electoral outcomes testified to a new spirit of civic consciousness. Yet vote-buying and electoral manipulation were more rampant than ever, and the credibility of the monitoring agencies such as the Election Commission was greatly undermined in the ensuing furore.[100]

[97] M Connors, 'Framing the People's Constitution', in McCargo, above n 20, at 55. See further, T Bureekul, *Citizen Participation in Politics: the Senate Elections 2000 Case* (Nonthaburi, KPI, 2002).

[98] Cf S Nogsuan, 'Party Elites in the Business of Conglomerate Model of Thai Political Parties' in N Rathamarit (ed), above n 29, at 103; D McCargo and U Pathmanand, above n 48, at 99 ff.

[99] Chantornvong, above n 20, at 211.

[100] McCargo, above n 20, at 17.

It appeared that

> the amount of money used by [TRT] for advertising, persuading politicians
> with local bases to defect from other parties and for buying votes in the run
> up to the election was probably unprecedented.[101]

The TRT Party was offering 300 baht per vote, 100 baht more than any
other party. It beat the opposition by outspending it. In addition, there
were many reports of MPs being offered huge sums to defect to TRT.[102]
After the 2001 General Election 30 candidates were summoned before
the ECT, and there were complaints lodged to it in 312 constituencies.

Nevertheless, it was somewhat ironic that TRT managed to construct
a manifesto that brought together an unlikely alliance of varying factions, including ex-left-wing activists and ex-right-wing thugs. In consequence, the new coalition was often victorious, and so many of the
blatantly corrupt mafia-like incumbent politicians failed to get re-elected
in 2001.[103] After their election MPs were routinely bankrolled by TRT,
receiving up to 200,000 baht per month.[104] It had been suggested that of
the total of 312 sitting MPs investigated by the ECT, as many as 66
would be disqualified. However, when the results of the investigations
were announced in January 2002, only two MPs received 'red cards'
resulting in immediate disqualification, while a further 12 received warn-
ings in the form of 'yellow cards'. It has been claimed that the failure to
elect impartial Commissioners clouded the outcome of painstaking
investigations.[105] Although the proceedings of the ECT were conducted
in secret and put beyond the reach of freedom of information laws, it
later emerged that the problem had been a failure by the Commissioners
to reach unanimous agreement as required by law. As a result of the
indecision, most of the perpetrators of malpractice escaped any punishment.[106]

---

[101] D McCargo, 'Thailand's 2001 General Elections: Vindicating Reform' in
McCargo (2002), above n 20, at 252. See the discussion of vote buying in S Sangwon
and J Gearing, 'Democracy at a Price: the Dirtiest Election Campaign in 20 Years',
Asiaweek, 1996.

[102] As was pointed out above, section VI, this practice is now unlawful.

[103] G Ungpakorn, 'From Tragedy to Comedy: Political Reform in Thailand'
(2002) 32:2 *Journal of Contemporary Asia* 191, 202ff.

[104] See Chantornvong, above n 71.

[105] W Katerenchuk, 'Thai Politics Monitor: Thai Politics Chronology November
2001–July 2003' in M Nelson (ed), *KPI Yearbook No 2 (2002/03)* (Nonthaburi, KPI,
2004) 510.

[106] *Ibid.*

The overwhelming win by TRT in the January 2005 election, in which Prime Minister Thaksin and his party took 370 of the 500 seats in Parliament, was equally unsatisfactory. It led to concerns over the further erosion of democracy. It was being claimed by the opposition that Thailand was on the path to becoming a one-party State.[107] The collapse of support for the opposition Democratic Party was greatly assisted by Thaksin's control over a substantial section of the media and by blatant vote-buying. It has been estimated that some 10 billion baht (US$260 million) was spent in bribes to voters during the campaign.[108] The performance of the ECT fell a long way short of the previously high expectations.

> Some observers accused the commission of laziness and inefficiency, while others went so far as to imply that the commission was biased in favour of Thai Rak Thai . . . The chairman of Poll Watch Foundation, General Saiyud Kerpol asserted that the election was plagued by violence and intimidation of voters and candidates.[109]

In response to claims of malpractice, there was very little evidence of positive intervention in the form of full investigations followed by firm action to eliminate continuing abuse. The degree of exasperation felt by many observers at the ECT's perceived impotence was encapsulated in an article published in *The Nation* (Bangkok):

> Following its final ruling on malpractice at the February 2005 polls, a monument should be erected in memory of the Election Commission. The monument might show a man with a stack of money in one hand, a gun in the other and a big smile on his face.[110]

Controversy continued to surround the ECT. As was discussed in section VI above, its decision to allow the election, which was held on 2 April 2006, to proceed was challenged in the courts. During the election itself, there were, once again, many allegations that votes were being bought on a widespread basis. The ECT failed to uphold objections to

---

[107] 'An Occasional Democrat', Editorial, *Guardian*, 8 February 2005.

[108] K Bowie, 'Vote-buying and Village Outrage in an Election in Northern Thailand: Recent Legal Reforms in Historical Context' (2008) 67:2 *Journal of Asian Studies* 469.

[109] W Katerenchuk, 'Thai Politics 2005: a Year in Review' in Rathamarit, above n 29, at 206.

[110] 'Two Fingers from the Election Commission', *The Nation*, Bangkok, 19 September 2005.

the results, and the King's intervention was required before the Constitutional Court eventually held the election invalid, having initially confirmed individual results which had been called into question. Further investigation of the conduct of the political parties (TRT and the Democratic Parties) in the elections of 2 April 2006 was expedited by the military government after the September 2006 coup. Although the complaint had originally been made to the ECT under the 1997 Constitution, the Constitutional Tribunal heard the resulting electoral fraud trial and disqualified former Prime Minister Thaksin and 110 TRT officials.[111] In addition, there was considerable criticism following the failure of the ECT to disqualify senatorial election candidates for having suspected party affiliations[112] and for the ECT's failure to prevent vote-buying in those elections.[113] In July 2006, three Election Commissioners were sentenced to four years' imprisonment for mishandling the elections.[114]

Further elections were held in December 2007, resulting in the now familiar scenario of a victory for the party supporting Thaksin amid widespread allegations of vote-buying. The ECT investigated 83 candidates for electoral fraud, and six candidates were handed 'red cards'. Three rounds of by-elections were held as a result of ECT intervention. Electoral fraud findings also led to the dissolution of the PPP in December 2008, and to the disqualification of the Speaker of the House of Representatives in February 2008.[115] It was then the turn of the Democrat Party to be investigated in respect of allegedly illegal donations.[116] The local elections of September 2009 also evidenced 'rampant' vote-buying according to the ECT itself, with votes being bought for 100–500 baht, or 2,000 baht in tightly-fought districts.[117]

---

[111]   See above, Section VI.

[112]   'Democrats Mull Suit against EC', *The Nation*, Bangkok, 7 April 2006.

[113]   'EC's Conduct Panned as "Inefficient, Incompetent"', *The Nation*, Bangkok, 20 April 2006; 'Major Party is "Buying" Likely Vote Winner', *The Nation*, Bangkok, 9 April 2006.

[114]   'Thai Court Convicts 3 for Election Missteps', *International Herald Tribune*, 26 July 2006. The main charge was allowing unqualified candidates to run. The three were also disqualified from politics for 10 years as well as losing the right to vote.

[115]   'Three Coalition Parties Bite the Dust', *The Nation*, 3 December 2008.

[116]   'EC Extends Democrat Funds Probe', *Bangkok Post*, Bangkok, 25 August 2009. Thirteen Democrat MPs lost their seats in Parliament as a result of ECT findings in July 2009: see <http://www.thaindian.com/newsportal/politics/thai-election-commission-disqualifies-13-lawmakers_100218870.html>.

[117]   *The Nation*, Bangkok, 7 September 2009. One candidate was said to have borrowed 500,000 baht from a loan shark.

Clearly, in spite of all the constitutional engineering, little has changed in the field of electoral malpractice.

VIII. THE NATIONAL ASSEMBLY: PROCEDURE AND POWERS

Thus far we have been concerned with the institutional structures, the actual composition of the two houses, and how these have changed over time. But how effective is the National Assembly in fulfilling the purpose originally envisaged of checking Executive power, policy and decision-making, and legislative agendas?

Political science and legal analyses have focused heavily on the politics of constitutional change, and on the oscillation between parliamentary and military rule since 1932. It is tempting to imagine that parliaments and senates have been replaced or marginalised from time to time by structures of authoritarian government because they have been ineffective. It is probably on the whole true that the political process within the legislative branch has been 'lacklustre' and that

> those in power [are] confident of their majority; those in opposition [know]
> their limitations and [wait] for an opportunity to open a no-confidence
> debate against ministers rather than giving weight to debate during legisla-
> tive sessions.[118]

However, this conclusion ignores the fact that the legislature, when actually functioning, has sometimes in fact shown clear signs of independence of the Government. For example, during the period 1968–71 Parliament often criticised the Government, delayed the passing of budgets and bills, and demanded more powers to control the Government. It was for this very reason that a coup was mounted by Thanom in 1971 and the entire political process suppressed. This in turn led to the democracy movement of 1973–76 and the uncertain lurch towards parliamentary government during the following decades. Coups are thus sometimes a sign of Parliament's independence rather than of its subservience. The real weakness of Parliament has rather

---

[118] L Dhiravegin, 'The Constitution – Political and Executive Reform', available at <http://www.kpi2.org/kpien/dmdocuments/RR_Reform.doc> (2003), at 12; see further, J Rüland, M Nelson, P Ziegenhain and C Jürgenmeyer, 'The Legislatures of Thailand, the Philippines, and Indonesia: Towards Greater Inclusiveness' in *KPI Yearbook No 2 (2002/3)* (King Prajadhipok's Institute, Nonthaburi, 2004) ch 2, 31, 45.

been in its failure in general to sustain a government in power for an extended period. To continue with the example of the turbulent 1970s, elections in 1975 and 1976 produced no clear result. Parliament expressed no confidence in the Democratic Party following the 1975 election, Prime Minister (PM) Kukrit Pramoj taking power for a few months leading a coalition of 16 parties; following the April 1976 election the Democrats under PM Seni Pramoj took power briefly with a highly fractious coalition of three parties; inevitably, in circumstances of extreme instability, a coup unseated this government the following October after the PM had resigned and then been reinstated a day later.

The actual performance of the National Assembly has therefore reflected the circumstances in which it has operated. During periods of genuinely representative, parliamentary government it has had a more political and less military membership, and has engaged in more extensive debates. In more authoritarian times members with a military background have predominated, and Parliament has acted as a rubber stamp to legitimise (when that was even considered necessary) and support without providing a real opportunity to criticise.[119] The period 1997–2000 probably represents the high-water mark of the National Assembly. During this period no fewer than 295 bills were passed, which included major new economic laws to deal with the economic crisis of 1997–98,[120] laws embodying social programs such as education, and organic laws to implement the 1997 Constitution and also decentralise government.

Under the present constitutional configuration the National Assembly is required to have at least one ordinary session and one legislative session in each year, and the former must be of at least 120 days' duration.[121] In some circumstances the two houses may sit together. However, when Parliament stands dissolved, the Senate may not meet except to fulfil its duties in relation to appointments. Sessions of Parliament are convoked, prolonged or prorogued by royal decree. The power of dissolution in the middle of a four-year parliamentary term lies with the King,[122] but may be exercised only 'once under the same circumstances'.

---

[119] Eg, Parliament had 62% military membership in 1972–73, but only 8% in 1973–74: Bunbongkarn, above n 44, at 65.

[120] Indeed a lack of effective representative structures has been blamed for contributing to the crisis: McCargo, above n 20, at 6.

[121] TC 2007 s 127. For provisions on legislative procedure discussed here, see ss 127–149; 163, 152–155, 170, 302.

[122] TC 2007, s 108, here acting on government advice.

The enactment of legislation is naturally the most important function of the National Assembly and may be done only by it; royal assent is also required. The Constitution prescribes different types of legislation (ordinary bills, organic bills, money bills and State administration bills). The legislative procedure differs somewhat according to which type of legislation is involved, although a requirement of three readings of a bill and its passing by a majority of both houses, followed by the royal assent and publication in the Gazette, are universal requirements, subject only to Parliament's power to affirm a bill which has not been passed, or has been amended, in the Senate. A bill also has to be introduced first in the House of Representatives, and the public must have convenient access to the bill. In some circumstances the two houses may sit jointly. In the following account of the different types of legislation, all bills should be seen as subject to the same procedure as for ordinary bills, except where otherwise stated.

A. Ordinary bills

Ordinary bills may only be introduced by the Government, 20 MPs or an independent agency where the bill concerns the administration of the agency. However, a unique feature of Thai legislative procedure is the provision for direct public participation in legislation. Under the 1997 Constitution, provision was made for 50,000 electors to submit a petition to the National Assembly requesting consideration of a bill which was attached to the petition; such bill had to relate to fundamental rights or directive principles of fundamental State policy. Although some use was made of this provision,[123] the collecting of 50,000 signatures proved a very onerous requirement, and the 2007 Constitution has made this public-participation process somewhat easier to negotiate in three respects. First, only 10,000 signatures are now required; secondly, the National Assembly must facilitate representatives of the petitioners to state the principles of the bill; and, thirdly, not less than one-third of the members of the committee considering the bill must consist of such representatives. Furthermore, there is a general right of both houses to

---

[123] An example of a law based on popular petition is the Community Forest Bill 2007, which although passed by the National Assembly did not however become law due to a successful challenge in the Constitutional Court (November 2008).

select and appoint standing committees (see section IX below) and *ad hoc* committees for the consideration of bills and consultation in connection thereto, *ad hoc* committees being normal for bills in the House of Representatives; and there is provision for the House of Representatives in considering a bill concerned with children, youth, women, the elderly, the disabled or handicapped, to appoint a non-standing committee including representatives of relevant private organisations (not less than one-third of the total, which also has to comprise equal numbers of men and women).[124]

Bills then proceed to the Senate, which must finish consideration of the bill within 60 days, although this period can be extended by the Senate for a further 30 days. If the Senate approves the bill it proceeds to royal assent; but if not then the bill is withheld and returned to Parliament, with or without amendment. If an amended bill is then approved by Parliament, it proceeds to royal assent; but if not, each House appoints an equal number of persons to constitute a joint committee (the number of members is decided by Parliament and these members may include non-members of the National Assembly). The joint committee considers the bill and reports to both Houses. If both houses then approve the bill it proceeds to royal assent; otherwise the bill is withheld. Withholding a bill after amendment or after a joint committee report means that the bill is returned to Parliament and may be reconsidered there no sooner than 180 days after it is returned: meanwhile no similar bill can be introduced. In such cases, if Parliament resolves to reaffirm the bill by the votes of more than half of the total number of MPs, the bill is deemed to have been approved by the National Assembly and proceeds to royal assent. In other words, in the final analysis the Senate can delay but not ultimately block legislation upon which Parliament insists.[125] This position, which is somewhat similar to that in other bicameral legislatures such as that of the UK, is desirable in that it prevents a constitutional impasse. This is particularly important considering the very different qualifications and appointment systems for the two houses as discussed above.

The royal assent is not a pure formality, and here the Thai notion of constitutional monarchy diverges slightly from the European precedents that have influenced its direction. When a bill is approved by the

---

[124] TC 2007, ss 135 and 152.
[125] TC 2007, ss 146–149.

National Assembly, the Prime Minister must present it to the King for his signature within 20 days, and the bill comes into force as an Act when it is published in the Government Gazette. However, if the royal assent is refused by the King returning the bill to the National Assembly, or if he simply fails to return it within 90 days, the National Assembly must reconsider it. If it resolves to reaffirm the bill by the votes of at least two-thirds of the total number of members of both houses then the Prime Minister presents the bill to the King for signature once again. If the King this time does not sign and return the bill within 30 days, it becomes law anyway by publication in the Gazette. This provision is similar to a procedure adopted in Malaysia at the federal level in 1984 (which was actually copied from Thai law) and is designed to acknowledge a legislative role for the King without giving him the power to block legislation upon which the National Assembly insists. This compromise seems uncontroversial, since it has never in fact been invoked by the King.

Following the introduction of the Constitutional Court in 1998, the Constitution offers a window for constitutional challenge both to legislation before it is submitted for royal assent and to draft rules of procedure made by the National Assembly or either house. This procedure can be invoked by one-tenth of the total number of members of both houses, or by the Prime Minister, on the grounds that the provisions or enactment of the bill are unconstitutional. If the Constitutional Court decides that the ground is made out, and that unconstitutional provisions of the bill form the essential element thereof, the bill lapses; if they are not essential then the provisions lapse but the bill itself proceeds to royal assent.[126]

B. Organic law bills

Organic law bills relating to elections, political parties and the independent agencies are mandated by the Constitution.[127] This requirement was introduced by the 1997 Constitution, which also prescribed time limits

---

[126] TC 2007, ss 154–155.

[127] See TC 2007, ss 138 and 302. Note that 'organic' laws are fundamental laws required by the Constitution in respect of certain matters (eg Election Commission, political parties, procedure of the Constitutional Court), which are passed by Parliament following a special procedure.

for the passing of such laws (two years in most cases). By this means the National Assembly was given a crucial role in the implementation of the 1997 Constitution. Impressively, the timetable was fulfilled, and this achievement also made compliance with the similar requirement under the 2007 Constitution comparatively simple, in that the organic laws were not rescinded by the abrogation of the 1997 Constitution and were in fact specifically continued in force under section 302. However, the independent agencies in question were required by the same provision to take action within one year (which was done) to secure, by organic law bills, compliance with the 2007 Constitution. However, organic law bills can be introduced only by the Government, by one-tenth of the number of MPs or members of both houses, or by the independent agency to which the organic law relates.[128]

The main difference from ordinary legislation is that such bills are subject to a limit of 120 days in Parliament, and 90 days in the Senate, for their consideration, and they must be passed by at least one-half of the total membership of each house. They are also subject to the requirement of scrutiny by the Constitutional Court, which examines them for their consistency with the Constitution during a prescribed 30-day period before the bill can be presented for the royal assent.[129] In the event that the Constitutional Court finds that provisions of the organic law are constitutionally invalid they will lapse; and if they are essential to the law itself, the entire law will lapse. In the former case the bill is returned to the National Assembly for amendment.

C. Money bills[130]

Money bills can be introduced only with the endorsement of the Prime Minister; they are defined as relating to State funds generally, taxes, estimates, loans and currency. The procedure is similar to that for ordinary bills, but money bills must be considered by the Senate within 30 days as opposed to 60 days for ordinary bills; and if returned to Parliament they must be reconsidered forthwith. Further special substantive requirements and procedural rules apply to appropriations bills, consideration

---

[128] TC 2007, s 139.
[129] TC 2007, s 141.
[130] See TC 2007, ss 143, 146, 166–169.

of which must be completed by Parliament within 105 days, otherwise the bill is deemed to be approved; and when it reaches the Senate the latter may only approve or disapprove the bill without any amendment and within 20 days, otherwise again the bill is deemed approved.

Interestingly, the Government is obliged to allocate adequate budgets for the autonomous administration of the National Assembly, the Constitutional Court, the Courts of Justice, the Administrative Courts and other 'constitutional organisations' (ie independent watchdog agencies). Thus far provision is similar to that made under the 1997 Constitution, but it now goes further to provide that in the consideration of the expenditure estimates of the above bodies, if any of these is of the opinion that the allocated budget is insufficient, it shall submit a motion directly to the finance committee, thus by-passing the Government. This enhances the constitutional position of the independent agencies.

D. State administration bills

The category of State administration bills derives from the enactment of the directive principles of fundamental State policies in the Constitution and the requirement that the Government formulate a plan to fulfil those policies (this will be discussed further in chapter three). The Government is obliged to state before the National Assembly its plan to fulfil the directive principles, and bills specified on that occasion are subject to a slightly more Executive-centred procedure compared to ordinary bills. If the bill fails but is disapproved by the votes of less than half of the total number of MPs, the Government can request a joint sitting of both houses whereby the National Assembly may constitute a committee for considering the bill further, preparing a report on it and submitting the bill to the National Assembly, whereupon the bill proceeds in the usual fashion.[131]

Bills of all kinds lapse when Parliament is dissolved or its term expires; but following an election the new Government may request further consideration of a lapsed bill within 60 days of the first sitting of the National Assembly if the latter approves.

---

[131] TC 2007, s 145.

Before moving on to consider Parliament's oversight function, it is worth emphasising certain features of the process. As well as relying on the lobbying of political parties and politicians to prompt government and individual parliamentarians into producing legislation, the attempt to further facilitate petitioning has sought to formalise wider public participation in the formation of law, even if such provision has been at best marginal in its effect. In regard to legislative procedure, we have seen that bills go through three readings in both houses before receiving the royal assent, which provides sufficient opportunity for the principles to be debated on the floor of each house. In terms of producing quality legislation there is, however, little attention in the Constitution to the routine function of committees in providing clause-by-clause scrutiny before legislation is finally enacted.

IX.   ACCOUNTABILITY OF THE EXECUTIVE BEFORE THE LEGISLATURE

Bringing the Executive to account is the other main analytical function of the National Assembly. Aspects of this topic are dealt with in chapter three; however, some other aspects are worth considering here in the context of the actual operation of Parliament and the political process more generally. Clearly, for example, the role of the parliamentary opposition is a crucial issue in relation to accountability. This is in fact officially recognised under the Constitution in a number of ways. When the Government is appointed the King also appoints as Leader of the Opposition the leader of the political party not holding any positions in the Government and having the largest number of MPs, being not less than one-fifth of the total number of members. If there is no such person then the opposition parties elect the Leader of the Opposition.[132] The office is also recognised constitutionally in other ways. The Leader of the Opposition sits as a member of the major selection committees for independent agencies.[133] He or she is also entitled to a salary prescribed in a royal decree on the same basis as Privy Councillors and other major office-holders.[134] The Constitution further requires the membership of parliamentary standing committees to be in proportion

---

[132]   TC 2007, s 110.
[133]   Eg TC 2007, s 206.
[134]   TC 2007, s 119.

to or in close proportion to the number of MPs of each political party or group of political parties.[135]

Parliamentary committees have been set up corresponding roughly to the various executive ministries. Following a government (not parliamentary) report in 2003, the committees were reduced in number even as the number of ministries was increased. Parliament has 15 and the Senate 13 standing committees. There are several difficulties in opposition and back-bench members and senators holding the Executive to account before these committees. Committees do not have the benefit of expertise to carry out the task effectively; parliamentary time is lacking; there is little opportunity to question senior officials; and corrupt practices are rarely revealed just by the paperwork but involve the need for careful inquiry appropriate to, for example, the National Anti-Corruption Commission. It is not the practice to hold joint committees of parliamentary and senatorial committee members. Moreover, increased effectiveness at the parliamentary level has not resulted in effective control of decentralised powers (see chapter four), there being less parliamentary expertise at the level of local representative bodies.[136] Committees play a modest role in the legislative process, being assessed as 'less visible and noisy' and affording 'limited space for supervision' compared with their regional counterparts,[137] but are of more significance in dealing with specific complaints by citizens against executive agencies.

Coalitions and factional mobility characterise governments in Thailand, and the same is true of the opposition. Parliament does not therefore usually embody a clear political debate conducted between two main parties with a fringe of minor players; rather it embodies an institutional setting in which parties, factions and individual politicians jockey for position in an ever-changing political situation. Since the emergence of TRT in 2000, however, Parliament has more than previously appeared to cater for something resembling a two-party system in which a Thaksin-orientated party and the Democratic Party seek to obtain or retain power. The rules under which this struggle takes place, however, seem far from what the Constitution envisages, and indeed the struggle has taken place mainly in the streets of Bangkok with rival demonstrations and demands

---

[135] TC 2007, s 135.
[136] See <http://www.cdi.anu.edu.au/CDIwebsite_1998-2004/thailand/thailand_downloads/Thai_JCPAA_report.pdf>.
[137] *Ibid* at 68.

occasionally threatening to spill over into violence. In this sense
Parliament, essential as it is, is not the main arena in which inter-party
conflict occurs. It is nonetheless undeniable that the Legislature, despite
all the political difficulties and constitutional manipulations of the mil-
lennial decade, has produced a large quantity of useful legislation, and in
many respects does in fact function as a legislature should.

The constitution-makers have indeed devoted much attention to role
of the Legislature in the general scheme of accountability and the balancing of powers. The 1997 Constitution made several innovations in
this area which are discussed below. For the moment we can note that it
was designed to embody a different idea of executive-legislative relations from that seen in previous constitutions in that, once chosen, the
Prime Minister and members of the Government had to resign their
seats in Parliament which were then filled by party-list MPs.[138] This was
not, as it proved, an effective method of providing parliamentary
accountability; indeed it rendered the office of Prime Minister in effect
more presidential than previously, while failing in any way to reduce the
significance of the Government enjoying a parliamentary majority.[139] It
was therefore no great surprise that in the 2007 Constitution the framers moved back to a more orthodox notion (in terms of Thai constitutional history) of parliamentary government. The Prime Minister must
now be and remain an MP; and the notion of ministerial responsibility
along the lines of a parliamentary form of government is clearly indicated in the Constitution, which gives MPs and Senators the power to
'interpellate' ministers on a weekly basis, and this power includes the
power to ambush ministers with questions, of the contents of which no
notice has been given, on any matter which involves an important problem of public concern, affects national or public interest, or requires
urgency.[140] The Senate also has power once in a session to require facts
or explanations from the Government if one-third of Senators submit a
motion to that effect before the Senate. Parliamentary privilege applies
to anything that is said in sessions of the National Assembly.[141]

---

[138] TC 2007 s 118(7), 204.

[139] McCargo and Pathmanand, above n 48, quoting *The Nation* at 121: '[T]he chief
executive has rarely shown up and is remembered only once for giving a brief
response during question time . . . he does not regard himself as being accountable
to the House'.

[140] TC 2007, s 157.

[141] TC 2007, s 130.

Parliament also has power to dismiss the Government by a motion of no-confidence[142] in the Prime Minister.[143] As was explained earlier, this power is controversial in view of the historically low survival rate of Thai governments, to which the no-confidence motion has made a large contribution.[144] There are therefore several restrictions designed to ensure that such motions are not presented frivolously and do not lead to uncertainty or a constitutional impasse. First, the submission of the motion has to be supported by one-fifth of the total membership of the House.[145] Secondly, the motion has to nominate the next Prime Minister. Thirdly, if the motion alleges the Prime Minister's unusual wealth, malfeasance in office or intentional violation of the Constitution or the law, it must be preceded by a petition for the Prime Minister's impeachment (under section 270, for which see below). Fourthly, the vote on the no-confidence motion must not take place on the date on which the debate concludes. Fifthly, the motion can only be carried by more than one-half of the total number of MPs. Sixthly, if the motion fails, the MPs who submitted it may not present another such motion within the same the session. Seventhly, MPs are not bound by party resolutions in relation to matters of confidence.[146] Lastly, a no-confidence motion can be introduced only during an ordinary as opposed to legislative session of Parliament, which usually means on only 120 days in the year.

Members of Parliament have a similar right to present a motion of no confidence in an individual minister.[147] There are some similar restrictions, except that the presentation of the motion has to be supported by one-sixth of the total number of MPs and the motion does not have to name the minister's successor. The debate cannot be avoided

[142] In early signs that the parliamentary system might take in Thailand, governments resigned in 1934 and 1944 following defeat on a major bill. PM Kriangsak Chomanan resigned in 1980 in anticipation of a no-confidence motion after blocking Parliament's reform proposals.

[143] TC 2007, s 158.

[144] The terms of office of 14 PMs have ended due to dissolution of Parliament; and 23 have resigned voluntarily; one was dismissed by Parliament; 8 were ousted by a coup; and two have been dismissed by a decision of the Constitutional Court (both in 2008).

[145] Under the 1997 Constitution this was two-fifths: s 185. The requirement modifies to at least half of the opposition members if their total is fewer in number than one-fifth of the total number of MPs, provided the Government has been in office for two years: s 160.

[146] TC 2007, s 162.

[147] TC 2007, s 159.

by transferring the minister to another portfolio. If the motion is passed, the minister is not under section 159 legally obliged to resign, but the motion may be linked with removal from office (see below) and his or her position will at the least become politically untenable. It has been commented that in view of the unsuccessful opposition attempt to unseat nine ministers by this means in 2003,

> the 'weapon' of a no-confidence motion may have been 'rationalized' to such a degree that it has become practically ineffective as a tool the legislature can use for holding the executive accountable.[148]

In spite of the fact that the Constitution embodies parliamentary rather than presidential-style government, there are also provisions for impeachment of the Prime Minister, and indeed other officials too,[149] which were introduced by the 1997 Constitution as a measure to deal with major instances of corruption and abuse of power. Here it is the Senate that has the all-important power of dismissal. Impeachment applies to the Prime Minister, ministers, MPs, Senators, judges (including Constitutional Court Justices), prosecutors, Election Commissioners, ombudsmen, State Audit Commissioners and high-ranking public officials. The grounds are

> being under the circumstance of unusual wealth indicative of the commission of corruption, malfeasance in office, malfeasance in judicial office, or an intentional exercise of power contrary to the provisions of the constitution or law, or serious violation of or failure to comply with ethical standards.[150]

The procedure can be invoked by one-fourth of the total number of MPs, 20,000 voters (a further example of the implementation of the principle of public participation) or one-fourth of the members of the Senate in the case of allegations against a Senator.[151] The procedure requires investigation by National Anti-Corruption Commission (NACC), which prepares a report submitted to the Senate, clearly stating its verdict on the matter. If the NACC passes a resolution by the votes of not less than one-half of the total number of the Commissioners that a prima facie case is made out, the accused person is automatically suspended and the matter is passed to the Prosecutor-General for insti-

---

[148]   Rüland *et al*, above n 118, at 46.
[149]   TC 2007, ss 270–274.
[150]   TC 2007, s 270.
[151]   TC 2007, ss 164 and 271.

tuting prosecution in the Supreme Court of Justice's Criminal Division for Persons Holding Political Positions. The matter is also considered by the Senate,[152] which may remove the person from office by a vote of three-fifths of its total membership. The person may not hold any political position or serve in the government service for five years thereafter.

X. BICAMERALISM AND THE SENATE

As is indicated in chapter one, the Senate has featured much more in Thailand's democratic constitutions than in its 'administrative charters',[153] and therefore in Thai thinking it is inextricably identified with democratic institutions, in spite of the fact that elections did not feature in the actual composition of the Senate until 2000. It seems extremely unlikely that the Senate would now ever be actually abolished on a permanent footing, but after the problems with political capture of a notionally independent body under the 1997 Constitution the challenge for the drafters of the 2007 Constitution was to produce a more independent body as a counter-balance to the strongly partisan and factional House of Representatives. The Senate as presently composed remains one of the most contested aspects of the present Constitution. Any further reform should be viewed against the background of a strong regional dimension to the current conflict between the 'Red Shirt' movement, based in the north and north east, and the 'Yellow Shirt' movement, strong in Bangkok and the south, coupled with the Islamic problem in the deep south. For what would be a legitimate objective of strong bicameralism to be realised, and to escape from accusations of cronyism, a constitutional amendment might be considered that would allow for a fully-elected Senate on a strongly regional basis for a term of years different from MPs, and this would of course need to be linked to a wider regional devolution of power. For all that, the question remains, in Thailand as elsewhere, what precise function is envisaged for the upper house and how it assists democracy. It has, after all, been entirely elected on only two occasions (in 2000 and 2006, under

---

[152] TC 2007, ss 273–274.

[153] Chambers, above n 15, at 5, writes that as of 2009 Thailand had experienced 36 years of bicameralism and 41 years of unicameralism.

the provisions of the 1997 Constitution, and the 2006 Senate never actually met[154]), and has generally consisted of elder statesmen and even members or former members of the military,[155] who have invariably remain Senators for six years: indeed the Senate has often, even during more democratic times, been the locus of military or royalist power, or for those who opposed a particular constitution and had to be appeased. Moreover, it has powers that may be used to thwart or delay the will of the elected parliamentary majority. This uncertainty has led to many changes relating to the Senate, even as Parliament itself remained a stable entity. Chambers identifies no less than eight different constitutional configurations among the 11 Senates formed since the institution was first introduced in 1946.[156]

The 1997 Constitution introduced fundamental changes in the nature and function of the Senate. Its composition was fundamentally altered so that it became a 'civil-society house' rather than an 'elder-statesman house' (it has since reverted to something between these two poles). It was also – crucially in the scheme of the 1997 Constitution – endowed with significant powers relating to the independent 'watchdog' agencies and impeachments, going far beyond its more traditional roles relating to scrutiny of bills and government performance, the royal succession and foreign relations. Although in some respects these powers are reduced under the 2007 Constitution, the 1997 Constitution's Ginsburgian 'afterlife'[157] is still apparent in the Senate retaining independence and powers over 'watchdog' appointments.[158]

The electoral system prescribed by the 1997 Constitution, which made it effectively impossible for candidates to campaign, thereby conferred electoral advantage on those candidates with prominent names and reputations. This proved the undoing of the Senate of 2000: power-

---

[154] This was due to difficulties completing the electoral process, for which see above, section VI. However, the elections resulted in interesting results: the number of female senators more than doubled, to about 23%; the number of military and police members reduced to zero; but Thaksin supporters were in a clear majority. Chambers, above n 15, 17–18.

[155] Currently five of the 14 appointed members from the government sector, and an estimated 23 of the entire Senate membership, have military backgrounds – still far fewer than in previous decades: Chambers, *ibid*, at 10, 27, 30.

[156] *Ibid*, at 7ff.

[157] T Ginsburg, 'Constitutional Afterlife: the Continuing Impact of Thailand's Postpolitical Constitution' (2009) 7(1) *International Journal of Constitutional Law* 83.

[158] See s 121. And chapter 1, section VI.

ful local elites were able to get elected because they were already well-known, or by substituting family members where they themselves were disqualified from standing. In the result the 'non-political senate' was actually easily identifiable before long as 'political' to the extent of about 75 per cent of its membership.[159]

The Senate of 2000, during its first three or four years before it was progressively 'Thaksinised', had nonetheless evinced a clear intention of using its powers to expose corruption and abuse of power. For example, it elected a controversial no-nonsense figure, Jaruwan Maintaka, as Auditor-General,[160] rejected the process for selecting the members of the National Telecommunications Commission, and accepted a petition from the Thai Journalists' Association alleging that Thaksin's Government had abused press freedom and the powers of the Anti-Money Laundering Office (AMLO) to harass journalists who were critical of the Government. Thereafter it was subject to executive interference, and played a far less important role in scrutiny of legislation and calling government to account, although committee investigations had proved quite useful. This experience indicates that far from being an unnecessary appendage to the legislative process, the Senate is potentially the house where the independence of the Legislature is felt.

XI. CONCLUSION

Since the inauguration of constitutional government and democratic elections with the overthrow of the absolute monarchy in 1932, Thailand's electoral politics have been tainted by corruption; the reputation of politicians, and therefore of Parliament and political parties, has thus deteriorated.[161] Due to this and other causes discussed in this book, Thailand has suffered grievously from political instability, so much so that constitutional innovation has been regarded as a form of crisis management rather than as a secure basis for reform.[162] For this reason, as with other aspects of the constitutional arrangements, there have been many difficulties, and many experiments with varied outcomes,

---

[159] Chambers, above n 15, at 12.

[160] For the full story of this matter, see chapter 5, section IX (E).

[161] One index of this is that MPs were excluded from the constitution-making processes of both 1997 and 2007.

[162] Kuhonta, above n 99; Ginsburg, above, n 157.

with regard to the configuration of the National Assembly and its support mechanisms such as the electoral system, policed by the ECT, and the various selection committees.

In spite of this instability, experimentation is better than rigidity, and can of course lead eventually to reasonably stable solutions to persistent problems. The military coups of 1991 and 2006 have not led to the demise of democratic institutions; on the contrary, they have been an aspect of the many changes in the last two decades which cumulatively have led to a more rather than less democratic National Assembly in terms of representation and accountability. At the same time it seems apparent that attempts to regulate electoral malpractice out of existence are doomed to failure, at least until such time as the political economy and legal culture of Thailand change dramatically. In this sense the resolution of the problem of electoral fairness is a function of the resolution of the large political problem that now confronts the country, which would appear to require some kind of a political rapprochement between what has for the moment polarised into two sides and agreement to proceed strictly according to agreed rules, particularly electoral rules, to be observed to the letter. Glancing towards the future, on the one hand, a bicameral legislature but with an elected upper house might seem to offer the best way forward in terms of the main arena for political process. On the other hand, a more stable resolution of Thailand's political problems might require agreement on the reconfiguration of a bicameral National Assembly to allow genuine representation for all of Thailand's sectors (political parties, monarchy, military, civil society, bureaucratic, professional, business, agricultural).

FURTHER READING

P Chambers, 'Superfluous, Mischievous or Emancipating? Thailand's Evolving Senate Today' (2009) 28:3 *Journal of Current Southeast Asian Affairs* 3.

S Chantornvong, 'The 1997 Constitution and the Politics of Electoral Reform' in D McCargo (ed), *Reforming Thai Politics* (Copenhagen, NIAS Publishing, 2002).

L Dhiravegin, *Wiwatthanakan Kanmu'ang Kanpokkhrong Thai* [Evolution of Thai Politics] 10th edn (Bangkok, Thammasat University Press, 2007) [in Thai].

N Eoseewong, *Rakya Sang Ban, Chonchan Klang Sang Mu'ang* [The Grassroots Build the Houses, the Middle Class Builds the Town] (Bangkok, Matichon, 2009) [in Thai].

F Ferrara, *Thailand Unhinged* (Jakarta, Equinox Publishing, 2010).

A Harding and P Leyland, 'Constitutional Design in Thailand: the Management of Electoral Process in an Emergent Democracy' (2010) 4(2) *The Journal of Parliamentary and Political Law* 299.

A Laothamatas, 'A Tale of Two Democracies: Conflicting Perceptions of Elections and Democracy in Thailand' in R Taylor (ed), *The Politics of Elections in South East Asia* (New York, Cambridge University Press, 1996).

—— *Song Nakkhara Prachathippatai* [The Two Democracies in Thailand] 6th edn (Bangkok, Khopfai, 2007) [in Thai].

P Phongpaichit and C Baker, *Thaksin: the Business of Politics in Thailand* (Chiang Mai, Silkworm Books, 2004).

N Rathamarit (ed), *Eyes on Democracy: National and Local Issues* (Nonthaburi, KPI, 2006).

J Rüland, M Nelson, P Ziegenhain, C Jürgenmeyer, 'The Legislatures of Thailand, the Philippines, and Indonesia' in M Nelson (ed), *Thai Politics: Global and Local Perspectives, KPI Yearbook No 2* (2002/03) (Nonthaburi, KPI, 2004).

N Setabutr, *Prasitthiphon Khong Ratthasapha Thai : Raingan Kanwichai Chabap Sombun* [Efficiency of the Thai Parliament] (Nonthaburi, King Prajadhipok's Institute, 2004) [in Thai].

X Somsakdi (ed), *Government and Politics of Thailand* (Singapore, Oxford University Press, 1987).

B Uwanno, *Botbat Læ Amnat Nathi Khong Wutthi Sapha Tam Ratthathammanun Hæng Ratchaanachak Thai, Pho So 2540* [Function and Power of the Senate in the 1997 Constitution] (Nonthaburi, King Prajadhipok's Institute, 2000) [in Thai].

3

The Executive Branch of Government

⬤

Introduction – The Formation and Succession of Government –
Parliamentary Scrutiny of the Executive – Directive Principles as
a Constraint on Government – Thailand's Civil Service –
Accountability and Thailand's Contracting State – Freedom of
Information – Anti-Corruption Strategies and the Civil Service –
The Throne and Armed Forces – Emergency Powers – Conclusion

I. INTRODUCTION

IN THIS CHAPTER we seek to accomplish two related tasks.
The first is to set out a picture of how Thailand is governed. We do
so by providing a survey of the institutional morphology of the
State to see how power is exercised. The second is to consider the many
constraints placed on the exercise of executive power that have been
introduced to ensure respect for the rule of law and to facilitate
conditions of good governance. The initial concern will be to outline the
effect of the constitutional provisions that deal with the formal position
relating to the formation and succession of governments, and then to
review the ways in which the Government is made directly accountable
to Parliament through a set of guiding principles that are intended to
underpin the policy-making process.

The second part of the chapter assesses the character of the civil
service by taking account of the history of its formation and then more
recent developments, including attempts to introduce new public management ideas to improve bureaucratic performance.[1] However, any

---

[1] See, eg, D Osborne and T Gaebler, *Reinventing Government* (New York, Addison
Wesley, 1992); C Hood, 'A Public Management for All Seasons' (1991) 69 *Public
Administration* 3.

assessment of the current role of the civil service in delivering policy must take account of the prevailing conditions of governance in Thailand, including the changing role of government and civil service as part of a 'contracting State'. Increasingly in Thailand, as in many other nations, both central and local government rely upon the private sector for policy delivery, and contracting becomes the primary method for controlling this method of delivery.

Having elaborated the fundamental structure of the executive branch of government earlier in the chapter, our attention turns to issues directly related to the promotion of constitutionalism as defined and discussed in chapter one. The remainder concentrates on the constitutional and legal provisions that have been introduced as mechanisms to eliminate corruption and to correct other forms of abuse and injustice. It will soon be clear that there has been a deliberate attempt to use the Constitution, related laws and codes of practice as a vehicle for inculcating ethical standards applicable to politicians and officials at every level. This effort has been supported by the introduction, under the 1997 Constitution, of a new set of watchdog bodies and courts (discussed in more detail in chapters 5 and 6).

II. THE FORMATION AND SUCCESSION OF GOVERNMENTS

In Thailand a government will normally be formed following an election. The House of Representatives must approve a suitable person within 30 days,[2] but the Constitution requires the King formally to appoint the Prime Minister (PM) and not more than 35 other ministers, constituting the Council of Ministers.[3] These ministers are chosen by the PM (once chosen) to head the ministries and departments. Appointment is subject to the requirement that all ministers must be university graduates without a criminal conviction and over 35 years of age. The stipulation in the Constitution[4] that the PM must be a member of the House of Representatives incorporates an important aspect of the 'Westminster' constitutional model. The device of the no-confidence motion[5] can be used to bring down the Government, but a

---

[2] TC 2007, s 172.
[3] TC 2007, s 171.
[4] TC 2007, s 171.
[5] For more details on the problem of no confidence motions, see ch 2, section IX.

no-confidence motion in the House of Representatives or the Senate can equally be filed against an individual minister.[6]

Contrary to most parliamentary systems of government, there is no requirement in Thailand that all ministers must be MPs: at the time of writing only 15 of the 35 ordinary Council members were MPs. Nonetheless, all Council members have the right to attend Parliament and, crucially, the PM and his or her government must continue to enjoy the support of Parliament.[7] In a wider sense the PM is accountable to Parliament for the policies introduced by the Government. Members of Parliament and Senators are entitled to question ministers concerning any matter that falls under their responsibility.[8] As might be expected in a constitutional monarchy, ministers can be dismissed by the King on the advice of the PM. This measure provides scope for ministerial reshuffling, which is a relatively common occurrence in Thailand. While the PM retains key powers, including acting as chair of cabinet meetings and the right to appoint and dismiss ministers, the 2007 Constitution introduced significant restraints on any PM in order to prevent an office holder assuming the dominance of Thaksin.[9] Not only is the office holder restricted to serving for eight years (a maximum of two terms), but also a no-confidence motion against the PM can be proposed by one-fifth of the members of the lower house.[10] Moreover, a PM is now expressly forbidden from having any commercial interests that might conflict with his official position.[11]

Any assessment as to whether the devices of accountability motions and questions operate as effective checks on the Government must take into consideration the extent to which MPs receive regular payment from their party leadership. Phongpaichit and Baker note that:

> In December 2003, party sources leaked that allowances paid to TRT MPs were being raised from 50,000 ($1600) to 200,000 ($6400) baht per month

---

[6] TC 2007, s 182.

[7] TC 2007, s 172 requires that the PM must be nominated by one-fifth of the votes in the House of Representatives and approved by one-half of the votes by open ballot.

[8] TC 2007, s 156; and see chapter 2, particularly section IX.

[9] V Muntarbhorn, 'Deconstructing Thailand's (New) Eighteenth Constitution', *Thailand Law Journal* 2009, Spring Issue 1, vol 20.

[10] TC 2007, ss 171 and 172.

[11] TC 2007, s 269 (something equivalent to a blind trust is proposed to deal with this eventuality).

with a bonus of 800,000 ($25000) baht for festivities during New Year and Songkran.[12]

This personal sponsorship by the party leadership calls into question whether individual MPs are capable of expressing a relatively independent, critical view of the matter in hand.[13] Moreover, the observation of recent events in Thailand discussed in chapters one and two, which permitted a change of government in late 2008 without an election, highlights the limited role of Parliament as a genuine forum for political debate, and raises the question whether the confidence requirement operates as part of a popular democratic process as envisaged by the framers of the 1997 and 2007 Constitutions.

III. PARLIAMENTARY SCRUTINY OF THE EXECUTIVE

As we observed in chapter two, the Constitution provides for parliamentary oversight of the Executive. To this end there are procedures within Parliament for questioning ministers and officials responsible for implementing government policy either before the whole elected chamber and/or before specialist committees. In other words, this system has been designed around parliamentary models of liberal democracy, where there is an assumption that governments are elected on the basis of a policy manifesto, for example, in the sense of making the economic and political system more welfare-based or more market-based. In an important sense there may be a lack of fit with these provisions. The problem arises because there is a virtual absence of ideology underpinning Thai politics, and this makes it difficult to apply scrutiny procedures designed to assess whether government policy is being pursued in line with declared objectives associated with manifesto commitments.

Moreover, it has been argued that the Thai case is distinct because of the relationship between the electoral process and the distribution of government posts.[14] Virtually all political systems based on elections, including Thailand, require a mechanism for the conferment of high

---

[12] P Phongpaichit and C Baker, *Thaksin* (Chiang Mai, Silkworm Books, 2009) 192.

[13] *Ibid*, 307.

[14] D McCargo and U Pathmanand, *The Thaksinization of Thailand* (Copenhagen, NIAS, 2005) 73.

office to the main movers and shakers of the victorious party or parties. However, it should be recognised that the approach to appointing ministers in Thailand has been heavily influenced by the benefits that the PM or any other minister might enjoy personally as a result of that particular government office. Party leaders who deliver the most MPs to the party or coalition will be the most handsomely rewarded. For example Ockey, reviewing the 1995 election, observed that:

> Chart Thai like other provincially-based parties relied on powerful local fig-
> ures for its electoral organization and most of its finances. When the party
> became core of the new government, these local figures sought their reward,
> particularly in the form of posts in the Cabinet.[15]

Ministries are rated by politicians not only according to size, but also according to whether they allow wide discretionary powers to be exercised in key policy areas, and whether they might allow bidding on projects by companies owned by the minister directly, or by his or her relatives or friends, and generally for their ability to generate extra income for the minister.[16] Such a culture of political power obviously has important implications for parliamentary scrutiny of the Executive, the point being that the political game is not normally about achieving a set policy vision but rather about obtaining political office at the highest possible level. The attainment of power is often regarded as a means for achieving a position to gain not only status and influence, but also financial enrichment for the office holder, his family and friends.

This tendency profoundly shapes political attitudes:

> [W]hen the Thai elite talked about undemocratic regimes or systems, what
> was meant most of the time was a rule or system that favoured their political
> opponents and, by inference, posed a serious disadvantage to their own
> political agenda.[17]

That political agenda is of course defined in terms of their own narrow self-interest. The upshot is a system dominated by what are described by

---

[15] J Ockey, 'Thailand: The Crafting of Democracy' (1997) *South East Asia Affairs* 302.

[16] B Bowornwathana, 'Thailand: Bureaucracy under Coalition Governments' in J Burns and B Bowornwathana, *Civil Service Systems in Asia* (Cheltenham, Edward Elgar, 2002) 291.

[17] K Suwannathat-Pian, *Kings, Country and Constitutions* (London, Routledge, 2004) 7.

the same commentator as 'greedy, self-centred and unscrupulous politicians and bureaucrats'. Although the 2007 Constitution sets out elaborate provisions to eliminate corruption (which are discussed Section VIII of this chapter and elsewhere in this book), it nevertheless also describes a conventional parliamentary system designed to work on the assumption that most MPs possess the motivation and expertise to partake in detailed scrutiny of the merits of any policy. This kind of in-depth technical debate rarely takes place in Thailand. The nature of criticism directed at government ministers and officials is very often in the form of personalised abuse.

Nonetheless, the Constitution also requires that an independent and impartial State Audit Commission (SAC), consisting of a Chair and six other members with relevant expertise in financial and fiscal matters, and having its own secretariat, is appointed to oversee the conduct of financial matters and to keep track of government spending. The SAC sets out the standards and rules of conduct in budgeting, and appoints an Independent Fiscal Disciplines Committee, which draws up additional budgeting criteria applying to all public bodies.[18] The decision to incorporate 'Directive Principles of Fundamental State Policies' as part of the Constitution[19] is an oblique way of addressing this problem, as it is intended to expose the Government to judicial as well as a formalised type of parliamentary scrutiny. Any government failing to take account of these overlapping principles would be susceptible to challenge before the courts.

IV. DIRECTIVE PRINCIPLES AS A CONSTRAINT ON GOVERNMENT

The Constitution clearly recognises that the initiative in policy-making rests in the hands of the Council of Ministers, which is responsible for the administration of State affairs. In a formal sense the Council of Ministers is made accountable to the National Assembly by first having to state what it intends to achieve during its period in office and then by preparing an annual report 'on the result of the implementation including problems and obstacles encountered'. The Council of Ministers is

---

[18] TC 2007, ss 252–254.

[19] TC 2007, ss 75–87, covering large areas of prescribed principles of government policy.

further required to make an annual plan for the administration of State affairs that is in conformity with the Directive Principles.[20]

Setting out these Directive Principles opens up the possibility of challenge to policy initiatives or legislative proposals before the Administrative Court or the Constitutional Court (see chapters six and five respectively) for failing to take account of what amount to prescriptive principles. Predictably, in view of the fundamentals of all Thai constitutions, there is a requirement under section 77 for the Government to uphold the monarchy, armed forces and State security. In addition, the following section of the 2007 Constitution specifies the attainment of sustainable social and economic development, and arranging administration of central, regional and local government in order to decentralise powers for the purpose of independence and self-determination.[21] In chapter four we shall assess the extent to which this aspiration has made inroads into a notoriously centralised State, with an ongoing insurgency problem in the South. The need to improve both the effectiveness and the moral virtue of the administration features as another principle. Given the generally low levels of remuneration granted to civil servants at the central and local levels, this ubiquitous concern to promote integrity and good governance should be considered alongside a requirement to implement a plan for fringe benefits for government and State officials. The enjoyment of free health care and education are among the benefits available to all public servants in Thailand. Some of the Directive Principles concern the administrative process. There is a requirement that expeditious, effective and transparent and participatory systems be introduced, and further, to ensure pursuit of the rule of law, government is required to implement a plan to ensure the independent functioning of legal oversight agencies (courts and watchdogs).

A further set of principles contained in the 2007 Constitution applies to specific policy areas and appear to impose prescriptive fetters on any elected government. These policy areas are religion, social relations, public health and culture; law and justice; foreign policy; economic policy; land natural resources and the environment; science, intellectual property and energy; and public participation.[22] The prescriptions

---

[20] TC 2007, ss 75 and 76.
[21] TC 2007, s 78.
[22] TC 2007, ss 79–87.

include a commitment to rule of law values, as government must prevent the rights and liberties of citizens from being violated, and secure the equal administration of justice. To date, Thailand does not have a welfare state funded from direct taxation, but, by virtue of these principles, government is nevertheless placed under a duty to promote the sustainable health of its people, and to develop the quality and standard of all levels of education in conformity with social and economic changes.[23] Further, in the realm of economic policy there is a duty

> to promote job opportunities for people of working age, protect women and child labour, to promote labour relations, and the tripartite system under which workers have the right to elect their own representatives . . . [24]

In stark contrast to this social emphasis, in relation to the development of the economy, government must promote a free and equitable economy through market forces, and sustainable development of the economy by refraining from enacting business control laws.[25] The problem is that there is no indication of how the pursuit of market-led policies in one area is to be reconciled with the commitment to protect social welfare objectives in others. The clarification of these issues must await policy initiatives or proposed legislation, which requires engagement with these principles. In sum, these principles are included in the Constitution to create a strong moral dimension on any government, both in a general sense and according to identifiable standards applicable to specific policy areas.

V. THAILAND'S CIVIL SERVICE

A. History

The Thai civil service originated from the bureaucracy that served the King.

> Members of the royal family and the aristocracy were appointed by the King to high positions in the bureaucracy. Bureaucrats were royal servants who

---

[23] TC 2007, s 80.

[24] Section 84(7). For further discussion, see A Brown and K Hewison, '"Economics is the Deciding Factor": Labour Politics in Thaksin's Thailand' (2005) 78(3) *Pacific Affairs* 353.

[25] TC 2007, s 84(1).

served the King. Siamese kings had absolute power to appoint, promote and dismiss all bureaucrats according to ancient laws and tradition.[26]

By the end of the Ayutthaya period[27] five departments had been established: the Ministry of the Interior, under an official who held the rank of Prime Minister for Civil Affairs; the Ministry for Capital Affairs, which was responsible for running Ayutthaya itself; the Ministry of Finance, which was responsible for collecting taxation and running the royal property; the Ministry of Agriculture; and the Ministry for the Royal Household. Given the distinct place occupied by the military in Thai society, it is significant that a separate bureaucratic organisation existed for military affairs even before the Chakri dynasty and the changes in administration introduced under it.

The main planks of the extensive reform of the entire system of government took place during the 1890s under Rama V. Reforms were undertaken in 1892 to replace the traditional government departments with western-style functional ministries. The new set of ministries comprised: Interior, Defence, Foreign Affairs, Justice, Finance, Public Works, Education, Agriculture, Metropolitan, Royal Household and Privy Seal. The heads of these ministries formed a cabinet. The high degree of centralisation that has characterised the Thai State up until this very day was consolidated by this structure, and the concentration of power in Bangkok can be linked to the particular influence of the Department of Interior. Some concessions towards decentralisation have in fact featured only as a part of very recent official policy (see chapter four).

Steps were taken to adopt modern techniques of administration by seeking to incorporate features that had already been identified in Europe, for example a move towards meritocratic recruitment. Moreover, the fiscal autonomy of each department was replaced by a new system whereby each department was required to submit estimates of expenditure for the coming year to the cabinet and the King for approval. For the first time officials were given fixed salaries and regular work hours.[28]

---

[26] Bowornwathana, above n 16, 282.

[27] This phase of Thai history (1350–1767) ended with the sacking of the old capital of Ayutthaya by the Burmese. Bangkok was established as the new capital in 1782 by Rama I. See B Terwiel *Thailand's Political History: From the 13th century to recent times*, 2nd edn (Bangkok, River Books, 2011), 43ff, 81ff.

[28] K Udyanin and K Suwanagul, 'Development of Thai Administration' (Kurenai, Kyoto University Departmental Bulletin Paper, 1965) 111.

There was a high degree of foreign influence from 1850 onwards, which meant that

> the administrative norms or ethics that emerged in Southeast Asia were largely influenced by the liberal democratic values of public administration found in developed nations, which included norms such as neutrality, equality, accountability, representation, fairness and so on.[29]

In addition, this outside influence manifested itself in a deliberate policy of employing Europeans and other foreign experts at the highest level of government from the 1890s. The contribution of Rolin-Jacquemyns, Strobel, Westengard and Sayre, to name but a few, have been well charted. These advisers were influential in foreign affairs and in drafting legal codes as part of the project of governmental and legal reforms launched under Rama V.[30] The revised order can be regarded as an integral part of the King's modernisation programme which sought to be in line with contemporary developments in governance. The foundation of a permanent, relatively independent, civil service recruited partly on merit was a crucial part of the King's legacy. In Britain the Northcote-Trevelyan report of 1854 stressed the enormous importance of a permanent civil service in the context of an expanding administrative State:

> It may safely be asserted that as matters now stand, the government of the country could not be carried on without the aid of an efficient body of permanent officers, occupying a position duly subordinate to that of the ministers who are directly responsible to the Crown and to Parliament, yet possessing sufficient independence, character, ability and experience to be able to advise, assist, and to some extent, influence those who are for time to time set over them.[31]

This set of transferable principles within the compass of the British Empire formed the backbone of the Indian civil service and colonial administrations around the world. Thailand took its cue from the trends in imperial administration, which meant that in effect

---

[29] M Shamsul Haque, 'Reforming Public Administration in Southeast Asia: Trends and Impacts' (2004) 4 *Public Organization Review: A Global Journal* 361 at 366.

[30] T Loos, *Subject Siam: Family, Law, and Colonial Modernity in Thailand* (Ithaca, NY, Cornell Press, 2006) 52ff; A Harding 'The Eclipse of the Astrologers: King Mongkut, His Successors, and the Reformation of Law in Thailand' in P Nicholson and S Biddulph (eds) *Examining Practice, Interrogating Theory: Comparative Legal Studies in Asia* (Leiden, Martinus Nijhoff, 2008), 319ff.

[31] P Hennessey, *Whitehall*, (London, Pimlico Books, 2001) 38.

the [bureaucratic] polity was thereby reorganised according to the pattern of colonial administration – the monarch taking the place of the colonial governor – while the economy, or an important part of it, was integrated into the international capitalist system.[32]

In sum, the effect of these reforms was to establish an autonomous Thai bureaucracy, and one that continued to operate after the transformation begun with the abolition of absolute monarchy in 1932.

However, despite these clear influences, it would be misleading to imply that the Thai civil service exactly replicated other models. In a well-known study, Riggs suggested that by the 1960s the Thai State was controlled by an elite that comprised civilian and military bureaucratic components. In other words, in this 'bureaucratic polity' not only was there no clear distinction between politicians and civil servants serving at the Cabinet level, or in the appointment to other senior posts in the public sphere, but the civil service itself comprised a combination of senior ex-military officers as well as career bureaucrats.[33] As part of this model of the State, the bureaucracy effectively constituted the political field but, as distinct from Western Europe and North America, the Thai bureaucratic polity did not gain legitimacy through appeals to electoral constituencies. Instead, it developed around a struggle between rival cliques within the civil service aiming at achieving parcels of State control. Apart from having an administrative function, the various layers of bureaucracy became an area for political rivalry. In an important sense Thailand lacked the institutional mechanisms of Western democracies because its bureaucracy operated around a system insulated from the outside world.[34]

A further dimension of great importance relates to the process of administration itself. This dimension reaches beyond the Cabinet and State bureaucracy, and involves personal ties that have been established between the civil service and business leaders.[35] More recently, the Riggs model outlined above has been criticised as being too simplistic. Rather, it

---

[32] J Girling, *Thailand: Society and Politics* (Ithaca, NY, Cornell University Press, 1981) 46.

[33] F Riggs, *Thailand: The Modernization of a Bureaucratic Polity* (Honolulu, East West Centre Press, 1966) 319.

[34] M Connors, *Democracy and National Identity in Thailand* (Copenhagen, NIAS Press, 2007) 11.

[35] J Ockey, 'State, Bureaucracy and Polity in Modern Thai Politics' (2004) 34(2) *Journal of Contemporary Asia* 143 at 144.

has been argued, the bureaucracy is dominated by financiers, provincial notables, retired government officials and professional politicians[36]; and each group has been able to gain access to government in different ways – for example, financiers have acquired large-scale concessions granted by the State, while retired officials are intimately familiar with bureaucratic patronage forming extensive networks of patron–client ties. It is against this background of complex financial relationships between the public administration and the private sector that the legal and constitutional constraints to protect the wider public interest have to be assessed. In an important sense then, '[t]ransparency, due process, accountability and public participation all serve to protect the integrity of the civil service'.[37] We shall see later that in redrafting the Constitution and in passing new laws related to the new constitutional measures (eg the Civil Service Act 2008) there has been a conscious attempt to reinforce the bureaucracy against politicians. But the next section of looks at the impact on the Thai public service of Thaksin's period in government (2001–06).

B. Modernisation and marketisation under Thaksin

The Thaksin Government launched substantial bureaucratic reform, and the public service was faced with three distinct types of transformation: an increased emphasis on the spoils approach to making appointments; a reorganisation of departments and agencies; and the introduction of a new form of internal managerialism based upon the philosophy of New Public Management (NPM).[38] In part, this was a response to a perception of inertia and resistance: Thaksin 'intimidated and politicised the senior bureaucracy while denigrating bureaucratic practice as inferior to the CEO culture of business'.[39]

First, the reforms were to be realised by following a deliberate policy of introducing a spoils system for the most senior appointments in the civil service and other public bodies, thus overthrowing the 'bureau-

---

[36] *Ibid*, at 151.

[37] D Nikomborirak, 'Civil Service Reform and the Quest for Better Governance: The Thai Experience' *TDRI Quarterly Review*, March 2007, vol 22, no 1, 7.

[38] For a discussion of NPM ideas in the context of public administration, see eg M Mulreaney, 'Economy, Efficiency and Effectiveness in the Public Sector: Key Issues' in T Hardiman and M Mulreaney (eds), *Efficiency and Effectiveness in the Public Domain* (Dublin, Irish Institute of Public Administration, 1991).

[39] Nikomborirak, above n 37, at 196.

cratic polity'. Executive intervention was extended into the bureaucracy to a much greater extent than previously. According to Connors, Thaksin 'attempted to break senior civil servant tutelage over the political executive and to turn the bureaucracy into implementing agencies'.[40] At the same time, he recognised the advantage in having a centrally-managed system of spoils distribution that could respond effectively to the political needs of the ruling party.

This trend was linked to a change in political culture that was meant to allow Thaksin's party, the TRT, to act as a vehicle for achieving progressive social policies such as the universal funding of healthcare (as well as the personal agenda of Thaksin). The introduction of a Chief Executive Officer with direct lines of control and formal accountability was an example of this trend. However, such appointments tended to be based on the capacity for political intervention rather than made on merit measured in terms of the competence and experience of the appointee.[41]

The introduction of outsiders into government occurred in a quite different way. At the highest policy level there was a deliberate use of spin-doctors and special policy advisers. Under Thaksin these policy gurus (including Suranan Vejjajiva and Pansak Vinyaratn) often assumed 'a combined role in strategic thinking for both party and government'. A team of 40–50 appointees was able to conduct performance checks on all policies approved by the Council of Ministers.[42] In other words, the employment of a team of adviser appointees amounted to a concentration of prime ministerial authority, and the capacity of these advisers to intervene without any claim to democratic legitimacy, took precedence over the wider constitutional mechanisms designed to make and oversee decision-making at the highest level.[43] The deliberate centralisation of decision-making power (including patronage) in the hands of Thaksin and his immediate circle has been identified as a central theme of the former PM's premiership, but 'this was achieved under the guise of creating a more performance-oriented public sector'.[44]

---

[40] Connors, above n 34, at 249.

[41] *Ibid.*

[42] McCargo and Pathmananand, above n 14, 93–99.

[43] See, eg, TC 1997, s 212, which required ministers to be 'collectively responsible to the National Assembly for the general policies of the Council of Ministers'.

[44] M Painter, 'Thaksinization or Managerialism? Reforming the Thai Bureaucracy' (2006) 36(1) *Journal of Contemporary Asia* 26 at 43.

In a secondary move, the departmental structure itself was modified to allow more effective control by the Government over policy. In October 2002 the Thaksin Government was responsible for the first major structural overhaul of departments and ministries since King Chulalongkorn. The new configuration, referred to subsequently as the 'big bang',[45] involved a change from 14 ministries and 126 departments to 20 ministries and 143 departments.[46] This process can be linked to the trend towards a spoils system, as it resulted in an increase in the number of agencies and top positions to be filled. It has been observed that 'lateral movement and reshuffling was the order of the day, with officials who fitted the new mould being rewarded by appointment to the most senior positions'.[47] The Thaksin Cabinet repeated the tactic of the previous administration by making many changes to senior bureaucratic appointments, but went further with a comprehensive reconfiguration of the bureaucratic structure. The PM was now in a position to make 'a large number of senior appointments, promotions and transfers'. Also, many businessmen were placed on statutory boards of government-controlled organisations. A number of officials identified themselves as TRT members in order to secure their promotion to senior positions.[48]

The third plank of the reform was directed at transforming the internal practice of Thailand's bureaucracy, confronting it with the prevailing influence of public-choice theory. This meant the adoption of a New Public Management (NPM) approach. The proliferation of market-driven State policies across the globe from the late 1980s onwards resulted in the restructuring of public services using a business model which had given rise to profound changes in the patterns of administrative ethics in both developed and developing nations.[49] The main objective was not only to lessen the profile of government, but also to improve its efficiency by adapting a business model for the public sector. Harlow and Rawlings provide a concise summary:

---

[45] *Ibid*, at 39.

[46] The Organisation of State Administration Act 1991 previously set out the bureaucratic structure of the State administration and recognised 14 ministries and 125 departments.

[47] Painter, above n 44, at 40.

[48] P Phongpaichit and C Baker, *Thaksin: The Business of Politics in Thailand* (Chiang Mai, Silkworm Press, 2004) 185.

[49] Shamsul Haque, above n 29, at 366.

Essentially, NPM is a managerial technique of administration, characterised by rules, accountability and qualitative audit. Two aspects of the package are especially relevant to administrative law. The first is a shift in dominant values associated with a more limited conception of government. The second is the shift from courts to auditors as external control machinery and the NPM methodology of standard setting, measurement and control evolving into 'value for money' (VFM) audit.[50]

Thaksin's NPM reform programme, introduced in March 2003 as the Strategic Plan for Thai Public Sector Development, followed in the wake of an ongoing failure from the 1990s successfully to introduce NPM. This policy had a similar agenda to that set out in the above quotation, but was now pursued with greater vigour than before. Ambassadors were recalled to Bangkok to join public servants attending seminars on business and management practices. The intention was to subdue the power of the traditional Thai public service, while at the same time harnessing a new form of authority for the common objective of centralising decision-making power in the hands of the PM. A Public Sector Development Commission staffed by Thaksin's appointees was established to oversee the implementation of this initiative.

Critics have observed that the attempt to introduce greater economy and efficiency as part of results-focused budgeting has been largely unsuccessful. In Thailand this critique resulted in

the superficial transplantation of NPM ideas and instruments produc[ing] ineffective and counter-productive hybrids without addressing many fundamental problems. Indeed, the common result was for the hybrids to be adapted to accommodate the dysfunctions rather than remedying them.[51]

In other words, the initiative has so far lacked substance, and it mainly amounts to the adoption of the latest managerialist rhetoric.[52] Furthermore, in a system where the bureaucracy enjoys more than usual power relative to the elected government ministers in office at any time, due to frequent changes in government and Cabinet reshuffles, this failure is attributed to a lack of political leadership. In an environment of top-down superintendence from those further up the bureaucratic hierarchy, rather than a results-based management style, far-reaching reform

[50] C Harlow and R Rawlings, *Law and Administration*, 3rd edn (Cambridge, Cambridge University Press, 2009) 59.
[51] Painter, above n 44, at 31.
[52] *Ibid*, at 43.

of this kind would have needed to be politically driven in order to over-come a general aversion to change.[53] In addition, it is significant, but perhaps not surprising given the desire to centralise power, that the aspects of NPM that emphasise decentralisation and autonomy were absent from the approach pioneered under Thaksin. However, as we shall see below, the values engendered in NPM remain in place under the current post-2007 constitutional framework.

C. The contemporary Civil Service

Before proceeding to consider the Civil Service Act 2008, it is useful to provide a breakdown of some data relating to the current service. According to recently published official statistics, there are approximately 1.3 million full-time officials in Thailand.[54] At national level there are about 380,000 ordinary civil servants; 470,000 school teachers; 56,000 university teachers; 219,000 in the police service; with a further 7,000 judges and 2,800 prosecutors. In addition, there are 225,000 local officials, a figure that includes a further 35,000 school teachers employed by the local administration. The largest civil service departments are Public Health (170,000); Interior (44,000); Agriculture (38,000); and Finance (32,000). Sixty-one per cent of full-time officials are female, but in the top two levels (10 and 11) the proportions of female officials are 7 per cent and 23 per cent respectively. Seventy-three per cent of full-time officials are university graduates.[55] Civil servants are prohibited from holding any political position.[56] Although civil servants receive modest salaries, they are entitled to a range of fringe benefits, including free health and education for their families. The total employment bill for the civil service has reached 80 billion baht, or approximately $2.54 billion per year.[57]

---

[53] G Dixon, 'Thailand's Quest for Results-Focused Budgeting' (2005) 28 *International Journal of Public Administration* 355 at 366.

[54] Ordinary Civil Servants in Thailand 2007, OCSC, p 2 (available from the OCSC website at <http://www.ocsc.go.th/ocsccmsen/View1/view.jsp>).

[55] The monarchy and the army are not included in these statistics.

[56] TC 2007, s 194.

[57] 'Thailand Government to Overhaul Medical Benefits for Civil Servants', *Thai Press Reports*, August 25, 2009.

In an attempt to restore some balance after the radical changes attempted under Thaksin detailed above, the Civil Service Act of 2008 (CSA 2008) places a strong emphasis on consolidating a permanent bureaucracy. The Thai civil service has retained its hierarchical structure, with each department being led by a permanent secretary. At a level below this, each government agency has its own head and deputy head. The next tier down consists of knowledge-worker positions that require graduate entry, and, in addition, general positions that do not require specific qualifications.[58] Recruitment to the service is conducted on the basis of merit from candidates with appropriate qualifications passing competitive examinations.[59] However, candidates for higher-level executive positions, such as the heads of departments and of ministerial level government agencies, are nominated by the relevant minister, and the nomination must then be approved by the Council of Ministers.[60] At the level below, namely higher executive or deputy head, nominations are submitted by the Permanent Secretary of the ministry or department. The PM submits names for royal assent, appointment of officials being to the age of retirement at 60; senior military appointments are subject to a similar approval process.[61] It is not surprising that technical expertise and/or specialist knowledge has become a necessary requirement for an increasing number of 'knowledge-worker' civil servants at professional, senior professional, expert or advisory levels.[62] However, the stipulation that an honours degree is required for many positions[63] is controversial, as this excludes at a stroke well over 90 per cent of the adult population. A perception of elitism is particularly felt by the rural population, for whom educational upward mobility is most restricted. In light of the evidence that previous questionable practices have continued, the framers of these laws would appear to have placed great reliance on university-educated technocrats. Notwithstanding the statutory selection procedure outlined here, and the constitutional mechanism prescribed for the various watchdog bodies discussed elsewhere, appointments to the highest positions in public sector institutions

---

[58] CSA 2008, ss 45 and 46.
[59] CSA 2008, ss 52 and 53.
[60] CSA 2008, s 57(1).
[61] TC 2007, s 194.
[62] CSA 2008, ss 55 and 56.
[63] Compare the position with regard to qualifications required for members of the National Assembly and the Senate discussed in ch two, section II.

continues to operate as a merry-go-round which has seen the same elite group of suitably qualified and experienced figures move from one position to another. The benefits of introducing so many new independent commissions and courts have been at the expense of wider popular participation in the running of public institutions.

The Thai Civil Service Commission (CSC) has a central role in overseeing the internal management of the service, and it is currently placed on a statutory footing by the CSA 2008.[64] It is chaired by the PM or a Deputy PM, and, in addition to the Permanent Secretary of the Ministry of Finance, the Director of the Budget Bureau, and the Secretary-General of the Office of the National Economic and Social Development Board (ex officio), it comprises between five and seven commissioners appointed for a renewable term of three years.[65] The CSC is responsible for advising the Council of Ministers on human-resource management policies, and for making recommendations to it in respect of salaries and other allowances. The CSC also sets out the grounds rules for management of staff; approves staffing plans of government agencies; oversees the performance of ministries and departments; and organises education and training, including the allocation of scholarships.[66] The CSC also performs a disciplinary role where a ministry, department or person has not acted in accordance with the CSA 2008 or guidelines issued under it.[67] A Merit System Protection Commission has recently been set up to work alongside the CSC to address human-resource management issues, including the issuing of rules and regulations, and consideration of appeals and complaints.[68]

The CSA continues to employ NPM language, which, as noted above, has exercised a significant influence since it was first pioneered in the 1990s. The emphasis is on what are termed in the Act as 'result-based outcome, efficiency and good value in the discharge of state functions'.[69] This wording, with an emphasis on results achieved, suggests that target-setting and judgement of performance will remain an inte-

---

[64] CSA 2008, s 6.

[65] With the exception of the PM or Deputy PM as chair, politicians are expressly excluded from membership.

[66] CSA 2008, s 8.

[67] CSA 2008, s 9.

[68] CSA 2008, s 31.

[69] CSA 2008, s 34.

gral part of management strategy. All government agencies are placed under a duty to implement actions to enhance the efficiency of and build motivation among civil servants, and this includes the introduction of performance evaluation schemes for officials.[70] Under this Act the goal is to produce a cadre of civil servants

> that possess quality, virtue, ethics, and have a good morale and quality of life, inspiration and enthusiasm in performing official functions to achieve the desired results-based outcome of the State's tasks.[71]

It has been argued that despite the pervasive vocabulary of NPM, in practice such reforms are largely inhibited by the highly centralised civil service budget system in Thailand.[72]

VI. ACCOUNTABILITY AND THAILAND'S CONTRACTING STATE

At this point we turn to consider briefly the interface between governmental bodies and the private sector. All governments must, to a greater or lesser extent, engage with the private sector in order to function. In one sense this involves the Government contracting for the supply of goods and services using a procurement process. In another, government or local-government bodies might contract with private-sector companies to fulfil functions that would otherwise be performed directly. In yet another sense it might involve a process of privatisation and regulation of State-owned enterprises which are floated on the stock market as private-sector businesses, with the imposition of a regime of statutory regulation to protect any public interest that might be adversely affected. The common denominator among these initiatives is the enormous sums of public money involved in transactions between government and the private business, and the potential for serious malpractice.

---

[70] CSA 2008, s 76.
[71] CSA 2008, s 72.
[72] Dixon, above n 53, at 356.

A. Public procurement

Modern governments possess extensive powers to enter into many different types of contractual arrangements, and these powers will be most important and sensitive when they concern the policy-implementation process. The reason for instituting a formal procurement procedure is to ensure that public contracts will be awarded in an open, fair and transparent manner. In addition, good procurement is often equated with getting value for money and in acquiring products that are fit for the intended purpose. The even more robust approach to media regulation discussed in chapter seven might be regarded as a response to sustained criticism over the lack of transparency and integrity associated with government contracting.[73] Concerns have been continually raised over the close nexus between civil servants, at the central and local levels, and business interests, and particularly in regard to large-scale prestige projects. One prominent example of abuse during Thaksin's premiership (2001–06) concerned the concessions relating to the operation of Bangkok's Suvarnabhumi International Airport. The US company Invision admitted in 2005 to paying money to officials and to a political party for the contract to supply the luggage scanners. Similar allegations have related to billions paid on the contracts for ground services, supply of luggage trolleys, provision of security services, concessions for car parking and advertising.[74]

The main legislation regulating public procurement in Thailand is referred to in short as the ROPMP,[75] but a separate law sets out the criminal offences and penal sanctions relating to bidding.[76] Of course this procurement legislation overlaps with the role of the NACC and other measures (see chapter five), which have been designed specifically

---

[73] *Curbing corruption and public procurement in Asia and the Pacific,* Asian Development Bank, Manila, Organisation for Economic Co-operation and Development, 2006. Available at <http://www.adb.org/Documents/Books/Public-Procurement-Asia-Pacific/default.asp>.

[74] Phongpaichit and Baker, above n 12, at 244.

[75] Office of the Prime Minister on Procurement 1992, as amended to No 6, 2002 (ROPMP). It should be noted that the ROPMP does not apply to State enterprises or local government.

[76] Act on Offences Relating to the Submission of Bids or Tender Offers to Government Agencies 1999.

to minimise corruption.[77] As part of the current procedure to help encourage participation while also making collusion more difficult, a strategy of increased transparency relating to the procurement process, coupled with the requirement that procurement opportunities have to be published widely, has been adopted. It is as yet too early to judge whether these laws and the strong commitment in the 2007 Constitution to the highest ethical standards will transform the practice of procurement in the way intended.

B. Privatisation of State assets

The Thaksin approach to economic management was to regard Thailand as if it were a private company in order to nurture rapid economic growth.[78] This approach was adopted to drag the nation onto its feet and out of the recession of the late 1990s. One commentator reminds us:

> A large number of state owned enterprises (SOEs) have been economically inefficient, incurred heavy financial losses, and absorbed disproportionate shares of domestic credit. Of particular concern has been the burden that loss-generating SOEs place on the hard-pressed public budgets of developing countries like Thailand.[79]

In pursuit of the creation of a more competitive environment there were attempts to dispose of some State-run enterprises.[80] Shares were sold as a means of raising revenues and promoting efficiency, but this approach was also regarded as a way of changing the complexion of the administrative State. While the inefficiency of existing structures may often have been manifest, the question was whether privatisation could be managed in the public interest as an alternative policy in the Thai context.

From the outset the way the process of privatisation was manipulated by the Government attracted strong criticism. In 2001, 30 per cent of

---

[77] See eg, TC 2007, s 279; Organic Act on Counter Corruption 1999; Royal Decree on Good Governance in State Administration 2003; Ethical Standards for Civil Servants.

[78] Phongpaichit and Baker, above n 12, at 101.

[79] J Blasko, 'Overcoming he Legal and Historical Obstacles to Privatization: The Telecommunications Sector in Thailand' (1998) 30 *Case Western Reserve Journal of International Law* 507, 517.

[80] Phongpaichit and Baker, above n 12, at 119ff.

the government petroleum company PTT was sold by a flotation on the stock exchange. Substantial holdings, obtained at rock-bottom prices, were left in the hands of relatives and friends of government ministers and party figures. There was also enthusiasm within the Government for some liberalisation and privatisation of communication services on the grounds of efficiency, but this approach was also favoured to secure access to the illicit revenues which had been accumulated on investments in the telecom sector.[81] Moreover, the regulation of the telecommunications industry has been regarded as an example of an oligopoly protected by government power. This is because

> the overall telecom industry is not governed by any set of regulations or real master plan. Rather, the industry is based on a series of deals hatched between a handful of state agencies looking for new revenue opportunities and a handful of businessmen looking for profits . . .[82]

By the time the Thaksin Government turned its attention to privatising the Electricity Generating Authority of Thailand (EGAT), it faced strong opposition from the labour unions as well as from many other organisations. The anti-privatisation campaign resulted in a successful Administrative Court challenge to the proposed flotation (see chapter six). The Court was prepared to quash the decision to go ahead on the basis that the Government had failed to consult adequately the parties likely to be affected under the hastily-drafted privatisation proposals. In fact this case might be regarded as a classic illustration of the potency of the new administrative courts in the face of an abuse of power.[83]

VII. FREEDOM OF INFORMATION

In a crucial sense the quest for accountability depends on transparency. If public institutions, including government, civil service and local government, are going to operate to serve a broader public interest, it is important to inculcate a culture of openness, and a statutory regime of freedom of information might be regarded as an important step in this

---

[81] *Ibid*, at 42ff.

[82] *Ibid*, at 197.

[83] P Leyland, 'Droit Administratif Thai Style: A Comparative Analysis of the Administrative Courts in Thailand' (2006) 8(2) *Australian Journal of Asian Law* 142.

direction. The Official Information Act 1997 (OIA 1997) was passed at the same time as the introduction of the 1997 Constitution.

In theory at least, this new law allowed citizens for the first time to request access to information that was previously restricted. The categories of information covered included resolutions of the Council of Ministers and contracts reached between SOEs and private companies.[84] Information would now be placed in the public domain, especially relating to sensitive issues such as these contracts. The reform would work on the assumption that the gaze of public scrutiny offers the prospect of uncovering malpractice; at the same time aggrieved citizens who believed they had suffered injustice at the hands of officialdom would be empowered to request the information they needed for resolution before an ombudsman or the Administrative Court.

In terms of formal limitations, there are many excepted categories under the Act[85] and the OIA 1997 allows the list of exempted categories to be extended by royal decree.[86] The implementation of the Act is overseen by insiders in the form of a senior minister and officials. An Official Information Board (OIB), presided over by a minister appointed by the PM and consisting of key permanent secretaries, is responsible for advising the civil service on the implementation of the OIA 1997.[87] However, where there is a refusal to disclose official information, an appeal may be lodged with an Information Disclosure Tribunal comprised of non-civil servants. These tribunals are empowered to determine finally whether or not the disputed information is to be published. It has also been pointed out that Thai laws often grant administrative authorities a wide margin of discretionary power in both interpretation and implementation of statute law.[88] This tradition has been likened to the writing of a blank cheque by the legislative body which is then handed over to the administrative body. Under such circumstances,

---

[84] Nikomborirak, above n 37, at 5.
[85] OIA 1997, s 14 states that official information that may jeopardise the royal family is exempted. Section 15 permits a State agency or an official to issue an order prohibiting disclosure. The exempted categories recognised under this section are broadly in line with other legislation of this type and include, eg: national security, international relations, national economic or financial security; prejudicing the efficiency of law enforcement; advice given within State agencies; medical information encroaching on a right to privacy.
[86] OIA 1997, s 15(7).
[87] OIA 1997, ss 27 and 28.
[88] Nikomborirak, above n 37, at 5.

transparency in administrative procedures becomes particularly vital in ensuring the bureaucracy uses its broad power in order to serve the public rather than to pursue personal interests.

A striking instance of the operation of this system was a case involving Kasetsart University. The parents of a student who failed the university entrance examination asked the university to disclose the results, but it refused to do so. The parents appealed to the OIB and their case was heard by the Information Disclosure Tribunal, which ruled that they had a right to see the examination results. However, the university refused to comply even with the tribunal decision, claiming that it had to consult the Council of State, the Attorney-General's Office and the Ministry of University Affairs first, for guidance as to procedure and standards. Finally, the OIB confirmed the tribunal's order for disclosure, with an added threat of disciplinary proceedings. The case contributed greatly to the educational system of the country. A commentator concludes that

> the examinations held by many institutions have been adapted in compliance with the Act, which brought about fair examination[s] and [a] transparent academic system.[89]

In practice, there have been many complaints concerning the implementation of this crucial law. One issue that has arisen is that the OIA 1997 fails to provide access to the record of communications within government, so that the proceedings of private meetings are not covered. More generally, ordinary citizens and investigative journalists have frequently experienced difficulty (as in the Kasetsart University case above) in enforcing their rights to gain access to official information. Some public bodies have refused orders to produce documents that have been requested; others have been so dilatory in their response that the information requested has lost its currency by the time of its release.

VIII. ANTI-CORRUPTION STRATEGIES AND THE CIVIL SERVICE

The values that have been identified with good governance for the Thai civil service should have a strong resonance in relation to any State

---

[89] N Serirak, 'Challenges of Thailand's Freedom of Information', available at <http://www.oic.go.th/content_eng/nsreport.html>.

bureaucracy. Directive principles set out in the Constitution recognise that the civil service should operate with transparency, due process, accountability and participation.[90] What should this mean in practice? Transparency involves the drafting of clear rules and procedures to ensure objectivity and impartiality; and as we have seen in relation to freedom of information, it demands disclosure and public scrutiny. Due process implies acting with fairness and impartiality – in other words, that all comers will be treated equally under the law. Accountability describes how far decision-makers in the public arena can be held responsible for their actions and decisions, and also for their general performance (for example under NPM, discussed in section V above). Lastly, participation is about expanding the democratic process more widely to allow those affected by policy to have more involvement in the management of their affairs.[91]

The 2007 Constitution seeks to impose these values through a set of rigorous ethical standards, supported by a battery of mechanisms of enforcement designed to prevent politicians or officials from abusing their position. This litany of virtue for civil servants, State officials and politicians is first set out in general terms,[92] and similar principles are then elaborated in related legislation and codes of practice. The Constitution provides that public servants are expected to stand up for what is right and adhere to the principles of correctness and justice. They must carry out their responsibilities honestly and responsibly, with the determination to fulfil duties to the best of their ability. Citizens must be treated fairly and equitably. Appropriate conduct must be displayed in their personal life. Further, public servants are placed under a duty to refrain from actions that would damage the reputation or integrity of the civil service.[93] While one might have anticipated, given the background to its drafting, the inclusion of some values and professional ethics in the 2007 Constitution, the language goes much further than any previous text; for example, it requires civil servants to act as role models, exhibiting qualities of fortitude and sacrifice. In addition, in order to expose any enrichment which might not otherwise be accounted for, the Constitution requires all public office-holders,

---

[90] TC 2007, s 78.

[91] Nikomborirak, above n 37, at 4 (paraphrased).

[92] TC 2007, s 279.

[93] See   <http://www.ocsc.go.th/ocscemsen/View1/view.jsp?categoryID=CAT0000140>.

including the PM, ministers, MPs, and central and local government officials, who take or vacate an official position, to submit an account of the assets and liabilities of themselves, their spouses and their children. This information will then be published.[94]

The robustness of any constitutional provisions needs to be set against recognised practice. We have already considered the scope for ministers to abuse their position. Notwithstanding the fact that Parliament has to pass laws, civil servants dominate the legislative process. Further, as we observe in chapter six when considering the role of the Office of the Council of State, officials are responsible for drafting the law and for developing the specific procedures required to apply the law. This includes dealing directly with client groups. In this capacity there has often been scope for malpractice, as Ockey indicates:

> Many provincial notables also hold government concessions and contracts in their regions . . . retired bureaucrats and officials are intimately familiar with the nature of bureaucratic patronage . . . They have tighter and more extensive networks of patron–client ties with active officials than do concessionaires, and can serve as an effective link between the two.[95]

To illustrate this point Ockey refers to kick-backs concerning officials in the Ministry of Agriculture. Attendant opportunities for patronage were traditionally left in the hands of bureaucrats, giving rise to endemic corruption.[96] Such instances describe one important aspect of the close nexus between commercial interests and public servants.

In order to establish the rule of law values contained in the text, the framers of recent constitutions recognised the need for rigorous enforcement. One of the most important features of the 1997 Constitution, as will be evident from the discussion in chapters two, five and six, was the reliance on a series of watchdog bodies,[97] as well as administrative courts and ombudsmen with formidable powers geared towards the elimination of corruption and malpractice.

---

[94] TC 2007, ss 259–264.

[95] Ockey, above n 35, at 152.

[96] *Ibid*, at 149–50.

[97] See, further the discussion of these in ch two, section VII, and ch five, section VIII.

IX. THE THRONE AND THE ARMED FORCES

Before we complete our discussion of the executive branch, it should be emphasised that there are two extremely powerful forces in Thailand – the Royal Household and the military – which fall outside current constitutional oversight mechanisms altogether. During his long reign an image of King Bhumipol has been constructed as a personification of national identity, standing above the conflict engendered in the political fray.[98] The rigorous application of the *lèse-majesté* law by factions behind the King suggests that any form of questioning of the status of the monarchy, or any criticism of the personal conduct of not just the King himself but also members of the royal family, will be interpreted as something tantamount to treason.[99] In line with its predecessors the 2007 Constitution recognises his supreme position as a figure of revered worship who is Head of State, and it provides that the King personally has unlimited power to make appointments to the Royal Household. Moreover, the personal intervention of the King in making calls for national unity after the bloody confrontations in 1974 and 1992 arguably demonstrates the 'absolute moral power and prestige of the throne' which might be seen as transcending the formal role defined under any Thai constitution (for further discussion of the Thai monarchy, see chapters one, seven and eight).[100]

On 17 occasions since 1932, as discussed in chapter one, the military, consisting of over 300,000 personnel spread over the three services, has constituted an obvious threat to democratic government as it has been directly responsible for overturning constitutional rule. Senior military figures have intervened on the grounds that they believed themselves to be sufficiently well trained as military academy graduates to be competent leaders, and that they possessed an advantage over weak, indecisive and short-lived civilian executives by being able to introduce strong government.[101] The military, represented by former senior personnel,

[98] Connors, above n 34, at 145.

[99] See P Leyland, 'The Struggle for Freedom of Expression in Thailand: The King, Citizen Politics and the Law' (2010) 2:1 *The Journal of Media Law* 115 at 122ff; and ch 7.

[100] K Suwannathat-Pian, *Kings, Country and Constitutions: Thailand's Political Development 1932–2000* (London, Routledge, 2004) 178.

[101] T Nakata, 'Political Culture: Problems of Development of Democracy' in S Xuto (ed), *Political Culture: Problems of Develpment Democracy in Government and Politics in Thailand* (Singapore, Oxford University Press, 1987) 174–75.

has a pervasive presence in the form of appointees to many official bodies. It retains of control of several television channels, which helps to ensure that it has a high institutional profile, as well as pursuing other business interests. McCargo has observed that:

> The Royal Thai army . . . is a uniformed bureaucracy that does not fight wars . . . The core pursuits of the Thai military are playing politics and engaging in business activities (including illegal activities such as smuggling); when the occasion arises commanders are not averse to killing a few dozen unarmed civilians.[102]

From the standpoint of constitutional accountability there has been clear evidence to suggest that the military command considers itself to be above the ordinary law. Rather, allegiance is owed directly to the King and to the greater interests of the nation (as defined by the military). The infamous Tak Bai incident (discussed in chapter four) in 2004, where 70 suspects suffocated in the back of a truck, is one alarming result of senior officers acting on their own initiative. More recently, there has been uncertainty under the 2007 Constitution over the willingness of the armed forces to intervene at the behest of the democratically-elected Government. Most obviously, long-running demonstrations originating around Parliament were allowed to cause violence and widespread disruption in 2008, culminating in the closure of both of Bangkok's airports, with the democratically-elected Government apparently unable to count on the military to disperse the demonstrators. On the other hand, in May 2010 the army was prepared to intervene in central Bangkok with the use of lethal force to remove Red Shirt demonstrations. The failure of the military to defer routinely to a civilian government of whatever complexion remains a matter of serious continuing concern.

The military coup of 2006 displaced the 1997 Constitution, which had been drafted after a process of genuine consultation. As previously, the generals responsible managed to secure their own immunity from prosecution under the Interim Constitution.[103] However, this intervention was very different from those on previous occasions. The coup leader, General Sonthi, made a pledge to restore democracy at the earliest opportunity. There has been criticism that the interregnum was used

---

[102] D McCargo, *Tearing Apart the Land: Islam and Legitimacy in the South of Thailand* (Ithaca, NY, Cornell University Press, 2008) 98.

[103] 'Thailand King Approves Interim Constitution, Absolves Coup Leaders', *Jurist Legal News and Research*, 1 October 2006.

opportunistically by the junta leaders, who appointed themselves and their associates to the boards of directors of several key State enterprises while at the same time approving substantial salary increases for themselves and a budget increase of 66 per cent over two years for the military.[104] Nevertheless, the pledge to return to democracy was honoured, with a new Constitution drafted after nine months and a return to civilian rule achieved within 15 months. This reluctance by the military to assume for more than a brief period the mantle of government would appear to be a highly significant development in Thai constitutionalism.

X. EMERGENCY POWERS

One final aspect of executive powers at the national level, which also relates to the military, is the use of emergency powers. Such powers have been a constant feature of Thailand's law and governance over several decades, and are provided for in the 2007 Constitution in the same terms as its predecessors of 1991 and 1997.[105] Under the 2007 Constitution,[106] an emergency decree may be issued by the King acting on the advice of the Cabinet when the latter is of the opinion that it is necessary for the purpose of maintaining national or public safety or national economic security, or averting public calamity. The decree must be submitted to the National Assembly without delay, and the approval of both houses is required for the decree to take effect. One-fifth of the members of either house can have the constitutionality of the decree referred to the Constitutional Court within three days. An emergency decree may also be passed if it is necessary to have a law on taxes, duties or currency, which, in the interests of State, requires urgent and

---

[104] C Charoensin-o-larn, 'Military Coup and Democracy in Thailand' in J Funston (ed), *Divided over Thaksin: Thailand's Coup and Problematic Transition* (Chiang Mai, Silkworm Books, 2009) 57.

[105] A Harding, 'Emergency Powers with a Moustache: Special Powers, Military Rule, and Evolving Constitutionalism in Thailand' in V Ramraj and A Thiruvengadam (eds), *Emergency Powers in Asia* (Cambridge, Cambridge University Press, 2009), ch 11; TC 2007, ss 184–186; TC 1997, ss 218–220; TC 1991, ss 175–177. Martial law, on the other hand, can be imposed without legislative scrutiny under the Martial Law Act 1914.

[106] Sections 184–188; the provisions are the same as in the 1991 and 1997 Constitutions.

confidential consideration.[107] These powers are here considered in conjunction with two other powers: martial law powers, and internal security powers.

As Kevin Tan, adverting to Thailand's chequered political history since 1932, observes, 'Thailand deals with exceptional political situations through coups d'état rather than through the invoking of emergency powers'.[108] Justifications based on emergency and national security considerations are frequently resorted to (although not invariably – constitutional breakdown and widespread corruption have also sufficed) by military leaders mounting coups d'état; the generals included in the justifications for their actions in 2006 a reference to a very imminent threat to law and order resulting from the protests against Thaksin and the acute polarisation of Thai society. In this sense an 'emergency' may be simply one of the recognised techniques of Thai governance.

On the other hand, emergency powers, in the strict sense of powers invoked constitutionally, have generally also been used for reasons connected with real issues of law and order or insurgency, as was the case with the controversial Decree on Public Administration in Emergency Situations 2005, which dealt with the insurgency in the Southern provinces. The Decree, ostensibly intended to consolidate several existing applicable laws, empowered the PM to order wire taps, censor the press, restrict freedom of assembly and movement, confiscate and destroy property, and preventively detain suspects in undesignated places without criminal charge; it also transferred all governmental authority in an area subject to an emergency declaration into the PM's own hands. These powers were expressed to be exercisable with no or minimal judicial oversight or access to justice, and to enjoy immunity from legal consequences. The Decree sparked extensive public debate about the role of emergency powers and the legitimate powers of the executive and the military. This debate continued in 2006–07, during which period a military coup (19 September 2006) overthrew the Constitution and the Government, and the interim legislature then passed the Internal

---

[107] This was extensively invoked during the economic crisis of 1998–2002; see ch 5.

[108] K Tan, 'From Myanmar to Manila: a Brief Study of Emergency Powers in Southeast Asia', *ibid* in V Ramraj and A Thiruvengadam, above n 105, ch 7 at 185. See Tan's chapter, further, for an historical overview of Thai constitutional history in comparative perspective.

Security Act 2008 (ISA 2008). The device of parliamentary scrutiny of emergency decrees[109] proved useful to some extent in 2005, as some of the most extreme measures had to be rescinded following parliamentary debate. A Bangkok newspaper headline even called the 2005 Decree 'the Decree with a moustache'.[110]

In raising the issue of emergency powers, however, it must be taken into account that in Thailand there are also standing martial law powers and internal security powers.[111] In both cases the powers exercised are potentially extremely wide. To a large extent, in practice the powers under the ISA 2008 replace emergency powers and were invoked in the May 2010 crackdown.

Martial law is normally proclaimed by the King, but can also be proclaimed by the military itself in a particular locality as an emergency measure. It is difficult to see why this constitutional provision (section 188) exists, given that in principle anything that could be done under a martial law decree could also be done under an emergency decree; yet a martial law decree does not require parliamentary scrutiny – or even in some cases scrutiny by any non-military arm of the Executive. There is, however, a Martial Law Act 1914 which prescribes the conditions for martial law rule. Martial law applied initially to the whole of Thailand following the coup of September 2006, and later to much of the country, and was only partially rescinded, being restricted to parts of 31, mainly border, provinces shortly before the elections of December 2007. It was then completely rescinded, except for parts of the three disturbed southern provinces, in April 2008.

The ISA 2008, on the other hand, essentially does the job of emergency powers, which would potentially involve both legislative and judicial scrutiny. The inspiration for this Act seems to lie in approaches that were taken during the 1970s and 1980s to deal with the threat of communist terrorism. The essence of this approach, which drew on the experience of British Malaya in dealing with a similar type of threat during the 1950s, was to deal with terrorism as a community issue, separating the terrorists from communities which were sources of sustenance, information, recruitment and logistical support.

[109] TC 1997, ss 218–220.

[110] *Thai Post,* 16 July 2005.

[111] 'Standing' in the sense that they can be invoked at any time and in any part of Thailand.

From the standpoint of civil liberties, the worrying aspect of the ISA 2008 is the extent to which it gives powers directly to the military, and that these powers are conferred not temporarily as an exception (as in the case of emergency powers) but on a permanent footing. It remains a matter of speculation whether this entrenchment of internal security powers relates to the precise situation in which the ISA 2008 was enacted – by an *interim* National Assembly *appointed* by the military-installed government under the Interim Constitution 2006, after the 2007 Constitution became effective but before the National Assembly elected under the 2007 Constitution was in session.[112] Democratic normality is contradicted not only by the Act's provisions, but even by the circumstances of its enactment. The Preamble to the ISA 2008 justifies the law on the basis of a need to guard against threats which may arise in times of normality, and to lay down measures to be used at times when a security threat has arisen in any area to regulate the use of power according to the level of seriousness of the situation, so that it may be resolved efficiently and with unity.

The ISA 2008 sets up an Internal Security Operations Board (ISOB) with the task of formulating national security policy, the policy being implemented by an Internal Security Operations Command (ISOC), which has power to give directions even to civilian public servants. In this capacity the Act imposes restrictions, potentially introduced simply by executive decision, on several fundamental rights protected by the 2007 Constitution.

The most significant provisions of the ISA 2008 give the PM as the Director of Internal Security responsibility for the execution of the Act, with the ISOC required to operate from within the PM's Office.[113] In the draft Act, the Royal Army Commander was responsible, which would have created an intolerable situation of giving vast and permanent powers to the military, and seriously disturbing the already problematic constitutional relationship between the civil and military powers.[114] In effect the draft law had the potential to create an entirely separate and parallel – military – government. While the PM possesses his powers under the ISA 2008 as head of the Government subject to

---

[112] For further discussion, see V Muntarbhorn, 'A Very Dangerous Precedent: Ten Reasons against Thailand's Proposed New Law on National Security', *Bangkok Post*, 5 November 2007, 6.

[113] ISA 2008, ss 4 and 5.

[114] It was a purpose of the 1997 Constitution to confine the military to the barracks. As we have seen, in this respect it was unsuccessful.

normal principles of cabinet government, the PM is also given authority to delegate his powers in writing to the Army Commander.[115] For the same reason as with the draft law, this presents an alarming prospect.

It is envisaged that the draconian powers available under this Act should apply to persistent situations falling short of the need for an emergency decree.[116] The ISOC has responsibility for maintaining internal security,[117] but it is also overseen by the ISOB, comprising senior members of government, civil service and military. This body lies at the head of a potentially vast administrative network comprising regional and provincial ISOCs, each advised by a board comprising persons trusted in all parts of the region or province in question.[118]

The powers and duties of the ISOC and the Director of Internal Security are breath-taking in scope; they include overseeing government agencies, if assigned this task by the Cabinet. Even more remarkably, in language redolent of the period of military dictatorship in the 1940s and 1950s, the ISOC has the power and duty to

> encourage people to be aware of their duty in upholding nation, religion, and king; to build love and unity among people in the nation; as well as to promote popular participation in preventing and overcoming various problems which affect internal security and the peace and order of society.[119]

More generally, the ISOC has powers to prevent, suppress, eradicate or mitigate a matter assigned to it; and, astonishingly,

> to order that any government official whose behaviour is a threat to internal security or an obstruction to the maintenance of internal security, be excluded from a designated area . . .[120]

which event requires the government agency in question to relieve the official of his or her duties. The Director has extensive powers to control movement and assembly, and to require government officials to perform or withhold performance of any action.[121]

---

[115]   ISA 2008, s 5.
[116]   ISA 2008, s 14.
[117]   Defined in ISA 2008, s 2 as 'operations to control, resolve, and restore any situation which is or may be a threat in order to restore normalcy for the sake of peace and order of the people, and the security of the nation, including prevention against such a situation.'
[118]   ISA 2008, ss 10–13.
[119]   ISA 2008, s 6(4).
[120]   ISA 2008, s 15(4).
[121]   ISA 2008, ss14 and 17.

Moreover, the Director of ISOC, in the name of the PM's Office, is empowered to prosecute or defend legal proceedings relating to the activities of the ISOC.[122] This provision has potentially alarming implications, as it takes control over prosecutions and security-related law suits away from the prosecution authorities and the Attorney-General, who are accountable, and gives it to the military, who are not. The ISA 2008 also, like the 2005 Decree, exempts any of its actions from administrative law,[123] and it creates legal immunity for any official acting in execution of his duty under the Act.

These provisions are worrying in many respects. The vagueness of many of the provisions granting powers to the ISOC, and the lack of recourse to the courts or even to normal procedures of criminal justice, create the potential for widespread abuse of power and human rights violations. The Act gives extraordinary powers to military as opposed to civilian personnel, thereby exacerbating the main problem that Thailand has been trying to deal with since 1992, namely defining a limited and appropriate role for the military. In sum, it is extraordinary that in Thailand there are three different regimes of exception which are to a large extent congruent with each other and all designed to deal with societal instability, however this arises.

One consolation is that the situation would have been worse still if the military had attempted to hold on to power in 2008 citing issues of national security. The ISA 2008 was amended in the course of its passage through the Cabinet and the Legislature to reassert control over the ISOC by the elected PM. While the Act gives extensive powers to the military – and that is a major concern – at least the prospect of exclusively military powers was avoided. The ISA 2008 could have contained even more draconian provisions with regard to freedom of expression, assembly and association, privacy and personal liberty. It does not, surprisingly, contain any provision for preventive detention. But these are small compensations. The Act moves Thailand further than before down the path of making the rule of law an exception, clothing the Executive and the military with legal immunity, and arming them to the teeth with a veritable panoply of security laws. The Government has indicated that it will implement the Act in disturbed areas to combat drug-trafficking, in place of the use of martial law.[124]

---

[122] ISA 2008, s 5.
[123] ISA 2008, s 22.
[124] 'End of Martial Law', *Bangkok Post*, 17 April 2008.

XI. CONCLUSION

At first encounter the Constitution appears to provide a conventional Westminster-inspired parliamentary system of government, where the Government is answerable to Parliament and where the maintenance of the Government depends upon it enjoying the support of Parliament. But the fact that political parties in Thailand are not founded on ideology but rather come to be directly controlled by one or more powerful individuals in exchange for payment, makes this resemblance misleading. The lack of commitment on the part of political parties to policy as such also helps to explain why prescriptive principles have been incorporated as part of the Constitution in order to provide general (and sometimes potentially conflicting) guidelines for any government.

The Thai civil service was fashioned under Rama V with the input of foreign advisers to provide the means to assert Bangkok's central authority, while also delivering the King's own reform programme. More recently, under Thaksin, the civil service, which provided a relatively autonomous administrative base for any government, was reorganised, and at the same time was exposed to outside advisers and a radical dose of managerialism in order to suit the personal agenda of the PM. However, this was undertaken in a very different constitutional climate. Both the 1997 and 2007 Constitutions were designed not only to establish a corruption-free environment for governance, but also to provide a bag of surgically sharp instruments, in the form of courts and watchdog bodies, with which to reach this objective. The EGAT case (discussed in chapter six) demonstrated that the administrative courts had retained their independence and have therefore remained an effective counterweight when faced with the abuse of executive power. In the current fraught political environment the other watchdog bodies have not preserved the same reputation for independence, and this perception has taken the edge off their effectiveness. The constitution-makers have provided a potentially useful set of instruments, but only if they remain in the hands of judges and public servants sufficiently detached from the political fray.

Lastly, the authority of this or any Constitution is potentially undermined by exempting the military and the monarchy from values of transparency and accountability which apply to all other constitutional players.

FURTHER READING

H Evers, 'The Bureaucratization of Southeast Asia' *Comparative Studies in Society and History*, vol 29, issue 4 (Oct 1987) 666.

A Harding, 'Emergency Powers with a Moustache: Special Powers, Military Rule, and Evolving Constitutionalism in Thailand' in V Ramraj and A Thiruvengadam (eds), *Emergency Powers in Asia* (Cambridge, Cambridge University Press, 2009).

D McCargo and U Pathmanand, *The Thaksinization of Thailand* (Copenhagen, NIAS, 2005), ch 4.

J Ockey, 'State, Bureaucracy and Polity in Modern Thai Politics' (2004) 34(2) *Journal of Contemporary Asia* 143.

P Phongpaichit and C Baker, *Thaksin*, 2nd edn (Chaingmai, Silkworm Press, 2009).

C Sawangsak, *Kan Khuab Khum Kan Chai Amnat Khong Fai Borihan* [Governing the Executive Power] (Bangkok, Winyuchon, 1997) [in Thai].

M Shamsul Haque, 'Reforming Public Administration in Southeast Asia: Trends and Impacts' (2004) 4 *Public Organization Review: A Global Journal* 361.

S Vallance, 'Performance Appraisal in Singapore, Thailand and the Phillipines: A Cultural Perspective' (1999) 58(4) *Australian Journal of Public Administration* 78.

W Wisarutphit, *Khor Khum Khit Lae Lukkan Phuen Than Nai Kodmai Mahachon* [Fundamental Principles in Public Law] (Bangkok, Nititham, 1997) [in Thai].

K Wongtrangan, 'Executive Power and Constitutionalism in Thailand' in C Sison (ed) *Constitutional and Legal Systems of Asean Countries* (Academy of ASEAN Law and Jurisprudence, University of the Phillipines, 1990).

4

Local Democracy, Southern Insurgency and Territorial Division of Power

⇒⊷∘⊷⇐

Introduction – Centralisation and the Evolution of the Thai State – The Structure of Local Government – Local Government Finance – Decentralisation and Participation – Promoting Good Local Governance – The Troubles in Thailand's Southern Provinces – The South under Thaksin – Devolution for the South? – Conclusion

I. INTRODUCTION

THAILAND HAS A number of levels and types of local government, but since its emergence as a modern nation in the 19th century it has been noted for having a highly centralised governmental system, with local government little more than an outpost of the Ministry of the Interior.[1] It will be suggested that the degree of centralisation, which has not been fundamentally addressed by recent constitutional or legislative reform, is being increasingly called into question in light of the troubles in the southern provinces and the current political polarisation between the Red Shirts and Yellow Shirts. This conflict also has a strong regional element to it, with the main support for the Reds being concentrated in the north and north east, while support for the Yellows tends to be concentrated in and around Bangkok and parts of the south.[2] Naturally, the place of sub-national

---

[1] M Nelson, *Central Authority and Local Democratisation in Thailand* (Bangkok, White Lotus Press, 1998) 26.

[2] D McCargo, 'Thai Protests: Military Crackdown Only Widens Divide', *The Guardian*, 19 May 2010; 'Bangok's Savage Conflict May be a Mere Dress Rehearsal', *The Daily Telegraph*, 19 May 2010.

government is considered here from a constitutional perspective. Both of Thailand's most recent Constitutions include a section headed 'Local Government', containing a general commitment 'to give autonomy to the locality in accordance with the principle of self-government according to the will of the people in the locality'.[3] In pursuance of this objective it is clearly indicated that local government status ought to be given to any local community that meets what are described as the 'conditions of self government'. The current Constitution also provides that forms of local government organisations should be autonomous and have a local assembly democratically elected every four years.[4] However, although there is repeated emphasis on progressive decentralisation,[5] there is no reference in the Constitution to any recognised form of federalism, devolution or regional government, neither is there any more detailed specification as to the structure, functions or powers of existing local government organisations or any such organisations that might be formed in the future. In this chapter the term 'local government' describes the elected institutions below the level of central government and the institutions at local level that have responsibility for policy implementation.

The first section of this chapter provides an overview of the structural features of the types of local government in Thailand while also considering the trends towards decentralisation and participatory democracy that have featured as part of the 1997 and 2007 Constitutions. In the last decade, there have been limited attempts to bring the delivery of local services closer to the citizen, and it is possible to observe how policy is being implemented at this level with reference to case studies in certain policy areas. Secondly, we evaluate the constitutional oversight mechanisms and related legislation that have been introduced in an attempt to promote good governance and eliminate corruption at this level. Lastly, having surveyed the framework of local government and the degree to which power has been concentrated in Bangkok, our attention turns to providing a contextual discussion of the long-running insurgency in Thailand's deep south, with a view to examining the constitutional implications which might be involved in reaching a viable settlement through a form of devolution.

[3] TC 1997, ss 282 and 283; TC 2007, s 281.
[4] TC 2007, s 284.
[5] TC 2007, s 283.

II. CENTRALISATION AND THE EVOLUTION OF THE THAI STATE

Viewed from an historical perspective, the reasons for the highly-centralised modern Thai State become apparent.[6] In essence, the creation of a relatively uniform nation in the period of King Chulalongkorn (Rama V), one that was able to resist the colonial ambitions of European nations, depended upon the implementation of administrative reforms which created a unified nation. Winichakul notes that the reform of provincial administration in Siam was

> first tested in the 1870s in Lanna and then developed and applied to the Lao region along the Mekhong, including Luang Phrabang and many other large and small tributaries. Finally, from 1893 onwards it was implemented in other regions including the inner provinces of Siam. It was a gradual process of displacing the traditional local autonomy . . . by the modern mechanisms of centralisation.[7]

The fundamental change in terms of administration was the replacement of local dignitaries with centrally-appointed civil servants who were loyal to the King or were members of the royal family. Ever since then, centralisation and territorial unity have been regarded as the essential conditions of Thailand's existence as a modern nation. The result is that

> Compared to many others, the Thai state is extremely strong and has effective reach into all provinces and districts, no matter how far they are from Bangkok. Although Thailand was never colonised, its provincial administration is reminiscent of the colonial apparatus of administration established by the British in India and the French in Indochina. It was designed to ensure effective control of rural areas . . . [8]

In assessing the trends towards decentralisation discussed below, it should also be stressed that there is a perceived danger of any

---

[6] M Nelson, 'Thailand: Problems with Decentralisation' in M Nelson (ed), *Thailand's New Politics: KPI Yearbook 2001* (Bangkok, KPI and White Lotus Press, 2002) 223.

[7] T Winichakul, *Siam Mapped: A History of the Geo-Body of a Nation* (Honolulu, University of Hawaii Press, 1994) 102.

[8] D Arghiros, 'Political Reform and Civil Society at the Local Level: Thailand's Local Government Reforms' in D McCargo (ed), *Reforming Thai Politics* (Copenhagen, NIAS, 2002) 225.

newly-formed units at local level becoming 'semi-independent States', reflecting the former system which existed before King Rama V's reforms. Indeed, in her study of the southern provinces, Loos identifies this imperialist narrative continuing into the present. She observes that:

> [t]he focus on Siam's endangered sovereignty is a red herring that ineluctably compels pursuers to follow the trail blazed by the monarch who heroically saved Siam [from its backward, chaotic and corrupt past], rather than a furtive path simultaneously taken by Siam's leaders who institutionalized an imperial juridical hierarchy in Pattani, Narathiwat, and Satan.[9]

In sum, the legacy of centralised absolute power at a local level of governance remains an element of crucial importance, except that now this power is mainly exercised through the Ministry of the Interior (MOI) rather than directly by an absolute monarch.

III. THE STRUCTURE OF LOCAL GOVERNMENT

Our point of departure is to set out the structural characteristics of local government in Thailand with reference to the various types of elected body, the methods of finance and the main form of local administration. Thailand is divided administratively into provinces, districts and sub-districts.[10] These are administrative areas under the authority of the provincial administration. At the same time there are geographical areas in which the various forms of local government function.

Local government in Thailand is organised in six different forms.[11] Three such forms are urban-based, with another three based in rural areas.

Urban-based forms of local government fall into the following categories:

---

[9] T Loos, *Subject Siam: Family, Law and Colonial Modernity in Thailand* (Ithaca, NY, Cornell University Press, 2006) 181.

[10] See <http://www.unescap.org/huset/lgstudy/country/thailand/thai.html>. This website provides a useful overview of Thailand's system of local government.

[11] See Act Changing the Status of Sanitary District to Municipality 1999, Provincial Administration Organisation Act (No 2) 1999, Municipality Act (No 10) 1999, Subdistrict Council and Subdistrict Administrative Organisation (TAO) Act (No 3) 1999, Municipal Government Act (No 12) 2003, Tambon Council and Tambon Administration Act (No 5) 2003.

a) The Municipalities (*Thesaban*) include a total 1,456 urban centres in the provinces. These comprise 25 cities (*Thesaban Nakhon*) with a population of over 50,000, which have 24 councillors; 118 towns (*Thesaban Mueangs*) with a population of more than 10,000 or a provincial capital, which have 18 councillors; and sub-district municipalities (*Thesaban Tambon*) with a population of more than 5,000 (these have largely replaced sanitary districts[12]), which have 12 councillors. Each of the above units has a council and a mayor elected every four years. The presidential-style mayor is the executive head of the authority, and the policies of the mayor are scrutinised by the council.

b) The Bangkok Metropolitan Administration (BMA). Bangkok has a Governor who is elected every four years. The Governor is both executive head of Bangkok province and chief executive of the Bangkok Metropolitan Administration In essence this is a presidential-style system, whereby the office-holder is scrutinised by a 57-member Bangkok Metropolitan Council, also elected every four years, which has limited legislative powers.

c) The City of Pattaya also has special status, and it partly resembles other municipalities and the BMA. The city authority is also headed by a Governor/Mayor elected every four years, who is responsible to an elected council of 24 members for making policies and running the city administration.[13]

Rural-based forms of local government include the following:

a) Below the level of central government the nation is divided administratively into 75 provinces. Other than in Bangkok and Pattaya, the Provincial[14] Administrative Organisation (PAO) administers local government at a provincial level. This comprises two bodies:

    i)   an administrative body headed by the provincial governor; and
    ii) an assembly of 24–48 members elected for a four-year term.

The Provincial Governor, renamed Chief Executive Officer (CEO), is elected from the council and is no longer appointed directly by the MOI. Provinces are divided administratively into a number of districts, headed by district officers who report to the CEO. At the provincial level the

---

[12] See Act Changing the Status of Sanitary District to Municipality 1999.

[13] See the Pattaya City Act of 1999.

[14] *Changwat* in Thai.

PAO is responsible for administering public services (see below) and for coordinating development projects.[15]

b) As observed above, the next tier down in urban areas consists of municipalities, but in rural areas 7,255 Tambon[16] Administrative Organisations (TAOs)[17] provide local government at the sub-district level. These TAOs govern an area with a relatively small population. Each one is headed by a sub-district chief (*Kamnan*). In rural districts a village headman is elected by popular vote once every five years. The local residents in each *Tambon* then elect a *Kamnan* from among these village headmen, who serves for a five-year term. Thus a *Tambon* can be broken down further as consisting of several villages (*Mooban*). Each village sends two representatives. Therefore the number of TAO councillors depends upon the number of villages. The *Kamnan* coupled with village heads have always been the prime linkage between the central State and the rural population. They have a mixed role as half civil servant and half representative. *Tambon* councils were only partially a structure for local government, but were previously firmly under the authority of the provincial government and did not have any law-making powers. These district councils have been replaced by TAOs which are more representative and are responsible for implementing citizen participation initiatives introduced under the 1997 Constitution. They continue to operate under the 2007 Constitution, as discussed in Section V below.

c) The *Sukhapiban*, or Sanitary Committee, is a local government unit in a rural centre, often referred to as a 'sanitary district'.

Competences which have been assigned to local government (Municipality, TAO and Pattaya City) under the Decentralisation Plan

---

[15] At provincial level the PAOs are responsible for: (i) provincial development planning with respect to the principle of economic growth and efficiency; (ii) the provision of large-scale public services, which are defined as services that cannot be executed by any other smaller localities within a province. Any benefit should apply to the entire province. For example, province-wide infrastructural projects, waste water treatment, solid waste disposal, and public transportation; (iii) human services for public education, health, social security and social welfare; (iv) natural resources and environmental protection relating to inter-local government activities; (v) promotion of trade and investment, tourism, culture and the arts; (vi) the provision of technical and financial support to lower-tier local authorities.

[16] May be translated as 'township'.

[17] Alternatively referred to as Subdistrict Administrative Organisations (SAO).

and Process Act 1999 fall under the main heads of: local and community planning and development; local public service provision for roads[18]; and social welfare provision.[19] Although a multiplicity of functions associated with the various tiers of local government are listed below, it should be remembered that in Thailand, State support for social welfare, pensions and advanced education is absent or offered only at a rudimentary level. The major exception is health care assistance, which is provided free in State hospitals under the 30 Baht Health Scheme, introduced after the 2001 election under the National Health Security Act 2002. This legislation made provision for local purchasing agencies, containing representatives from health institutions and from local government. A devolved scheme was established by introducing a National Health Security Office, separate from the Ministry of Public Health, which could channel the funding through contracting units at the point where primary care is provided.[20]

Local authorities were required by organic law promulgated under the 1997 Constitution to promote democratic values, civil rights, public participation, law and order, and conflict resolution. Further, there has been a constitutional requirement since 1997 to empower local government organisations to promote and maintain the quality of the environment in the preservation and exploitation of natural resources, and this requirement is exactly replicated in the 2007 Constitution.[21]

IV. LOCAL GOVERNMENT FINANCE

Local government in Thailand is financed in four ways:

a) local revenue from taxes, fees, charges and permits (10.78 per cent);

---

[18] Also including walkways, public transportation, traffic control, public markets, ports and docks, waste treatment, water, drainage, public utilities, parks and recreation, refuse collection, pet control, food hygiene, protection of the environment and natural resources, disaster control and cremation services.

[19] This includes education, social welfare for children, the elderly and disabled, primary health care, medical services, housing and restoration, art and culture.

[20] D Hughes and S Leethongdee, 'Universal Coverage in the Land of Smiles: Lessons from Thailand's 30 Baht Health Reforms' (2007) 26(4) *Health Affairs* 999; K Damrongplasit and G Melnick, 'Early Results from Thailand's 30 Baht Health Reform: Something to Smile About' (2009) 28(3) *Health Affairs* 457.

[21] TC 1997, s 290; TC 2007, s 281.

b) local revenue collected by central government agencies (VAT, excise duty, vehicle fees, land registration) (33.07 per cent);

c) shared taxes (18.25 per cent); and

d) grants from central government (37.9 per cent).

This expenditure comprises 22.5 per cent of central government's total revenue.[22] Municipalities and *Tambons* are allowed to borrow subject to certain conditions.[23] In regard to most forms of local, regional or devolved government, the financial arrangements are of pivotal importance in determining the degree of local autonomy. Although a substantial proportion of funds is raised locally, expenditure is largely determined by central government as local authorities cannot control their own tax policy. It has been observed that:

> Local governments have limited authority to set priorities and make expenditure allocation decisions. Local budgets must still be approved by the provincial governor (or district council), and central agencies monitor spending financed by general and specific subsidies. Most of the central government's transfers are tied to specific functions/programs, thereby restricting local government's autonomy.[24]

These restrictions on the financial capacity of local government were also designed to restrict the scope for financial misfeasance at the local level. The difficulty has been that the high level of dependency on central government for revenue tends to undermine the autonomy of local government. Furthermore, it has been widely recognised that these grants tend to be distributed in an unsystematic and highly politicised manner but with a high proportion of local expenditure allocated to health and education programmes. The Decentralisation Plan and Process Act 1999 to some extent tackled these issues. The Act stipulated that by 2006 the proportion of total revenue devoted to local government should be at least 35 per cent. This measure was designed to prevent central government economising by squeezing the block grants and tax-raising powers given to local authorities. To date, the provisions of

[22] W Krueathep, 'Fiscal Strategies of Thai Local Governments during the Decentralization Movement: A Preliminary Exploration of Characteristics and Causes', *ILGI Working Paper 01-2549*, May 2006. The breakdown is for the fiscal year 2004.

[23] See Decentralisation Plan and Process Act 1999, s 28.

[24] S Amornivivat, *Fiscal Decentralisation: The Case of Thailand* (Ministry of Finance, Thailand, 15 February 2004) 4. See <http://www.econ.hit-u.ac.jp/~kokyo/APPPsympo04/FiscDect%20_Thailand.pdf>.

the 1999 Act allowing decentralisation have been implemented unevenly, with only limited progress achieved in most relevant policy areas.[25]

V. DECENTRALISATION AND PARTICIPATION

A. Local administration

The various layers of local administration and provincial administration outlined above overlap to some extent. In addition, until very recently there was no regional apparatus for administration in Thailand. Administration at local government level was placed under the command of provincial governors and district officers who operated as the representatives of central government in the provinces. The Department of Local Administration, operating under the MOI, is responsible for the implementation of provincial as well as local administration. As a result of this capacity to intervene, administrative power at the local level has been highly centralised. Moreover, many other central government departments also have branch offices in the provinces. The provincial administration superimposes its own authority on local government. Essentially, it acts as an appointed agent of central government, through the MOI. To a large extent, the administrative power of local government in the provinces has been exercised under these central government agents, ie governors and district officers.

The relationship between these levels of government has clearly reflected the high degree of centralisation. The Community Development Department (CDD), which was established in 1962, encouraged the idea of local development focused on village leaders. The King initiated the project so that villages could develop self-reliance and self-governance. It was aimed at rural development on the basis of 'aided self-help'. King Bhumiphol stated that

> a true Thai-style democracy was one in which people understood the word 'enough' or 'appropriate', and in which people thought comprehensively (of all interests) such that the homeland was secure and the people were considerate to each other, and one where problems were addressed with cool-headedness.[26]

[25] *Ibid*, 18.
[26] M Connors, *Democracy and National Identity in Thailand* (Copenhagen, NIAS Press, 2007) 65.

In their unreformed condition the *Tambons* had little power in relation to the State administration. They served as vehicles for bureaucratic power, rather than as a form of local government involving genuine representation and participation. Progress towards achieving decentralisation had been held back by the existing bureaucracy, which was reluctant to cede power. In part this was because sub-district heads and council members were in a position to cream off a proportion of any contracts they commissioned. In their reconstituted form, the *Tambons* have two elected representatives from each village, and were intended to emerge as genuine forums for advancement of local interests.[27] In the absence of adequate oversight mechanisms, the grant of more autonomy, coupled with greatly increased grants and revenues, also had the potential to result in a systemic bureaucratisation under the control of the MOI.[28] Moreover, it has been pointed out that the approach of the Thaksin Government (2001–06) was not directly to support the devolution of authority.[29] Rather, under its policies, the culture and status of bureaucracy at the local government level (as also for central government) was to be transformed by injecting techniques of managerialism and by exposing the CEOs at PAO level to the ideas of business, risk and profit (see chapter three). Although operating in the public domain CEOs have been charged with responsibility for promoting the economic growth of their regions. In practice, the resulting business plans have mainly relied on growth through an expansion in tourism. The 2007 Constitution indicates that administration at local level will be reformed by giving local government officers the status of national civil servants and allowing for transferability between officials, through the introduction of committees that are independent of central government control; and by the introduction of an ethics committee to oversee the adherence to ethical values.[30]

In a different sense E-Government[31] offers the potential of changing the relationship between the governors and the governed, and in particular bringing service delivery closer to the people. One commentator states that:

[27] Arghiros, above n 8, 228.

[28] *Ibid*, at 231.

[29] P Phongpaichit and C Baker, *Thaksin: The Business of Politics in Thailand* (Chiang Mai, Silkworm Books, 2004) 187.

[30] TC 2007, s 279.

[31] E-Government refers to the range of initiatives by government at central or local level directed at providing information and/or services on line.

In Asia today, there is growing evidence that E-Government can lead to an improved business environment, greater citizen access to government services and information, and reduced levels of corruption.[32]

There have been plans to develop the government information and technology service to tackle poverty and increase contact with the outside world by providing information through the government web portal. At the same time there has been opposition by some vested interests to the wider introduction of E-Government, because the new technology will inevitably lead to greater transparency and reduce the unchecked exercise of discretion. However, the prevalence of E-Government at all levels in Thailand is dependent on general access of the community to computers.[33] The importance of bridging the digital divide applies to the 7,250 *Tambons* in order to be able to promote modern communication networks throughout rural Thailand.

B. Decentralisation: subsidiarity Thai-style or devolution?

Although Thailand is described as indivisible in section 1 of the 1997 and 2007 Constitutions, there has also been a constitutional commitment to decentralisation:

> The State shall decentralise powers to localities for the purpose of independence and self-determination of local affairs and encourage the provinces which have the potential to develop large-scale administrative organisations by placing emphasis on aspirations of the people in such provinces.[34]

In the context of the European Union, a similar concept referred to as *subsidiarity* addresses the difficult question of what is best achieved in the application of European law and policy at European level, and what is best achieved at national level, but the principle is not prescriptive of

[32] T Parks, 'A Few Misconceptions about eGovernment', Asia Foundation, 17 August 2005, 2.

[33] S Wangpipatwong, W Chutimaskul and B Papasratorn, 'Factors Influencing the Adoption of Thai eGovernment Websites: Information Quality and System Quality Approach', *Proceedings of the Fourth International Conference on eBusiness*, 19–20 November 2005, Bangkok; P Bhattarokosol, 'IT Direction in Thailand: Cultivating an E-Society', *IT PRO*, September/October 2003, 16–20.

[34] See TC 2007, ss 77(3) and 283.

the internal organisation of Member States.[35] Any action by the (now) Union should not go beyond what is necessary to achieve the objectives of the Treaty. In Thailand the State is required under the Constitution to give autonomy to localities in a way that reflects local demands. An equally important feature of the two most recent Constitutions is a section which requires the passage of subsequent law setting out the division between State and local government, and which introduces a progressive procedure to achieve this aim.[36]

The Decentralisation Plan and Process Act 1999 was passed to implement this constitutional provision designed to loosen the grip of central government on local government. As noted above, financial changes have been introduced to increase local government autonomy, but the main aim of democratic decentralisation is to transfer power from unelected civil servants and the local economic elites, who have tended to dominate the administration of policy at local government level, and to give additional powers to locally-elected representatives of the people. These changes would mean that the power formerly exercised by the MIO and provincial governors would be weakened through a redefinition of the role of PAOs and a progressive transfer of functions, budget and personnel to the TAOs. At the same time, this change was intended to encourage organisational uniformity between the units of administration at the *Tambon* level.[37]

Although the latest Decentralisation Plan of 2008 is currently being implemented as government policy, a number of concerns have arisen over the manner in which it is being introduced. In the first place, the task of introducing the initiative has been left in the hands of the MOI. The Department of Local Government Promotions attached to the MOI has been placed in charge of transferring responsibilities to other local administrative bodies. Given that for over 100 years the MOI has been recognised as the traditional agency for the tight imposition of the authority of the Thai State based in Bangkok, its commitment to the project might be called into question.[38] Secondly, in the absence of any constitutional or legislative clarity there is a lack of consensus over the

---

[35] Art 5 of the Treaty Establishing the European Community following the Treaty of Nice 2003.

[36] TC 2007, s 298.

[37] Nelson, above n 6, at 222.

[38] W Tanchai, 'Thailand's Case' published conference paper *Local Public Finance and Governance* (Bangkok, KPI, 2009) 27.

distribution of powers and functions between the various levels of government. For example, should PAOs be developed mainly as a tier of service delivery in relation to clearly-defined functions devolved to provinces, or should they be refashioned as strategic planning agencies with a mainly coordinating role?[39]

In view of the track record of PAOs as representative bodies as representative bodies, the issue of accountability arises as a third concern. Thailand has experienced a top-down local politics largely without political parties, where the widespread practice of vote-buying has allowed powerful cliques to predominate. Further, the candidates elected to councils at PAO level have tended to have personal business interests, and at the same time a high proportion of the budget allocated to PAOs tends to be spent on large-scale infrastructural projects. In consequence, it has been observed that:

> [t]he degree of accountability demonstrated by Provincial Councils and individual members to the electorate remains extremely poor. Councils tend to serve the collective and individual interests of members more effectively than those of the electorate.[40]

And of course success in local politics might provide a convenient stepping-stone to national politics. Apart from the general promotion and enforcement of ethical standards, there are no simple ways of transforming political culture to attract candidates who more broadly represent their community and to encourage the wider involvement of civil society in the form of non-governmental organisations (NGOs). Moreover, as we shall see at 137ff below, the dearth of female representatives in political office has been identified as a further problem that has yet to be addressed adequately at local government level.

The recognition of such deficiencies and the acknowledgement of the lack of expertise at the base levels of local government might be regarded as the prelude to establishing a credible reform programme. Indeed, the next step in achieving a more participatory form of decentralised democracy is to undertake, with the assistance of NGOs and academic institutions, a comprehensive programme of 'capacity building'. This might include the provision of education and training for

---

[39] D Webster, 'Implementing Decentralisation in Thailand: The Road Forward' in M Nelson (ed), *Thai Politics: Global and Local Perspectives, King Prajadhipok's Institute Yearbook No 2 (2002–2003)* (Bangkok, KPI, 2004) 492.

[40] Arghiros, above n 8, at 238.

politicians and officials in the theory, and particularly in the practice, of local governance.[41] The reluctance of the MOI and the Bangkok establishment to confer genuine empowerment on these institutions, in part, might have been justified because these practical challenges have not yet been surmounted, but a desire for the retention of authority at the centre is also a reflection of a view within the ruling elite that any further loosening of control over budgeting and policy implementation will simply increase the potential for abuse and lead to more endemic corruption at a lower level of government. From a different perspective, however, it is apparent that the political fault lines that have emerged between the Red Shirt and Yellow Shirt factions have a very strong regional dimension to them, and that in particular the current conflict is accentuated by the 'winner takes all' outcome of any power struggle in Bangkok. The failure to achieve sufficient decentralisation means that the Government in Bangkok exercises direct control over policy for the entire nation, including those regions where it enjoys little electoral support. For example, since the change over of power in December 2008 there has been hostility to the Government in the Red Shirt strongholds in the north and north east, but the main levers of political power remain with Bangkok. On the other hand, it could be argued that a radical revision of the Constitution to introduce a form of devolution for the nation, or for parts of the nation, would help ameliorate such tensions by reducing the capacity of the centre to impose its domination to the perceived detriment of any region.

C. Decentralisation: policy initiatives

In addition to innovations in the organisation and administration of local government alluded to above, there have been decentralisation initiatives at the micro-political level of policy delivery. Education is a crucial policy area where widespread decentralisation of administration and management was set out under existing education legislation, but the implementation has been sporadic and uneven.[42] There have been concerns over the management of primary and secondary schools, and regarding the provisions for their funding. In view of the difficulties in

[41] Nelson, above n 6, at 261.
[42] See the National Education Act 1999.

capacity and training, a staged process of decentralisation has been put in place. It was reported that 10 schools had already been transferred to local control, and a further 292 schools followed suit by May 2008.[43] Likewise, it has been noted that:

> If social services are to be delivered by local government . . . large-scale and effective capacity-building will be needed. Local government cannot just be given responsibility for relatively complex functions such as primary health care, vocational training, social services delivery etc, without grounding in the basic principles and approaches.[44]

On the other hand, there are many individual instances of the transfer of power to local control. One such example concerns the provincial sports centre in Phrae, a province in Northern Thailand, which was transferred from the Sports Authority of Thailand to the PAO under the Decentralisation Plan and Process Act of 1999.[45] In addition, a concept of EU-style subsidiarity has been discernible, with a wider trend towards delegation downwards of decision-making.

> A total of 245 responsibilities were transferred from the central and regional government to local organisations, involving 50 departments in 11 ministries. In this transfer the important dimension was not just the local organisations' increased responsibilities that affected people in all directions, but also their increased power of discretion as issuers and enforcers of laws and regulation[46]

Further, PAOs are meant to promote democratic decentralisation but, to date, the policy has been applied unevenly. It does not rely on any general popular participation and substantial powers have yet to be devolved to these bodies.

D. Public participation

The 1997 and 2007 Constitutions have encouraged participation in national and local government by placing a duty on the State through directive principles to promote public participation in laying down

---

[43] 'Locals Take Charge of Problem Schools', *The Nation*, 4 July 2007.

[44] Webster, above n 39, at 485.

[45] Krueathep, above n 22, at 229.

[46] O Kokpol, 'Conflict of Interest in Local Government' in N Rathamarit (ed), *Eyes on Thai Democracy: National and Local Issues* (Bangkok, KPI, 2006) 138.

policies, in decision-making, and in the formulation of economic and social development plans. For example, the State is required to implement a public participation policy to encourage people to participate in forming socio-economic development policies and plans at both local and national levels, and in the making of political decisions.[47] The Constitution further provides that people in a local area have the right to participate in the administration of the activities of local government organisations, and that such organisations must provide the method for them to do so.[48]

This initiative is based on the assumption that democratic values will be more easily embedded if the wider population is drawn into policy implementation and the decision-making process.[49] In theory, this means that citizens should be granted the right to be involved in the process of policy-making, but the evidence available to us suggests that public participation is not yet part of general experience; rather, these experiments in various Thai forms of participatory democracy have been realised in a number of test-bed schemes in a variety of contexts. For example, the Khon-Khan project in an urban environment might be taken as representative of one approach. Khon-Khan is a city of 130,000 inhabitants. Citizen participation has involved focus-group meetings for discussions between members of the community and municipal administrators. The input of the local community might allow the environmental and societal impact of infrastructural development to be registered relatively informally at these discussions, while Town Hall meetings are used for broader policy-related discussion. Participatory techniques have in this instance been employed as a means of developing a form of policy dialogue at a number of levels.[50] By way of contrast, the Nong Ko Development Council of Maharsarakhan Province is an example based on a much smaller rural community. It depended on the Council pooling resources and building up carefully managed cooperation to deliver infrastructural benefits of water sup-

---

[47] TC 2007, s 87.

[48] TC 2007, s 287.

[49] See, eg, J Habermas, *Moral Consciousness and Communicative Action* (Cambridge, MA, MIT Press, 1990) 66; and see M Deflem (ed), *Habermas, Modernity and Law* (London, Sage, 1996) 9.

[50] Krueathep, above n 22, at 222. Other more radical participatory models, including the civil forum and the local development planning forum, are also discussed by Krueathep.

plies, road construction, transport provision, etc to enhance the economic strength of the community. Part of the process has involved the modification of regulations and developing techniques of dispute-resolution at this level of government.[51] Another well-known project has been the Community Forest Network of the Upper Ping River in Chiang Mai Province, which has been developed to allow the local community to self-manage the local forest while also protecting and conserving it in the interests of the local community. Despite predictable difficulties in implementing such initiatives, commentators have generally reported positively on their outcome. However, any success of these pilot schemes must be qualified by the recognition that they have depended on generous funding and intensive professional support from academics and from NGOs.

A crucial area where the call for wider participation has not been adequately addressed concerns the involvement of women and women's groups in the political and social arena at the local level. Women are under-represented, with only 6 per cent of elected positions in local government and no female mayors.[52] There have been strong traditional prejudices for women to overcome before they could consider entering public space to pursue a political agenda. Women voicing political demands tended to be regarded as unwomanly and were accused of endangering the unity of the family.[53] Despite the emergence of a number of civic women's groups there has been a virtual exclusion of women from representative government, which reflects prejudice and ignores the need for positive discrimination. For instance, it has been argued that legislation is required that would require a quota of seats to go to women.[54]

The discussion so far has concentrated on the constitutional and legal path to increased decentralisation. A central aim envisaged by the

---

[51] T Bureekul, 'Participation of Civil Society in Decentralisation in Thailand: Lessons Learned from Natural Resource Management and Community Economic Development' in Rathamarit (ed), above n 46, at 80.

[52] A recent detailed study revealed that women are under-represented. The national figures show that women make up only 5.8% of local elected councillors. At PAO level 3.6% of Chief Executives are female and 12% of other representatives are female. Only 6.6% of councillors are female; 4.4% of TAO and 6.7% of councillors are women. See W Tanchai, O Kokpol, P Phosuwan and P Achariyapanya, *Local Democracy in Thailand: Representation in Decentralised Governance* (Bangkok, KPI, 2007) 123.

[53] P Doneys, 'Political Reform through the Public Sphere: Women's Groups and the Fabric of Governance' in McCargo (ed), above n 8, at 167.

[54] Arghiros, above n 8, at 234.

designers of the 1997 Constitution was to re-invent local government as an agency for the redistribution of wealth, tackling the obvious discrepancy between rural and urban communities. The grant of additional autonomy to local government has obvious pitfalls in the light of the widespread evidence of malpractice and corruption at this level of government, and the inadequacy of existing mechanisms to contain it.[55] In part, these dangers explain the reluctance of politicians and officials to devolve power downwards. The thrust of Thaksin's leadership when he was Prime Minister (2001–06) with an overwhelming majority in Parliament, was based on 'strong centralised leadership'. At local level this meant conferring increased powers on local governors as CEOs. In other words, the Thaksin Government was pulling in exactly the opposite direction from that envisaged by the framers of the 1997 (and 2007) Constitution. Despite the success of Thaksin's party (TRT) at the national level, the party leadership was not able to dominate local party politics, which is organised around traditional cliques. Nelson has explained that:

> Local politics is a largely exclusive affair. Political parties are basically absent at the provincial level; they have hardly any branch offices at the local level that could support the political participation of citizens. Instead we find informal cliques (*phuak*) of people who are active as national and local politicians. These cliques are based on a variety of relationships, for example family ties, friendship, business interests, or patron client ties.[56]

Essentially, there was a conflict of interest between local MPs, associated with local interests, and the newly-appointed and powerful CEOs carrying out the policy of central government. Success in local elections, however, has remained dependent on vote-buying and established canvasser networks. Lacking these assets, TRT failed to achieve comparable success in local government elections. The initial reaction to the defeat of many of the TRTs candidates for elected mayorships in 2004, and elections for village headmen, was for the PM to float proposals (later dropped) to recentralise power and abolish elections at this level.[57]

We can conclude this section by noting that despite the constitutional commitment to decentralisation and participation (which has continued

---

[55] Kokpol, above n 46, at 169.
[56] See Nelson, above n 6, at 259.
[57] D McCargo and U Pathmanand, *The Thaksinization of Thailand* (Copenhagen, NIAS Press, 2005) 103ff.

under the 2007 Constitution), trends in this direction have been limited. Further progress towards centralisation might be achieved by a rationalisation of local administration linked to an improved capacity for service delivery and improved oversight mechanisms. However, apart from overcoming the resistance of politicians and central government officials to further decentralisation, the reduction of corruption at a local level remains the most important obstacle to surmount, and this issue will now be addressed.

VI. PROMOTING GOOD LOCAL GOVERNANCE

A. Elimination of corruption

The elimination of corruption has been a constitutional priority in recent years. Under the 1997 Constitution, the Election Commission of Thailand (ECT)[58] was made responsible for controlling and conducting elections for local assemblies and local administrators under the Local Elections and Local Administrators Act 2002, as amended in 2003.[59] This task covers all stages of the electoral process, from having responsibility for determining the demarcation of constituency boundaries at the provincial level, keeping the electoral register and establishing eligibility to vote, to the organisation of balloting and the counting of votes. In addition, the role of the ECT in overseeing the expenditure of candidates not only involves setting the amount candidates are allowed to spend according to the size of the geographical area, but it also specifically includes the elimination of vote-buying. The ECT is required to conduct investigations if there are disputes over the conduct of an election, and it must do this before announcing the result. The ECT is further empowered to order a re-run of the election if it finds evidence of irregularities.[60] The 2002 Act does not prevent individuals under contract with the municipality from standing at elections. Provincial Councils and TAOs are rarely representative of the local electorate. The manifest prevalence of vote-buying at the provincial and sub-district

[58] See P Leyland, 'Thailand's Constitutional Watchdogs: Dobermans, Bloodhounds or Lapdogs?' (2007) 2(2) *Journal of Comparative Law* 151, at 160ff.
[59] See website of ECT at <http://www.ect.go.th/english/localelection_f.html>.
[60] Local Elections Act 2002, s 95.

levels has meant that elected bodies are dominated by local economic and political elites and business interests, mirroring this same trend in national politics.

In practice, there has been considerable scope for corruption in local government. At the provincial level, where the PAO is dedicated to allow democratic decentralisation, this is particularly serious, because members often have privileged access to development budgets which have been intended for infrastructural development, typically earmarked for construction of roads, dams and irrigation channels.[61] In many regions there have been widespread problems concerning conflicts of interest.[62] Many different types of malpractice have been reported in considerable detail. For example, self-dealing is a common form of conflict of interest which occurs when members of local councils or administrators, or their families, are involved, or become involved, in a construction company or other company which is awarded a contract by the local administration. There have been cases where payment has been received for a project without any work being carried out. Another abuse has involved the direct use of public funds for personal benefit, or for canvassing votes.[63]

These abuses have continued despite numerous statutes that attempt to outlaw corruption. The Organic Law on the Prevention and Suppression of Corruption 1999 bans any such conflicts of interest and expressly forbids any connection with private companies. It allows for inspections to take place and prevents the acceptance of gifts or rewards. A jail sentence of up to three years and/or a fine may be imposed for breach of these rules. In addition, the Municipal Act 1953, as amended in 1999, forbids the mayor and members of councils and administrators from having vested interests, directly or indirectly, in any municipal contract. Infringement of the regulation is a cause for termination of membership. The Tambon Council and Tambon Administrative Organisation Act 1994, the Provincial Administrative Organisation Act 1985, and the Bangkok Metropolis Administration Act 1985 enact similar provisions relating to their respective types of local government authority. However, it has been

---

[61] Arghiros, above n 8, at 235.

[62] There has been a raft of legislation on the issue of banning conflicts of interests relating to councillors and administrators. See, eg, Municipal Act 1953 plus amendment (No 10) of 1999; Tambon Councils and Tambon Administration Organisations Acts 1994 and 1999; Bangkok Metropolis Administration Act 1985.

[63] Kokpol, above n 46, at 144ff details the various kinds of malpractice.

pointed out that a major loophole in the law is that the Prevention and
Suppression of Corruption Act 1999 does not apply to local government.
This allowed the majority of local politicians to escape from having to
declare their assets, thus concealing conflicts of interest.[64] It would appear
that there is an urgent need to consolidate these various statutes to draw
up clear rules that would apply to all levels of government. Also, the system of petitioning for the removal of alleged miscreants from office can
be activated on a reduced number of signatures.[65]

B. Ethical standards and declaration of assets

In terms of its drafting, the 2007 Constitution is even more clearly
directed towards the elimination of corruption than its predecessor. It
seeks to patch many of the most obvious loopholes that were apparent
in the previous Constitution.

A specific commitment to an ethical code that applies to all persons
holding political positions, government officials and State officials at all
levels, including local government, is a novel feature of the 2007
Constitution.[66] The ombudsman is expected to advise on the drafting of
the moral code and then promote awareness of the code that is adopted.
Once it is in place, the ombudsman has an oversight function in investigating and disclosing violations of the code, the most serious of which
are to be referred to the National Anti-Corruption Commission
(NACC). The ombudsman has powers to investigate, to refer and to
report, but the office is not able to disqualify miscreants. In addition,
stringent provisions are included elsewhere in the revised Constitution
to prevent conflicts of interest at all levels, and local administrators and
members of local assemblies are required to submit accounts showing
particulars of their assets and liabilities, and those of their spouses and
children.[67] If malpractice is identified by the NACC, on referral to the
Constitutional Court for confirmation as required under the 2007
Constitution and the related organic law,[68] any person who fails to

---

[64] *Ibid*, at 158ff.
[65] TC 2007, s 276.
[66] TC 2007, s 270.
[67] See generally TC 2007, ss 250–255.
[68] Organic Act on Counter-Corruption 1999, s 34.

comply with these provisions will be subject to an immediate five-year ban from holding any political position or public office.[69]

This emphasis on ethical values can be linked to provisions designed to achieve greater transparency. Local authorities will be required to publish annual reports detailing their budgeting, spending and performance, thus allowing these aspects to be monitored and scrutinised more systematically.[70]

VII. THE TROUBLES IN THAILAND'S SOUTHERN PROVINCES

Thailand has a serious political problem in the extreme south of the country. This is the region where the minority Malay/Muslim population is concentrated, and it will soon be apparent that, although the origins of the insurgency can be traced back historically, the policies of recent governments have contributed to the escalating violence since 2004 which has resulted in more than 3,500 deaths. The level of insurgency suggests that a radical political initiative will be required to break the cycle of violence. The 2007 Constitution follows the pattern of previous constitutions by stating that Thailand is an indivisible kingdom.[71] Indeed, given that Thailand has been forged as a highly centralised State, it might be suggested that a form of devolution specifically designed to meet the demands of the local population in the south might contribute to a political settlement.[72]

Before floating possible constitutional solutions it will be instructive to attempt to set this problem in the context of Thai history and recent politics. The extreme south shares a border of more than 600 km with Malaysia. A substantial proportion of Thailand's nearly 5 million Muslims (comprising over 5 per cent of the total population) lives in the south,[73] particularly the provinces of Yala, Narathiwat and Pattani,

---

[69] TC 2007, s 254.

[70] TC 2007, s 278(3).

[71] The same system of local government for urban and rural areas (described in section III above) applies to all of Thailand, including the troubled southern provinces.

[72] See P Leyland, 'Thailand's Troubled South: Examining the Case for Devolution from a Comparative Perspective' (2009) 11(1) *Australian Journal of Asian Law* 1.

[73] See <http://www.state.gov/g/drl/rls/irf/2003/24323.htm>.

where Muslims account for 1.3 million of 1.8 million inhabitants.[74] Although these mainly Malay-speaking regions form part of modern Thailand, the southern border of Siam was disputed in the early to mid-19th century. As the western colonial power with an interest in the area from the end of 18th century, the British sought to negotiate treaties with Siam in order to set clear territorial boundaries. The Anglo-Siamese Treaty of 1909, which incorporated these southern provinces as part of Siam, also transferred the 'Malay' States of Kedah, Kelantan, Perlis and Terrenganu to the British.[75]

However, it has been argued convincingly that Siamese involvement cannot be understood merely in terms of border claims and what is an essentially European definition of State sovereignty. Winichakul's intricate survey explains that:

> A history of the geo-body of Siam is not a chronological description of boundary demarcations and the events which led to the making of Siam's map.[76]

Rather, this was a region of self-governing tributary kingdoms that owed allegiance to a supreme overlord as part of the Theravada Buddhist notion of righteous kingship. The King in Bangkok, to consolidate his power, had to fight to expand his umbrella of merit and righteousness, *dharma*. In effect this meant that as far as possible he needed to bring lesser kingdoms under the protection of his supreme merit. This relationship was not understood merely in terms of territory. Rather, these tributary provinces were bound to Bangkok by a ritual of submission, involving periodic payments to renew the allegiance, and with it the expectation of protection. Whenever the Thai royal capital was weak, local rulers often revolted by refusing to send tribute, and this in turn prompted military intervention from Bangkok.[77] Despite attempts during the 20th century to integrate the south, varying degrees of resistance have been displayed, with phases of insurgency during most of the 20th century and beyond.

---

[74] U Pathmanand, 'Thaksin's Policies Go South', *Far Eastern Economic Review*, July 2005, 8.

[75] See D Wyatt, *Thailand: A Short History*, 2nd edn (Newhaven, Conn, Yale University Press, 2003) 180 and 190.

[76] T Winichakul, *Siam Mapped: A History of the Geo-Body of a Nation* (University of Hawaii Press, Honolulu, 1994) 56.

[77] Loos, above n 9, at 77.

The complexion as well as the intensity of the unrest has fundamentally changed over time. The three main competing groups in the south of the previous generation were the Patani National Liberation Front (BNPP), the Patani United Liberation Organisation (PULO) and National Revolutionary Front (BRN). Each was established with an Islamic dimension reflecting the religious belief of its supporters, but primarily to campaign for an independent homeland for Thai citizens of Malay origin.[78] Although in the 1990s PULO was responsible for a low-level conflict resulting in the death of more than 100 Thai soldiers, it operated on the fringes of society and failed to gain wider support. The BRN still exists as a secret organisation responsible for the dissemination of separatist ideas geared towards the founding of an independent Patani State.[79]

International terrorism has certainly exerted some influence in the tactics and ideas that have been prevalent in the southern provinces, but there is some debate as to the extent to which separatist and religious groups have clear links with transnational extreme Islamicist groups and have managed to attract external assistance, particularly support from rich Middle-Eastern nations.[80] Latterly, it has been claimed that religion has become a prime motivator for militant Islamic groups with a radical Islamicist social agenda associated with fundamentalist organisations such as Tabliqhi Jamaat and Wahhabism. There were reports in 2009 by the Brussels-based International Crisis Groups that recruits were systematically indoctrinated with radical Islam and prepared for *jihad*. For groups under the influence of Salafism, the attempt to reach a state of pure Islam in any locality is achieved not by winning hearts and minds of local people, but by intimidating moderate fellow Muslims who are warned against any form of interaction with the Thai State. But commentators have been careful to qualify the influence of militant Islamicism:

> Rather than demonstrating a resurgent, aggressive Islam, wielding arms with confident flourish, the renewed violence reflects a disappointed, dissenting, and divided Malay-Muslim community, whose most capable leaders have been captured by Bangkok. Where Malay-Muslims have turned to militancy,

---

[78] Z Abuza, *Conspiracy of Silence: The Insurgency in Southern Thailand* (Washington, DC, United States Institute of Peace, 2009) 16.

[79] T Khanthong, 'The Battle to Win Hearts and Minds in the Deep South', *The Nation*, 30 June 2009.

[80] Abuza, above n 78, 145ff.

it has been because their own leaders have experienced a parallel loss of spiritual, moral, and political authority.[81]

This shift from having recognisable organisations associated with prominent individuals to having multiple religious groups, often without clearly identified political as opposed to religious leaders, presents a problem for the authorities when seeking to have negotiations that engage all the relevant factions.

There is an important economic and social dimension to this problem.[82] These provinces are also among the poorest in Thailand, and over a prolonged period going back over a century they have experienced spells of intermittent rebellion directed against the Thai State which tended to be violently repressed, as in the case of Muslim tax rebellions of 1922 and 1923.[83] After the Second World War the policy of the military governments was to attempt to resettle and integrate Buddhists from the north east (one estimate puts the figure at 102,000), while at the same time suppressing the separatist elements of southern Muslims. Although a substantial proportion of both the Muslim and Buddhist populations migrated to the region relatively recently, sizable minorities have also left the region, partly in response to the upsurge in violence. It has been noted that 'the insurgency has never just been about this economic marginalization. There is a strong sense of internal colonialism and relative deprivation.'[84] Although the majority group in Thailand as a whole, the Buddhist minority (roughly 20 per cent) in the southern border provinces of Pattani, Yala and Narathiwat has enjoyed a privileged position. By controlling most businesses and occupying the majority of senior bureaucratic positions, Buddhists have exerted a disproportionate degree of economic and administrative power in the southern border provinces. For example, the discrimination perceived by the Muslim majority has been apparent in their alienation from the mainstream educational system, which is regarded as being of poor quality. The vast majority of the Muslim population have abandoned State education at secondary level in favour of their own Islamic schools. In turn, these

[81] D McCargo, *Tearing the Land Apart: Islam and Legitimacy in Southern Thailand* (Ithaca, NY, Cornell University Press, 2008) 20.

[82] S Jitpiromsri and P Sobhonvasu, 'Unpacking Thailand's Southern Conflict: The Poverty of Structural Explanations' in D McCargo (ed), *Rethinking Thailand's Southern Violence* (Singapore, NUS Press, 2007) 96.

[83] Abuza, above n 78, at 12.

[84] *Ibid*, at 30.

schools, with their teachers often educated in Egypt, India, Pakistan, Saudi Arabia and Sudan, might become recruiting grounds for Islamic insurgents. Further, as manifestations of the State, schools and teachers have been systematically targeted for attack by militants. [85]

The pattern of people's ordinary lives has changed in response to the violence. Recent studies have revealed

> a number of critical themes touching on the broader question of how neighbourhoods and the individuals within them manage survival and trust in the face of an unseen enemy, an often ineffective state and the pressures (from both local and national contexts) to divide into ethnic and religiously polarised 'communities of fear'. [86]

In the place of the rule of law and State protection, village headmen in rival Buddhist and Malay-speaking villages undertake responsibility for the protection of the respective communities; but these individuals have also become prime targets for the extremists. At the same time the increasingly assertive conduct of the Muslim majority has also made the Buddhist population feel further marginalised and under threat.[87] Nevertheless, an enlightened approach has often been adopted by the Thai Government, with the intention of integrating the Muslim community by increasing the number of appointments to provincial positions and by increasing educational opportunities.[88]

During the 1980s the Thai governments in power managed to establish a delicate balance within this region because leaders such as Prime Minister Prem Tinsulanond recognised and built upon the established power structure. These provinces were an enclave of military power and privilege, supported by local government officials who were overwhelmingly loyal to the royalist Democrat Party. This included elevating some local Muslims to influential positions as local officials, for example district officers. This approach was a working microcosm of the national-level political networks comprising a complex mixture of monarchism,

---

[85]   McCargo, above n 81, at 40ff and 52.

[86]   M Askew, 'Landscapes of fear, horizons of trust: Villagers dealing with danger in Thailand's insurgent south', *Journal of Southeast Asian Studies*, 40(1), February 2009, 59 at 85.

[87]   D McCargo, 'The politics of Buddhist identity in Thailand's deep south: The demise of civil religion', *Journal of Southeast Asian Studies*, 40(1), February 2009, 11 at 14.

[88]   A Harding, 'Buddhism, Human Rights and Constitutional Reform in Thailand' (2007) 2(1) *Asian Journal of Comparative Law* 1 at 11.

moralism and structural corruption. In addition, local military commanders were given full responsibility for securing the Malaysian border. From a different perspective, we can see that any success this policy enjoyed depended upon a formal strategy of institution-building. The Southern Border Provinces Administrative Centre (SBPAC) was established in 1981 as a forum for the military, Muslim leaders, religious teachers, local officials and an agency to channel support for local projects. This body was recognised as performing a useful task as an intermediary between the various manifestations of the Thai State and the Muslim community.

A. The South under Thaksin

The sharp escalation of violence since 2004 in particular has been attributed, in part at least, to the policies pursued by former Prime Minister Thaksin Shinawatra.[89] From his political standpoint the south was viewed as home territory for the opposition Democrat Party, and he sought to bring this region within the scope of his political influence. He sent in some of his acolytes to report back on the situation. The key representatives of the old power group were identified and then transferred out of the region. The existing power structures were staffed with new Thaksin loyalist officials. Also, the police were given an enhanced role in a new power structure.[90] Moreover, it is particularly significant that Thaksin abolished the SBPAC in May 2002; this was because of its association with the Democrat Party. Its eventual replacement, the Southern Border Provinces Peace-Building Command (SBPPC), failed to gain the confidence of Muslim leaders. These changes resulted in key figures who enjoyed local trust being replaced by Thaksin appointees who possessed little or no experience of the south. In effect, the existing power structure was dismantled; and at the same time there was an intention to eliminate violence directly by strengthening the hand of the security forces. It has been pointed out that

[89] See S Jitpiromsi and P Sobhonvasu, 'Unpacking Thailand's Southern Conflict: The Poverty of Structural Explanations' (2006) 38:1 *Critical Asian Studies* 95.

[90] D McCargo, 'Thaksin and the Resurgence of Violence in the Thai South: Network Monarchy Strikes Back?' (2006) 38:1 *Critical Asian Studies* 46.

the far south's unique position as a cultural enclave under semi-colonial rule meant it was uniquely sensitive to the Thaksin government's centralization of power [and this upsurge of Islamic consciousness] renewed stress on Thai culture, and rehabilitation of the military . . . as security forces became more concerned over possible links with militant Islam, the frequency of searches and seizures increased.[91]

Rather than recognising that separatists might have their own political agenda, Thaksin sought to portray the southern violence as attributable to 'bandits' or to organised crime in the form of drug trafficking.[92]

This recent trend towards polarisation should be viewed against a long tradition of interaction and coexistence between the two communities that included Muslim patronage of local Buddhist temples (*wats*). It is particularly significant that the conflict has recently assumed a strong religious dimension in the Buddhist community, with *wats* increasingly employed as military bases. Since 2002 temples have become associated with the military as military personnel work and live within the confines of a *wat*. The buildings have often been fortified with raised outer walls and stretched barbed wire around the perimeter to offer protection from observation and from attack. These tactics have impacted on the traditional role of Buddhism in the south. As Jerryson goes on to observe:

> The State's appropriation of Buddhist space has altered the southern Thai wat's spatial significance. Serving as a home base for the military, wat have lost some of their sacrality in exchange for a strident nationalism.[93]

There has been a covert introduction of military monks operating under cover. This militarisation means that rather than representing a religious quest for enlightenment as Buddhists, the *Sangha* in these southern provinces have tended to become a manifestation of the Thai State. In consequence, it is not surprising that monks have featured increasingly as a target for Muslim terrorists.

Of course, this trend towards militarisation of monks is highly controversial among many Thai Buddhists, as it flies in the face of the Buddha's basic teaching, which prohibits military ordination. On the

---

[91] Phongpaichit and Baker, above n 29, at 236.

[92] U Pathmanand, 'Thaksin's Achilles' Heel: The Failure of Hawkish Approaches in the Thai South' (2006) 38:1 *Critical Asian Studies* 77.

[93] M Jerryson, 'Appropriating a Space for Violence: State Buddhism in Southern Thailand' *Journal of Southeast Asian Studies*, 40(1), February 2009, 33 at 43.

other hand, the need for the Buddhist minority to stand up and resist the insurgency has been stressed. No lesser figure than the Queen has called on Buddhists in the south faced with recurrent vicious sectarian attacks not to be driven from their homes, but rather to defend themselves and learn how to shoot. Such calls have encouraged the formation of militias such as the Or Ror Bor (civil volunteers for village protection).[94] In anticipation of wider civil conflict, the arming of locals has been accompanied by the formation of some separate and gated communities with checkpoints at night to prevent indiscriminate attacks.

This trend towards militarisation and separation is compounded by an ultra-conservative Thai Buddhist discourse which trades upon demonising Islam and, at the same time, exaggerating the threat to the Thai State by the demographic spread and growth of the Muslim population.

A growing terrorist problem was first associated with an increasingly militant Islamic separatist movement which from 2004 has been responsible for a catalogue of brutal murders and bomb attacks, targeted not only at the army and police, but also at monks, teachers and civilians. The murder of a monk in Bacho, Narathiwat, on 22 January 2004 was the first of a series of such killings. As the situation developed the groups involved in violence have changed, and there have been atrocities on both sides, often on a tit-for-tat basis. In April 2004 international human rights organisations were already calling into question the oppressive use of force by the Thai army and policy when it was reported that 107 alleged assailants, mostly between 15 and 20 years of age, had died in nine hours of clashes.[95] The Tak Bai Incident was certainly the most notorious example of heavy-handedness associated with the Thai authorities.[96] It occurred on 25 October 2004, when around 2,000 Muslim protestors encircled a police station. More than 1,000 arrests were made. Those detained were bound and forced to lie in the street, and were then packed into trucks to be taken to a detention centre for interrogation. Seventy-eight of those subsequently transported in these appalling conditions died of suffocation. Despite the unqualified defence of the military made by Thaksin as Prime Minister, the

---

[94] McCargo, above n 87, at 25.

[95] 'Thailand: Probe Use of Lethal Force in Muslim South', *Human Rights Watch*, 28 April 2004, available at <http://www.hrw.org/en/news/2004/04/28/thailand-probe-use-lethal-force-muslim-south>.

[96] See Harding, above n 88, at 9.

victims' families were offered limited compensation, and a report by an independent commission set up by the Government later directed blame at the military commanders. Predictably, a series of revenge attacks by Muslim militants followed in the wake of this event.

The verdict of the electorate in the south in the February 2005 General Election was ample testimony to the failure of this policy of repression and the growing polarisation in these provinces. Despite a landslide victory in much of Thailand, Thaksin's TRT Party was decisively rejected, losing 52 of the 54 seats that were contested in the region's 14 provinces to the opposition Democrat Party. Moreover, it was well known that the palace was opposed to the Thaksin policy of military force, and to the division of the south into zones as way of rating the extent of the threat posed by insurgency.

Whether prompted by royal intervention or, as some have suggested,[97] in an attempt to undermine royal authority, Thaksin suddenly changed his tune. His public pronouncements became relatively conciliatory, and he reinstated a representative body in place of the SBPAC to bring the parties together and prepare the ground for a negotiated settlement. The National Reconciliation Commission (NRC) was set up by the Thaksin Government under the chairmanship of Anand Panyarachun, former Prime Minister, with a brief to look into the conflict and recommend solutions.[98] A few southern Muslims were recruited to the Commission, but only one Buddhist monk representative, who favoured inter-faith dialogue, leading to a perception among elements in the Buddhist community that the body was pro-Muslim. At this point Thaksin acknowledged that 'violence could not be solved by violence'. However, the potential of this new body was undermined by a number of factors. Representatives from the south were reluctant to become involved, as this would expose them to the prospect of personal attack by militants. At the same time Muslims felt further alienated from any official overtures as a result of Thaksin's declaration of a state of emergency in July 2005, which gave unprecedented and draconian powers to a civilian Prime Minister.

When it reported in March 2006 the NRC made an important set of policy recommendations containing elements that might form the basis for an eventual settlement. These included proposals for the decentrali-

---

[97] McCargo, above n 90, particularly at 58ff.
[98] McCargo, above n 81, at 10.

sation of political power and mechanisms for enhanced participation in policymaking, coupled with proposals for the introduction of a new regional administrative body (Peaceful Strategic Administrative Centre for Southern Border Provinces (PSAC)) which would assume responsibility for policy administration in the area. There were also plans to address perceived deficiencies in the courts and judicial system. However, more radical were proposals further to strengthen Islamic law, improve Islamic education and adopt Malay as a second 'working' language.[99] As McCargo points out, a settlement on such terms was doomed to failure as

> [t]he NRC had become the de facto opposition, representing a set of values and ideas comprehensively opposed by the Thaksin government. While the formal membership of the NRC included a number of bureaucrats and Thaksin associates, by October 2005 most of the core participants were people aligned with the NGO sector.[100]

In making such proposals the NRC was out of touch both with the Thaksin Government and with mainstream Thai opinion. Any settlement of this problem will have to confront the upsurge in Buddhist chauvinism that emerged in Thailand during Thaksin's premiership (2001–06). The Yala attack of March 2007, in which Islamic militants executed eight Buddhist minibus passengers, is an example of a shocking incident that has inflamed the extreme popular responses to the violence in the south. A new form of hard-line nationalist discourse and anti-Muslim sentiment has become an increasingly overt and mainstream element of Thai Buddhist identity.[101] Nevertheless, after the bloodless military coup in September 2006, the military government sought to court the Islamic community by distancing itself from Thaksin's southern policy. Prime Minister Surayad Chulanont made a public apology in November 2006 for the excesses of the previous government, while dropping criminal charges against some protestors and making a formal legal commitment to recognise the practise of Sharia law. (It should be remembered that Islamic family courts set up by Siam's leaders have dispensed Islamic marriage, divorce and inheritance law for more than a century in Thailand's southern provinces.) The emphasis was now not only on upholding the rule of law, but on achieving some

[99] Abuza, above n 78, 130.
[100] McCargo, above n 90, at 65.
[101] McCargo, above n 87, 32.

form of reconciliation. The main feature of the interim government's policy was an economic development plan and a resuscitation of a reconstituted Southern Border Provinces Administration Centre (SBAC) which now included Justice Ministry officials. It has been pointed out that in this form the SBAC is 'firmly subordinated to the security apparatus of the Internal Security Operations Command (ISOC)'[102] and thus it might be perceived as 'acting as a development organization to support military-security policy'.[103] Despite this change of tone by the junta, a high-profile military presence continued in the border provinces and no agreement was reached. In fact, there was another surge in the number of violent attacks, particularly a series of beheadings and bombings directed mainly at Buddhists. The attacks have continued with varying ferocity since the restoration of an elected government under the 2007 Constitution in January 2008.

The awareness in some circles of the need for a political settlement has already led to proposals to modify the approach to governance of the southern provinces.[104] The main plank of one initiative has been to develop the SBAC further, in preference to the Interior Ministry, as the basis for a newly-fashioned administrative structure.[105] This would be achieved by releasing this body from its current links with the military under the ISOC and, at the same time, granting the body more autonomy as a regional agency under the office of the Prime Minister. The agency would be run at a political level by an elected MP from the region, and at an administrative level by a permanent secretary together with the governors of Pattani, Yala and Narathiwat as deputy secretaries. It has been pointed out that:

> The main benefit of creating the new ministry would be to ensure that the problems of the South were directly addressed by a powerful agency with a direct line to the prime minister and cabinet . . . [106]

---

[102] For further discussion of emergency powers, see ch 3 of this book.

[103] M Askew, 'Thailand's Intactable Southern War: Policy, Insurgency and Discourse' (2008) 30(2) *Contemporary Southeast Asia* 186 at 198.

[104] J Funston, 'Governance in the South: Is Decentralization an Option?' in J Funston (ed), *Divided over Thaksin: Thailand's Coup and Problematic Transition* (Chiang Mai, Silkworm Books, 2009) 124.

[105] See S Jitpiromrsi and D McCargo, 'A Ministry for the South: New Governance Proposals for Thailand's Southern Region' (2008) 30(3) *Contemporary Southeast Asia* 403.

[106] *Ibid*, at 416.

This proposal suffers from the fundamental limitation of lacking any commitment to extending popular democracy at a regional level. Rather than introduce a directly-elected governor and/or assembly, the main popular input would come from a Chamber of the Southern Border Provinces, which would be consultative body composed of religious leaders, teachers, health professionals, business representatives, administrators and security officials. Essentially, it would exercise a policy oversight function. Representatives for this body would be elected not from the wider electorate but from these groups. Existing local government structures would remain in place. At present any proposals that appear to weaken the authority of the Thai State inevitably encounter establishment resistance. The spectre of new institutions falling under the control of Islamic militants is foreseen, with the current threats to national security still looming large as the insurgency continues; while for those who support the grant of greater autonomy the measures do not go nearly far enough. In particular, the consultative components have been perceived to have a tokenistic quality to them. The most important aspect of such a proposal, contested as it may be, is that it draws attention to the need to investigate political solutions for the southern provinces. The path to reaching any form of accommodation will be extremely difficult. It is not only a matter of confronting increased hostility between the communities, but also the fact that the Islamic side is no longer represented by separatist groups with identifiable agendas and leaders. Rather, Islamic insurgency appears to lack clear political objectives, and it has become increasingly fragmented. The task ahead is to produce a formula that will go far enough to satisfy a substantial majority of the Islamic community, while at the same time providing reassurance to Buddhists who reside in this region.

B. Devolution for the South?

Forms of federal, devolved or regional government have been introduced in many nations to contribute to a political settlement where there have been strident popular calls within a sovereign State for a significant degree of local self-government by powerful minorities concentrated in a particular area, or where a particular region has a different ethnic, religious or linguistic profile from the remainder of the nation.[107]

---

[107] For more detailed discussion of devolution proposals, see Leyland, above n 72.

This is not to underestimate the methodological issues raised by any side-by-side comparison between legal systems. For example, the concept of legal transplants has been recognised as more problematic when it comes to comparing matters of public law because of the difficulty in accounting for crucial variables relating to the configuration of the State in each nation, including accounting for similarities and differences in both the arrangements for the separation of powers between State institutions, and the distribution of power between individuals and organised groups at many different levels.[108] In neighbouring Indonesia the Government granted a form of special autonomy to the Aceh region in response to nearly 30 years of armed conflict, with immediate benefits in terms of reducing the levels of violence.[109] Following a realisation by the Thai authorities that an imposed solution based on military force is most unlikely to be successful, it would appear that a form of devolution with power-sharing features comparable to those introduced in Northern Ireland,[110] or granting greater autonomy as in Aceh, might have obvious advantages from the perspective both of the Bangkok government and of the local population in the south.[111]

In the first place, under devolution sovereignty is retained by central government while considerable autonomy is granted to a particular nation, State or territorial entity. Indeed, it is particularly relevant to observe that devolution has been used as a countervailing strategy in what were previously regarded as strongly centralised systems. In the second place, the devolved governmental arrangements can be tailored to suit local conditions, so that the form of devolution represents a political settlement following a process of negotiation.[112] At the very least, devolution would provide an intermediate level of government on

[108] See O Kahn-Freund, 'On Uses and Misuses of Comparative Law' (1974) 37 *Modern Law Review* 6.

[109] M Morfit, 'The Road to Helsinki: Aceh and Indonesia's Democratic Development' (2007) 12(1) *International Negotiations* 111.

[110] P Leyland, *The Constitution of the United Kingdom: A Contextual Analysis* (Oxford, Hart Publishing, 2007) 195.

[111] A Pattani Metropolis (Mahoha Nakhon Pattani), proposed by Chavalit in 2004 as an upgraded form of provincial administration including Pattani, Yala and Narathiwat, would have been a limited step in the direction of devolved government. See J Funston, 'Governance in the South: Is Decentralization an Option' in Funston, above n 104, 132.

[112] As part of the 'Langkawi process' in 2006–07, Malaysian-brokered peace talks were held with insurgents to reach a political settlement. See Abuza, above n 78, at 197; McCargo, above n 81, at 187.

a territorial basis between national and local government. A swathe of southern Thailand would have a directly-elected parliament or assembly. This regional division would certainly include Yala, Narathiwat and Pattani, but it could possibly extend to other parts of the south in order to provide greater overall balance between the Islamic and Buddhist communities. Also, from the standpoint of public administration, the region would have its own devolved government with a first minister and cabinet. Policy would be implemented at this devolved level by the local administration. Thirdly, devolution has been used where the underlying conflict has a supra-national dimension linked to strongly divergent national, religious and cultural aspirations. In order to address the concerns of Malay-speaking Muslim separatists, the peace-brokering might have a Malaysian element, or alternatively the involvement of the UN or (ASEAN) in this capacity. Furthermore, to meet in part the aspirations of both communities in these provinces, a body with Thai and Malaysian inter-governmental representation, but also with regional representation from neighbouring parts of Thailand and Malaysia, could form part of any agreement. Such a body would be designed to perform a function similar to that of the North South Ministerial Council and the British Irish Council as part of the Northern Ireland peace process.[113] Lastly, any devolution arrangements might be supported by customised human rights oversight bodies (such as the Human Rights Commission and the Equality Commission for Northern Ireland) to ensure that the principles worked out in an agreement, including any commitments to equality of treatment, are put into practice.

In sum, it can be argued that to stand a realistic chance of being successful a negotiated devolution package would need to cover: policing and internal security in these provinces; a separately elected parliament or assembly and its law-making capacity; the functions that would be administered at this level of governance; the financial parameters of the settlement; the recognition of ethnic and religious rights, and the mechanisms for protecting such rights; and some kind of agreement which draws in the neighbouring State of Malaysia.

---

[113] See V Bogdanor, 'The British-Irish Council and Devolution' (1999) 34(3) *Government and Opposition* 287.

X. CONCLUSION

Although it has tiers of elected local government, Thailand has been characterised as being a very centralised, unitary State with most policy implemented directly from Bangkok. In some respects there has been a consolidation of power, with an emphasis placed (certainly under Thaksin's premiership) on central government assuming a strongly centralising role. This approach offers the advantage of the relatively uniform delivery of public services throughout the country. At the same time a language of decentralisation and citizen participation has been widely employed in recent years, signifying a fundamental shift in approach. The architects of constitutional change and legislators have set in place provisions for power to be exercised at the lowest possible level, and for various types of citizen participation to be introduced. In this discussion we have noted that there have been some positive experiments in this direction. Nevertheless, resistance to these trends is understandable for a number of reasons. For example, first, from a practical standpoint, the administrative capacity for policy delivery at local level has been identified as generally inadequate. Secondly, to achieve meaningful local democracy further progress needs to be made in order to transform the nature of politics at local government level, in particular to reduce the influence of narrow cliques and to facilitate the distribution of wealth to local communities. Thirdly, a more serious but related objection concerns the potential for corruption if funding is channelled down to smaller units without effective oversight and audit mechanisms in place at local government level.

In the discussion above it was argued that the commitment to a highly centralised system of governance may have contributed to the deep-seated problems in the south of Thailand, and that a form of devolution for the southern provinces might form the constitutional basis for a possible solution. In fact the prospect of devolution for the south draws our attention to a broader question, namely, that the political conflict between the Yellow Shirt movement and the Red Shirt movement has a strong regional dimension to it. The Democratic Party which forms the kernel of the Yellow Shirt movement has traditionally been strong in Bangkok, where it has enjoyed support from the educated middle and upper classes, and more generally in Thailand's southern provinces. On the other hand, the support for Thaksin and the Red

Shirts has been strongly concentrated in the north and north east of Thailand. A winner-takes-all outcome is one of the effects of a system where power is heavily concentrated at the centre. In effect, any government holding power in Bangkok is placed in a position to exercise a high level of control over the entire nation. This leaves little scope for outlying regions, with different political loyalties and interests, to pursue divergent policies. The introduction of a form of devolution, or a more potent system of regional government on a wider basis, could ensure that locally popular politicians have responsibility for forming and implementing policy at this level, and in turn this might assist in reducing the intensity of the present conflict.

FURTHER READING

Z Abuza, *Conspiracy of Silence: The Insurgency in Southern Thailand* (Washington, DC, United States Institute of Peace Press, 2009).

D Arghiros, 'Political Reform and Civil Society at the Local Level: Thailand's Local Government Reforms' in D McCargo (ed), *Reforming Thai Politics* (Copenhagen, NIAS, 2002).

M Askew, *Culture and Electoral Politics in Southern Thailand* (Bangkok, KPI, 2006).

N Boramanun, *Kan Pok Khrong Suan Tongthin* [Local Administration] (Bangkok, Winyuchon, 2009) [in Thai].

S Lertpaithoon, *Kodmai Kan Pok Khrong Tongthin* [Law on Local Administrative Law] (Bangkok, Expernet, 2007) [in Thai].

P Leyland, 'Thailand's Troubled South: Examining the Case for Devolution from a Comparative Perspective' (2009) 11(1) *Australian Journal of Asian Law* 1.

D McCargo (ed), *Rethinking Thailand's Southern Violence* (Singapore, National University of Singapore Press, 2007).

—— *Tearing Apart the Land: Islam and Legitimacy in Southern Thailand* (Ithaca, NY, Cornell University Press, 2008).

M Nelson, *Central Authority and Local Democatization in Thailand* (Bangkok, White Lotus Press, 1998).

—— 'Thailand: Problems with Decentralization' in M Nelson (ed), *Thailand's New Politics: KPI Yearbook 2001* (Bangkok, KPI and White Lotus Press, 2002).

C Sathaanan, *Pandin Jintanakan* [Imaginary Land (Re Southern Conflict)] (Bangkok, Matichon, 2008) [in Thai].

S Wallipodom, *Fai Tai Lua Ja Dab* [How the Southern Fire Can Stop] (Bangkok, Matichon, 2007) [in Thai].

5

The Constitutional Court and Constitutional Enforcement

The Constitutional Court under the 1997 Constitution – The
Constitutional Court under the 2007 Constitution – Powers of the
Constitutional Court under the 1997 and 2007 Constitutions –
Appointments – Gateways – Interpretation – The Criminal Law,
the NACC and the Fight Against Corruption – Constitutional
Jurisprudence – Conclusion

I. INTRODUCTION

This chapter concerns the role of the judiciary and the criminal law
in interpreting and enforcing the Constitution. This entails extensive
coverage of the Constitutional Court, which since 1998 has been the
principal body entrusted with that task. Supportive roles are also played
by the ordinary courts, especially the Supreme Court, and the
Administrative Courts (discussed in chapter six). In this chapter we also
include consideration of the National Anti-Corruption Commission
(NACC), which plays a crucial role in policing constitutional provisions
concerning public corruption, especially assets declaration and conflicts
of interest.

The importance of the judiciary goes back at least to the reforms of
King Chulalongkorn (Rama V) which reached their culmination a century ago. Before that the courts were not independent and were ham-
pered by the extreme complexity of the system of appeals. The King
made the courts independent of royal authority, and improved their
organisation, competence and supervision. The reforms also introduced
the civilian codes for personal, private and criminal law matters, and a

Ministry of Justice. Since that time the Thai judiciary has generally enjoyed high status, and is renowned for its competence and its independence from the Government.

Modern Thailand has a highly articulated and complex judicial sector, with civil and criminal courts of first instance and appeal both centrally and at regional level. It has many special courts, for example juvenile, military, labour, tax and intellectual property courts. These are all ultimately supervised by the Supreme Court. In addition the Administrative Courts exist at first instance, regionally, with final appeal to the Supreme Administrative Court; and these are independent of the ordinary courts and of the Constitutional Court. Thus it can be said that Thailand has in a sense three supreme courts, since the three superior courts are truly independent of one other.

Constitutional enforcement, however, became relevant only after the introduction of a written constitution and the fall of the absolute monarchy in 1932, but it has been discussed frequently since then. A Constitutional Tribunal appears in some of the 1997 Constitution's forerunners since 1945,[1] although these bodies enjoyed neither the monopoly on interpretation nor the wide powers that characterise their successors since 1998. It was only with the 1997 Constitution that constitution-makers in Thailand gave the final say over interpretation to a constitutional court, which can be seen as the keystone of the entire constitutional edifice of 1997. A constitutional court creates what has been called a 'centralised' as opposed to 'decentralised' system, or a 'European' as opposed 'American' system of judicial review.[2]

The challenge has been not simply to create a counterweight to the abuse of executive power and to the conduct of politicians by placing power in the hands of judges, but to create a respected institution insulated from the political fray and providing a reflective and reasoned judgment.[3] The Constitution Drafting Assembly (CDA) of 1997 placed great faith in a cohort of judges finally to determine many of the most

[1] N Setabutr, *The Constitutional Court and Society's Expectations* (Bangkok, KPI, 2000).

[2] A Harding, P Leyland and T Groppi, 'Constitutional Courts: Forms, Functions and Practice in Comparative Perspective' in A Harding and P Leyland, *Constitutional Courts: A Comparative Study* (London, Wildy, Simmonds and Hill, 2009).

[3] A Harding , 'A Turbulent Innovation: the Constitutional Court of Thailand, 1998–2006' in A Harding and P Nicholson (eds), *New Courts in Asia* (London, Routledge, 2009); B Uwanno and W Burns, 'The Thai Constitution of 1997: Sources and Process' (1998) 32 *University of British Columbia Law Review* 227.

important constitutional questions. James Klein emphasised the significance of the Constitutional Court in the Thai constitutional context:

> Thai politicians, the military and senior civilian bureaucrats have always reserved for themselves the power to interpret the meaning of law and the intent of the constitution. The 1997 Constitution seeks to remedy these problems by reversing the course of Thai constitutional law. It establishes the Constitution as the basis for all law, thereby reducing the power of politicians and bureaucrats to subvert constitutional intent.[4]

Indeed, familiar rationales that often motivate constitution-makers in creating a constitutional court were evident in debates concerning the 1997 Constitution. First, it was reasoned that such a court would ensure adherence to the Constitution and its protection against legislative majorities. Secondly, it would provide unity and finality in interpretation, avoiding the possibility of different courts adopting different interpretations of the Constitution. Thirdly, the court would stand as a visible symbol of constitutional progress. And fourthly, the advent of a constitutional court offered the prospect of reversing a trend of judicial deferentialism, which may have characterised previous regimes of judicial review.

Despite strong historical links with France in the field of law and law reform, both public and private,[5] it was in fact the German and Austrian models of the court that influenced the CDA most. Thailand is by no means alone in East Asia in putting its faith in a specialist court of this kind.[6]

II. THE CONSTITUTIONAL COURT
UNDER THE 1997 CONSTITUTION

The proposal to create a constitutional court proved highly controversial. The judiciary, particularly the Judges of the Supreme Court, had expressed

---

[4] J Klein, 'The Battle for the Rule of Law in Thailand: the Constitutional Court of Thailand' in A Raksasataya and JR Klein, *Constitutional Court of Thailand: the Provisions and the Working of the Court* (Bangkok, Constitution for the People Society, 2001).

[5] See eg B Bhalakula, *Pridi and the Administrative Court* (Bangkok, Office of the Administrative Courts, 2003) (on file with the authors).

[6] C Durkop and Y Hui Bin (eds), *Present Status and Future Development of Constitutional Jurisdiction in Asia* (Singapore, Konrad Adenauer Stiftung, 2003); T Ginsburg, *Judicial Review in New Democracies: Constitutional Courts in Asian Cases* (New York, Cambridge University Press, 2003).

opposition to it on two grounds of principle: first, that the power to interpret the Constitution was a quintessentially judicial power that should be exercised by the ordinary judiciary; and, secondly, that the proposal involved the appointment of political scientists to the proposed court, thus diluting the primacy of legal logic in the task of interpretation. The constitution-makers were, however, of the view that a constitutional court would be more likely to take a broad as opposed to a narrow view of its function based on legal interpretative techniques, and that there was merit in having a flagship institution with responsibilities only in respect of the Constitution. Influential members of the CDA clearly did not think that the judiciary had proved itself equal to the task of interpretation, given the sea-change in Thai constitutionalism that was contemplated. Even so, the CDA conceded something to the judiciary in that seven of the 15 judges of the new Constitutional Court were to be drawn from the ranks of the ordinary judiciary, and only three political scientists, instead of six as had been contemplated, would sit on the court.[7]

The creation of numerous new jurisdictions[8] in 1997 also opened up the possibility of turf wars between the respective bodies.[9] The Constitutional Court under the 1997 Constitution was designated the final arbiter of such constitutional questions and, as a result, it had a clearly-defined function at the core of the entire constitutional system. For example, as a judicial safeguard the findings of certain watchdog bodies such as the NACC (see section VIII below) required confirmation by the Constitutional Court before a decision had binding effect. Most crucially, the decisions of the Constitutional Court were made explicitly binding on all State institutions and individuals.[10] In order to establish the rule of law it was therefore essential that all the constitutional players fully complied with the judgments laid down by the Court.

The constitutional watchdogs were rapidly recruited and operational. The early signs until 2001 were encouraging. The Election Commission of Thailand (ECT) and the NACC in particular prosecuted constitutional abuses with considerable vigour. However, as will be apparent from the discussion of performance of the Constitutional Court which follows, the failure of the combined strength of the watchdogs and the

[7] TC 1997, s 255.

[8] See ch 1, section VI.

[9] See eg, 'Watchdog, Judges in Turf Battle: Administrative Court Claims Jurisdiction', *The Nation*, 2 October 2002.

[10] TC 1997, s 268.

Constitutional Court to achieve compliance with constitutional norms by the political leaders, including the Prime Minister, was a major contributory factor that prompted the military coup of 2006.

With the revocation of the 1997 Constitution and the adoption of the Interim Constitution by the Royal Decree of September 2006 following the military coup, the Constitutional Court ceased functioning. The military junta in introducing the Interim Constitution was careful to replace the Constitutional Court with an (interim) Constitutional Tribunal in order to prevent challenges concerning the legitimacy of the coup, and any possible adverse implications under the 1997 Constitution for those responsible for engineering the coup.[11] However, all cases pending from the previous Constitutional Court were transferred under section 35 of the Interim Constitution to the Constitutional Tribunal consisting of nine judges.[12]

Undoubtedly, the Constitutional Tribunal's most significant judgment, delivered on 30 May 2007, related to the investigations into the alleged misconduct of the two main political parties (TRT and the Democrat Party) during the elections of 2 April 2006.[13] The Democrat Party was acquitted, but TRT and its most senior officials were unanimously found guilty on charges of bribing small parties to compete in the election, in order to fulfil the 20 per cent minimum turnout requirement. The Tribunal sanctioned the dissolution of TRT and also banned 111 of its senior members, including its leader, former Prime Minister Thaksin Shinawatra, from politics for a period of five years. This outcome was welcomed in some quarters as a reasoned judgment which responded to evidence presented before the court; but given the undemocratic prevailing constitutional circumstances, the generals ousting Thaksin and the TRT being still in charge, the result could hardly be regarded as a triumph for the rule of law.

---

[11] Constitution of the Kingdom of Thailand (Interim) BE 2549 (2006) ('TC 2006'), ss 35, 37. See further, AJ Harding, 'Emergency Powers with a Moustache: Special Powers, Military Rule and Evolving Constitutionalism in Thailand' in V Ramraj and A Thiruvengadam (eds), *Emergency Powers in Asia* (Cambridge, Cambridge University Press, 2010); and ch 1, section VII.

[12] The interim court comprised the President of the Supreme Court as President; the President of the Supreme Administrative Court as Vice-President; five other Supreme Court Justices; and two other Supreme Administrative Court Justices.

[13] 'The Constitutional Tribunal Disbands Thai Rak Thai', The Nation, 30 May 2007; 'Summary of the Decision of the Constitutional Tribunal: Thai Rak Thai', The Nation, 6 June 2007.

III. THE CONSTITUTIONAL COURT
UNDER THE 2007 CONSTITUTION

The CDA of 2007 was in effect required to take the 1997 Constitution as the basis for what became the 2007 Constitution.[14] The constitution-drafters clearly saw the need to enhance the powers of the Constitutional Court. Indeed, a revamped Constitutional Court was established under the 2007 Constitution, comprising a President and eight other judges.[15] A quorum of five judges must preside over any case brought before the Court[16] and the Court may decide matters by majority vote. The decision of the Court must at least consist of the background or allegation; a summary of facts obtained from hearings; the reasons for the decision on questions of fact and law; and the provisions of the Constitution and the law invoked and resorted to. Under both the 1997 and 2007 Constitutions the Constitutional Court is granted final authority over all matters of constitutional interpretation.[17] This jurisdiction arises under many provisions of the respective Constitutions, but principally by reference to the Court from an ordinary civil or criminal court, where a constitutional question arises;[18] or by a reference from the National Assembly or the Prime Minister before an impugned bill becomes law.[19] However, the Supreme Court and the Supreme Administrative Court retain their jurisdiction as final appellate courts regarding all other questions of law and fact in their respective fields.

---

[14] The process laid down by TC 2006 required the Drafting Committee to justify any deviation from the provisions of TC 1997. Moreover, in the event of the draft not being approved by the prescribed referendum, the Government was empowered to bring into effect any previous constitution with appropriate amendments.

[15] TC 2007, s 204.

[16] TC 2007, s 216.

[17] TC 1997, s 268; TC 2007, s 154.

[18] TC 1997, s 264; TC 2007, s 211. The Court is given discretion to reject the case if it considers that it would have no bearing on the decision of the ordinary court.

[19] TC 1997, s 262.

IV. POWERS OF THE CONSTITUTIONAL COURT UNDER THE 1997 AND 2007 CONSTITUTIONS

There are several typical or possible adjudicatory functions of a constitutional court, so that 'constitutional jurisdiction' may cover a number of different aspects. Table 1 below indicates the extent of powers enjoyed by the two Constitutional Courts (1997 and 2007 versions) against the full possible range of such powers.

Jurisdiction

Constitutional Court Jurisdiction 1997 and 2007	1997	2007
Strike down a constitutional amendment	No[1]	No
Strike down legislation (ex ante)	Yes	Yes
Strike down legislation (ex post)	Yes	Yes
Strike down decisions of the legislature	Yes	Yes
Strike down decisions and acts of the Executive[2]	No	No
Strike down emergency decrees	Yes	Yes
Hear petitions from individuals alleging a violation of rights	No	Yes
Rule on references from the courts as to constitutionality	Yes	Yes
Impeachment proceedings against holders of public office	Yes	Yes
Consideration of criminal cases in respect of official corruption[3]	No	No
Consideration of qualifications to hold public office	Yes	Yes
Hear disputes as to the competence of organs of State	Yes	Yes

[1] But it could propose constitutional amendments.

[2] This power is given to the Administrative Courts, but not in relation to emergency decrees.

[3] This power is given to the ordinary courts. Under the 1997 Constitution and beyond a new chamber of the Supreme Court was empowered to decide criminal cases involving holders of political office.

Control over the constitutionality of regulations made by bodies established under the constitution	Yes	Yes
Dissolution/ merger of political parties and control over constitutionality of their actions	Yes	Yes
Decide on the legality of elections and election results	Yes	Yes

Some conclusions may be drawn from this: first, that both Courts were given comparatively wide powers; secondly, that neither Court was given powers over executive actions; thirdly, that the only significant change in 2007 was the introduction of an individual right of petition. Given that it is often in relation to executive rules and regulations that real issues arise regarding fundamental rights, the role of the Administrative Courts is possibly at least as important as that of the Constitutional Court.[20]

V. APPOINTMENTS

The enormous faith placed in the Thai judiciary to decide crucial issues was identified by some critics as *the* 'dominant theme' of the 2007 Constitution.[21] Both the 1997 and 2007 Constitutions include numerous provisions to guarantee (in theory at least) the institutional independence of the Court. Not only must the Office of the Constitutional Court have autonomy in its personnel, administration and budget, but it must have its own autonomous secretariat, with a Secretary-General responsible to the President of the Court and nominated by the President with the approval of the Court's judges.[22] The judges hold office for nine years from the date of their appointment[23] and may serve only for a single term.[24] Conflicts of interest are expressly forbidden, as judges serving on the Constitutional Court are prohibited from having any governmental position, business interests or engagement in any

---

[20] P Leyland, 'Constitutional Problems and Constitutional Reform: The UK, Thailand and the Case for Preservation as well as Change', in A Harding and T Bureekul (ed), *Constitution Reform: Comparative Perspectives* (Bangkok, KPI, 2008) 69.

[21] 'Judicial Role in the Constitution: From People's Charter to Judges Charter', *The Nation*, 30 April 2007.

[22] TC 2007, s 217.

[23] TC 2007, s 209.

[24] TC 2007, s 208.

profession.[25] Furthermore, politicians, judges and members of other independent agencies under the Constitution are specifically excluded from serving on the Court.[26]

Above all, the judicial appointments system is clearly of pivotal importance. On the one hand, the selection process under both the 1997 and 2007 Constitutions reflected the requirement that the composition of the Court needed to draw upon the existing pool of professionally-trained judicial talent, the assumption being that selection to the Court would be on grounds of seniority, experience and merit. Currently, more than half of the nine members of the constitutional bench are chosen from serving judges. The Supreme Administrative Court nominates two judges, while the Supreme Court nominates three judges (as compared to two and five respectively of the 14 judges under the 1997 Constitution). On the other hand, in regard to the appointment of the other four members of the Court with expertise in political science or law, the robustness of the intricate selection process has come under close scrutiny.

The Constitutional Court in its 1997 version consisted of a President and 14 judges, appointed by the King on the advice of the Senate, and comprising: five judges elected by the Supreme Court Justices from amongst their own number; two judges elected by the Supreme Administrative Court from amongst their own number; five persons qualified in law; and three persons qualified in political science. The judges held office for one nine-year term, or until 70 if this age is reached earlier.[27]

The process for electing the members of the Court in the last two categories was complex, and in fact several appointments, especially some of the initial ones, gave rise to sharp differences between the Senate and the Supreme Court over the Senate's investigation of the backgrounds and qualifications of proposed justices, in particular the then Vice-President of the Supreme Court, Amphorn Thongprayoon, Supreme Court Justice Jumphol na Songkhla and former President of the Parliament, Ukrit Mongkolnavin. These differences resulted in several rulings by the Constitutional Tribunal, which exercised jurisdiction during 1997–98 while the Constitutional Court was being established; these rulings alone indicate the necessity of having a body empowered

[25] TC 2007, s 207.

[26] TC 2007, s 205(3).

[27] See TC 1997, ss 255–268 for provisions on the composition and procedure of the Constitutional Court.

to adjudicate divisive issues arising between organs of State, even where one of those is the higher judiciary.

First of all a Selection Committee was chosen, consisting of:

a) the President of the Supreme Court;
b) four Deans of law and four Deans of political science chosen from amongst their own number; and
c) four MPs representing parliamentary political parties, each party having one representative and such representatives electing four from their own number.

The Committee, by a resolution supported by three-quarters of its members, nominated 10 persons qualified in law and six qualified in political science; the final choice was made by the Senate, the first five lawyers and three political scientists on the list receiving at least one half of the votes.

The revised procedure under the 2007 Constitution also requires a Selection Committee to be formed,[28] but this time it comprises the President of the Supreme Court, the President of the Supreme Administrative Court, the President of the House of Representatives, the Leader of the Opposition in the House of Representatives and a further representative elected from amongst their own number by the independent organisations established under the Constitution. Thus political interference with appointments is rendered more difficult compared with the previous selection process. Persons selected by this Committee who consent are nominees to the President of the Senate, but the selection resolution must be by open vote and must be by a two-thirds majority of the existing members of the Selection Committee.[29] A special sitting of the Senate is then called within 30 days by the President of the Senate to pass by secret ballot a resolution approving the appointment of the selected persons. If the nominations are ratified, the names will be presented to the King to be appointed. If the nominations are rejected, wholly or partly, the matter is referred to the Selection Committee for re-selection. At this point, contrary to the procedure prescribed in 1997, when the Senate had the final say, the Selection Committee can *re-affirm* its original nomination of candidates

---

[28] TC 2007, s 206.
[29] For a decision to be valid at least half of the Committee must be present. Assuming all are present, this means 4 out of 5 must be in favour.

selected unanimously, which will result in the names of those selected being forwarded by the President of the Senate for appointment by the King. The Selection Committee dominated by judges and professionals thus has the final say rather than the Senate. If the Selection Committee does not reaffirm unanimously there must be a re-selection process within 30 days. Under the Constitution the three judges elected from the Supreme Court judges select a President of the Court from amongst their own number.[30] A quorate bench can be formed from any five judges of the panel of nine.

The explanation for the reduced role of the Senate in the selection processes is that the elected Senate under the 1997 Constitution was designed as a politically neutral body which had a key role in many constitutional appointment processes, but in practice it was gradually captured by TRT, the ruling party (2001–06), and was therefore able officially to approve a number of highly controversial appointments.[31]

The complexity of the selection process has important ramifications. For example, under the 1997 Constitution the delay in replacing the President of the Court, Kramol Tonghamachart, following his mandatory retirement on his 70th birthday, had a number of knock-on effects. It left a situation where there could be an even number of judges and therefore no casting vote. Selection committees for other important constitutional bodies were also invalid as the Constitution required the President of the Constitutional Court to be a member.[32]

VI. GATEWAYS

Access to a court tends to determine in significant ways the extent of its jurisdiction and the nature and practical incidence of its powers. In determining the extent of access to a constitutional court, a balance has to be struck between ensuring that relevant issues that arise falling under its jurisdiction are referred for determination, and finding a means of protecting the court from being inundated with frivolous claims.

---

[30] TC 2007, s 204.

[31] Sharp differences arose under the TC 1997 between the Senate and the Supreme Court over the Senate's investigation of the backgrounds and qualifications of proposed justices.

[32] 'Lack of Head for Top Court Creating Lots of Problems', *The Nation*, 10 November 2005.

Cases alleging lack of compliance with the Constitution may be brought before the Constitutional Court under the 2007 Constitution in ways similar to the position under the 1997 Constitution. The principal methods are as follows:

a) There is the possibility of reference to the Constitutional Court from an ordinary civil or criminal court where a constitutional question arises, such as the unconstitutionality of a law under which an accused person has been charged.

b) A bill may be challenged by members of the National Assembly or the Prime Minister before it becomes law. One-tenth of the total membership of the National Assembly (or the Prime Minister acting alone) has the power, if of the opinion that a bill which has been passed by the Assembly is inconsistent with the Constitution or was enacted contrary to the provisions of the Constitution, to have the bill referred to the Constitutional Court for its opinion.[33] The same threshold applies when requiring the Constitutional Court to consider violations of the Constitution through the misappropriation of public funds.[34] In the case of a bill for enactment of an organic law, this power of reference can be exercised by 20 Members of the Assembly. If the Constitutional Court rules that provisions of the bill are unconstitutional then, if the unconstitutional provisions formed the 'essential element' of the bill, the bill lapses; otherwise only the unconstitutional provisions lapse and the bill goes for the royal assent. Also one-fifth of the Members of each house of the National Assembly may refer an emergency decree to the Constitutional Court on grounds of unconstitutionality.[35]

c) A law may be challenged by reference from the Ombudsman.[36]

d) Various provisions relating to control of the constitutionality of political parties and their operation allow a reference to the Constitutional Court.

e) In the case of a dispute as to powers and duties of State organs, a reference may be made by such organs, or by the Prime Minister or the President of the National Assembly.[37]

---

[33] TC 2007, ss 154–155.

[34] TC 2007, s 168.

[35] TC 2007, s 185.

[36] See TC 1997, s 198 and the Ombudsman Act 1999, s 17. Under TC 2007, the Ombudsman's role has been extended (eg, in relation to investigating the ethical standards of politicians and officials): TC 2007, ss 245, 270–271.

[37] TC 2007, s 214.

f) References may be made in respect of legislative procedure and membership of the legislature; by reference from the NACC for further decision as to disqualification from office for failure to declare assets; in respect of the qualifications of members of independent agencies, including courts; or regulations made by the NACC and the ECT.

It is interesting to note that individual citizens adversely affected did not previously have any right to petition the Court, except indirectly through the Ombudsman or by reference by the court in a civil or criminal case.[38] This perceived defect was corrected in the 2007 Constitution. Now any citizen who considers that his or her rights have been violated by any 'State organ or State agency' is able to make a challenge on grounds of constitutionality before the Constitutional Court. This constitutional provision potentially opens up the system to widespread challenges, but this right of referral has been made a remedy of last resort, to the extent that the claimant must have first exhausted all other existing remedies, which might include the right to take a case to the Administrative Courts.[39]

VII. INTERPRETATION

Interpretive techniques and the style of the rendering of judgments in the court are critical to establishing the legitimacy of constitutional courts, and the Thai Constitutional Court of 1998–2006 was required to give a decision setting out the allegations, facts, reasons of law and fact, and the legal provisions relied upon;[40] and the decisions of the Court and of each judge were required to be published in the Gazette. Dissenting opinions were allowed and were actually quite frequent in practice, an interesting development in a civilian jurisdiction, where

[38] For examples of instances where the lack of an individual right of petition has worked detrimentally on fundamental rights, see Asian Human Rights Commission, 'Thailand: What Can be Done When a Constitution Cannot be Enforced', available at <http://www.ahrchk.net/statements/mainfile.php/2006statements/427/>; Asian Human Rights Commission, 'Thailand: Somchai Case Reveals Flaws in Thai Constitution', available at <http://www.ahrchk.net/statements/mainfile.php/2006 statements/418/>.

[39] TC 2007, s 212.

[40] TC 2007, s 267.

dissenting judgments are not usual. Formalistic, French-style judgments were given, which avoided elaboration as to the reasoning processes, creating the impression that the decisions were somewhat arbitrary and unrelated to each other. This impression needs to be moderated, however, by certain other considerations. First, all justices were obliged to enter individual judgments. Secondly, dissents were allowed and became a regular feature of the decisions, which were often split ones in important cases. Thirdly, the Constitutional Court made some reference to its own previous decisions in an attempt to provide a consistent and rational jurisprudence; it also consistently consolidated cases raising similar issues.[41] Lastly, the Constitutional Court can refuse to accept for review a specific provision of law on which it has previously issued a decision.[42]

VIII. THE CRIMINAL LAW, THE NACC AND THE FIGHT AGAINST CORRUPTION

Before we proceed to assess more generally the contribution of Thailand's Constitutional Court in fulfilling its role under the 1997 and 2007 Constitutions, it is important to recognise the intended contribution of the ordinary criminal courts and customised watchdog and enforcement agencies in upholding the rule of law. As we shall observe shortly, these specialist institutions were designed to root out misconduct, but at the very pinnacle of the legal system the Constitutional Court was required to act as the final arbiter by sanctioning the decisions that were made to impose far-reaching penalties.

In many ways Thailand has a conventional system of criminal law. Criminal prosecutions relating to the Thai Penal Code of 1956 and other criminal law statutes are heard in *Kwaeng* courts if relatively trivial, or otherwise are referred to the Bangkok or regional criminal court.[43]

---

[41] Eg, a large number of cases involving changes in bank interest, brought in 1998–99.

[42] TC 2007, s 215.

[43] *Kwaeng* courts for quick trial have jurisdiction only for offences punishable by a maximum of 3 years' imprisionment, or a 60,000 baht fine. Appeals from both criminal and civil cases go first to the Court of Appeal, or to one of 9 Regional Courts of Appeal. The Supreme Court, as Thailand's highest judicial court, acts as the final court of appeal from the ordinary courts (as opposed to Administrative and Constitutional Courts). See <http://www.lexadin.nl/wlg/courts/nofr/oeur/lxct-tha.htm>.

However, the quest to entrench ethical values through constitutional rules and under the ordinary law has been of particular relevance in view of the fact that in Thailand

> public sector corruption remains a major problem, and is perceived as such. This problem falls into two parts. First, there is bribe solicitation, often on a large scale, confined to a few offices which have authority over transactions of money and property – namely the customs, land and tax, offices – plus the police. . . . Second there is a major problem of corruption in the political system.[44]

For many years this high level of endemic corruption has been singled out as a matter for concern,[45] and of course the propensity for the abuse of political power – together with constitutional and legal attempts to contain such abuse – has been one of the themes of this book. Such unlawful conduct might be considered as falling under conventional criminal law. It is not surprising, then, to discover that the Thai Penal Code includes an exhaustive list of offences to prevent corruption, including: offences against officials, malfeasance in public office, other abuses of authority for personal gain, offences relating to justice, offences against judicial officials.[46] However, many of these laws have been undermined by notorious loopholes. For example, the 'gifts of good will' principle (*sin nam jai*) has been successfully pleaded, and this prevents an official from being successfully prosecuted for accepting a bribe for performing any of his or her legitimate functions. Moreover, given the accusations of widespread corruption within the police force itself, understandably there has been limited confidence in the established agencies of law enforcement as a vehicle to combat such abuses.

The introduction of a radically overhauled NACC under the 1997 Constitution,[47] alongside a battery of other watchdog bodies (see chapters two, six and seven), may be regarded as a crucial part of a coordinated strategy to eliminate corruption at all levels in Thai society.[48] In

---

[44] P Phongpaichit, N Treerat, Y Chaiyapong and C Baker, *Corruption in the Public Sector in Thailand: Perception and Experiences of Households* (Bangkok, Political Economy Center, Chulalongkorn University, 2000) 57.

[45] See P Phongpaichit and S Priiyarangsan, *Corruption and Democracy in Thailand* (Chiang Mai, Silkworm Books, 1999).

[46] Sections 143–144, 148–150, 151–155, 167–199 respectively.

[47] CT 1997, ss 297–308 and Organic Act on Counter Corruption 1999.

[48] P Leyland, 'Thailand's Constitutional Watchdogs: Dobermans, Bloodhounds or Lapdogs' (2007) III:2 *Journal of Comparative Law* 151.

particular, the NACC and the Anti-Money Laundering Office (AMLO), both of which have continued to operate in the same capacity under the 2007 Constitution,[49] were designed to perform the role of specialist criminal investigatory bodies, with powers to prosecute and to award penalties, including immediate removal from office subject to confirmation. The jurisdiction of the NACC ranges over the political and administrative domain. In discharging its duty to eliminate corrupt practices the NACC was granted the task of formulating codes of conduct requiring the disclosure of assets, which applied to the Prime Minister, ministers, politicians and public officials at all levels of government.[50] In common with the ECT, the NACC was given wide-ranging powers to investigate not only where there was suspicion that an individual was unusually wealthy, but also where it found that a person had failed to disclose assets, or had attempted to supply false information; in such circumstances it could order that person from office with immediate effect for a period of five years. However, as a safeguard to protect anyone accused from suffering injustice, this power to issue what has been termed a 'red card' had first to be approved by the Constitutional Court.[51] Also, a matter may be referred to the NACC by the President of the Senate to determine if there is a prima facie case under the petitioning procedure for the removal from office of politicians, judges and other public figures suspected of unusual wealth or malfeasance in office, which is triggered by a motion supported by a minimum of 25 per cent of members of the House of Representatives. If the NACC decides that grounds for a prosecution exist, the person will immediately be suspended from office and the matter will be referred to the Prosecutor-General for the purpose of prosecution.[52] The process of rooting out corruption is brought to the attention of the public, as the revamped NACC has been required to submit an annual report to Parliament on its overall performance and on the results of its investigations.[53]

The office of NACC has been granted autonomy under the Constitution in the way it organises its personnel, administration and

---

[49] TC, ss 246–251.

[50] Parliamentarians were prohibited from receiving State concessions or monopolies, and ministers must transfer corporate holdings into blind trusts.

[51] Organic Act on Counter Corruption 1999, s 34.

[52] TC 2007, ss 270–279.

[53] See TC 1997, s 301; Organic Act on Counter Corruption 1999, s 7.

budget,[54] but the effectiveness of the NACC has been compromised because the impartiality and reputation of its commissioners has been repeatedly called into question by both main political factions. In common with the Constitutional Court and the other watchdog bodies introduced under the 1997 Constitution, an elaborate selection process was conceived for the nine NACC Commissioners, with the express purpose of providing a high degree of independence,[55] but the attempt to insulate the NACC from political interference by relying on a supposedly politically neutral Senate finally to approve nominations failed. Notwithstanding the preliminary short-listing by a dedicated selection panel, after 2001 the covertly pro-Government Senate was able to vote for its own preferred candidates. The commissioners selected subsequently during Thaksin's premiership spectacularly destroyed any credibility that the organisation still retained when they awarded themselves a massive increase in salary without first gaining parliamentary approval. All nine commissioners were sentenced by the Supreme Court to a two-year suspended jail term for this blatantly unlawful conduct.[56] In order to reduce partisanship, a constitutional amendment had been proposed in 2005 to remove party politicians from the preliminary selection panels for the NACC and other watchdog bodies,[57] and under the 2007 Constitution the role of the Senate in making selections was revised so that it was only granted the power to reject nominations for specified reasons. Any such rejection now results in the re-running of the selection procedure.[58] But in the polarised political environment of recent years, changes to the method of appointment have failed to remove the perception that the governing party can influence the selection process, even if indirectly.

To date, at best the NACC has made a marginal contribution to constitutional enforcement and the reduction of corruption in public life in Thailand. In fact the Constitutional Court's failure in 2001 to uphold the NACC's finding of corruption against Thaksin despite overwhelming evidence might be regarded as the defining moment.[59]

---

[54] See TC 1997, s 302 and TC 2007, s 251.

[55] CT 1997, s 297 and ss 257 and 258.

[56] 'Is There No Shame Among the Guilty?', *The Nation*, 27 May 2005.

[57] See 'Time May Run Out Before NCCC Chosen', *The Nation*, 4 June 2005; 'Chamber Won't Confine Itself to NCCC Selection-panel Clause', *The Nation*, 6 June 2005.

[58] TC 2007, s 206(2).

[59] Leyland, above n 48, 169.

This case (discussed in detail in section IX below) demonstrated the continuing difficulty in securing convictions against the most prominent figures in public life, despite the increased resources and powers available; and more recently Samak's removal as Prime Minister in 2008 for a trivial breach of the rules has tended to highlight the unpunished excesses of the Thaksin premiership. In the absence of high-profile investigations and prosecutions, the NACC adopted in 2010 what it calls its National Anti-Corruption Strategy.[60] This campaign is mainly based on inculcating values of integrity across the entire public service by visiting individual government offices to familiarise staff with the law and relevant codes of practice. The prospect of these exhortations, however well meant, making a substantial impact is extremely unlikely in view of the low levels of remuneration received by the vast majority of civil servants and police officers.

IX. THAILAND'S CONSTITUTIONAL JURISPRUDENCE

We can assess the performance of the 1997 Constitutional Court during the period 1998–2006, which has a complete record. The Constitutional Tribunal of 2006–07 made only one really significant decision (relating to TRT), which is discussed in section II above. At the time of writing, the 2007 Constitutional Court has been in operation for a little over three years. In 2008 it made two highly controversial decisions, those relating to Prime Minister Samak and the Puea Thai Party.[61] As for the Court's impact in other areas, it is probably too early to assess this. The discussion below therefore principally relates to the Court's first iteration of 1998–2006 and is organised into categories, relevant cases decided by the 2007 Court being added where relevant.

A. Human rights cases

As a preliminary point, any analysis of the contribution of the Constitutional Court to the enforcement of human rights should take into account not only the decisions of the Court itself, but also the larger human rights milieu and the enforcement role of other institu-

---

[60] See <http://www.nacc.go.th/ewt_news.php?nid=939>.
[61] See ch 2, section IV.

tions, such as the National Human Rights Commission (NHRC). In light of this, it is apparent that the role of the Constitutional Court was not as significant in this field as a reading of the 1997 Constitution would suggest it ought to have been. A large number of important human rights issues have arisen in Thailand in recent years, but the Constitutional Court has made virtually no contribution to their resolution. This point will be made clear in chapter seven which is devoted to human rights. In a few cases, discussed below, the Court gave rather negative and unimpressive judgments. Part of the explanation for this is the absence of a right of individual petition. When the Constitutional Court did consider directly a matter of alleged unconstitutionality of legislation, it was nevertheless slow to enforce the fundamental rights set out in the Constitution.

Disappointing examples of what appears to be an unduly deferential approach that elevated existing legislation over the 1997 Constitution (despite the clear provisions of the Constitution indicating otherwise) occurred in two 2002 cases where the Court considered the rights of the disabled.[62] In the first of these, the Ombudsman, who was empowered to submit petitions on behalf of citizens, petitioned on behalf of two lawyers, disabled as a result of childhood poliomyelitis, who had applied to become an assistant judge, but had been rejected following physical and psychological examination; in the second, the Central Administrative Court submitted a complaint on behalf of a similarly rejected candidate for a position as State Attorney (public prosecutor). The plaintiffs in both cases had been rejected on the ground of their disability. The relevant statutes[63] prohibiting persons with physical disabilities from taking the relevant examination. It was argued that the statutes were unconstitutional in that they contravened section 30 of the Constitution, which prohibited discrimination 'on the basis of physical or health conditions'. The Court, in a highly controversial majority decisions, ruled that the statutes were constitutionally valid, basing its decisions on assumed prevailing cultural norms relating to the public perception of judges and public prosecutors rather than a progressive ideal of inclusiveness. This decision sent a signal

---

[62] Cases 16 and 44/2002. See also Case 3/2001, where the Court failed to enforce fundamental rights provisions in favour of an accused who had been subjected to an ankle restraint for 28 months; and Case 11/2001 on presumptions in drug-trafficking cases.

[63] The Rules on Judicial Officials Act 1978, and the Rules on State Attorney Officials Act 1978.

that, despite the constitution-makers' intention that the Constitutional Court should exercise its jurisdiction in a transformative manner, the Court on the contrary saw its position as maintaining the status quo. Interestingly enough, this decision was quite specifically countermanded by provisions of the 2007 Constitution, so all is not lost on this issue.[64]

A further example may be seen in the area of freedom of religion. The overtly secular nature of the State in Thailand was modified under the 1997 Constitution by the fact that Buddhist monks, novices and clergy were prohibited under the Constitution from voting for or standing as candidates for (or from continuing to sit as members of) the House of Representatives or the Senate.[65] Muslim *imam, ulama,* Catholic monks, nuns and clergy, and so forth, were not subject to the same restrictions. The Court refused to hold unconstitutional a statutory provision disqualifying a man who became a Buddhist priest from continuing as a member of a local authority, despite the fact that the Constitution at section 38 guaranteed the liberty of a person

> to profess a religion, a religious sect or creed, and observe religious precepts or exercise a form of worship in accordance with his or her belief, provided it is not contrary to his or her civic duties, public order or good morals.

In exercising this liberty, the section continued, a person was

> protected from any act of the state, which was derogatory to his or her rights or detrimental to his or her due benefits on the grounds of professing a religion, a religious sect or creed or observing religious precepts or exercising a form of worship in accordance with his or her different belief from that of others.

Also, section 29 laid down the principle that the restriction of rights and liberties as recognised by the Constitution should not be imposed on a person except by virtue of provisions of the law specifically enacted for the purpose determined by the 1997 Constitution, and only to the extent necessary, and provided that it should not affect the essential substances of such rights and liberties (this section did not apparently suffice to give any priority to the rights of the disabled in the cases mentioned in the previous paragraph). The Constitutional Court held that the law was not unconstitutional as it was saved by the fact of its pre-dating the

[64] TC 2007 extensively recognises the rights of disabled persons in ss 30, 40, 49, 54, 80 and 152.

[65] TC 1997, ss 106(2), 118(5), 109(3), 126(4), 133(5).

Constitution.[66] Part of the argument, however, was that the prohibition did not actually cause the local authority member to lose his right of freedom of religion, as that right still existed despite the prohibition. This part of the decision seemed to fly in the face of sections 29 and 38, as clearly his right had been abridged at the very least, and it could be argued that, in terms of section 38, it was in fact his civic *duty*, if anything, to continue to serve as a member of the local authority. The Court, however, considered the other sections of the 1997 Constitution that had the effect of prohibiting Buddhist priests, novices, monks or clergy from voting or standing as a candidate as stated above. Thus, in approximating the position of a member of a local authority to that of an elected member of the National Assembly, the Court privileged the principle of religious disqualification over that of religious freedom, and in a sense implicitly downgraded constitutional human rights as well as civic duty, in the process bringing Buddhism closer to the constitutional entrenchment which some monks have been demanding.

Sometimes, however, the Court has upheld fundamental rights. In a 1998 case the Court asserted the right to vote, and struck down a regulation of the ECT that purported to deprive of State assistance those who had failed to cast a vote in an election. The ECT had powers to prescribe punishments for failure to vote, but the Court held that the punishment was in effect prescribed by the 1997 Constitution itself, which at section 68(2) stated that citizens who failed to vote lost only their right to vote but could suffer no other penalties; further sanctions could be imposed only by an Act of Parliament.[67] In another case the Court ruled unconstitutional a law requiring a married woman to assume her husband's surname, on the grounds that such law was gender-discriminatory.[68] The same principle, however, was not applied to a law which allowed the wives of Thai men to acquire Thai nationality automatically but did not accord the same status to husbands of Thai women, who were simply told by the Court that they could acquire Thai nationality by other means.[69]

In a somewhat different context, the Court upheld the principle of judicial independence and restricted the powers of military courts when it held that a military judge could deliver judgment only if he presided over the case; and that where the military court sought to impose a sen-

[66] Case 44/1999.
[67] Case 15/1998.
[68] Case 21/2003.
[69] Case 37/2003. Cf Case 48/2002 and Case 45/2003.

tence heavier than that prescribed in the ordinary law, the case should be referred to the local civil court.[70] Other cases failed to assert the rights of traditional communities to have their interests taken into account with regard to development projects.[71]

It is crucial to remember that a strong emphasis on the protection of individual rights was a fundamental concern of the 1997 Constitution; and whereas the NHRC possessed only general investigatory powers, by way of contrast the Constitutional Court was placed in a position to enforce these human rights norms by robust intervention. The above selection of cases suggest that the Court's performance in this area has been at best patchy, the road to vigorous enforcement of the 1997 Constitution remaining one on which the Court apparently feared to tread.

B. Cases concerning corruption

The other main group of cases concerns issues of direct political interest relating to official corruption. The case of Sanan Kachornprasart in 2000 was an indication that the anti-corruption function of the Court was producing results. Sanan was the second most important politician in Thailand, being Deputy Prime Minister, Minister of the Interior and Secretary-General of the (then ruling) Democrat Party when he was investigated on corruption charges in 1999. He resigned from his ministerial offices immediately after being indicted in March 2000 for falsification of his declaration of assets and liabilities. In August 2000 he was found guilty by the Constitutional Court, was barred from political office for five years and resigned his party political office.[72]

However, in another of its major early cases, concerning the then Prime Minister Thaksin Shinawatra in 2001, the Court damaged its standing irrevocably. The pivotal decision under the 1997 Constitution occurred when the Constitutional Court failed to uphold the findings of the NACC in 2001 after the election of Prime Minister Thaksin Shinawatra. The case was of enormous political importance. It involved an investigation of claims that before becoming Prime Minister, Thaksin had concealed most of his fortune as part of a dishonest

---

[70] Case 24/2003.

[71] Case 59 and Case 62/2002.

[72] See 'Thai Minister in Corruption Scandal', BBC News, 10 August 2000, available at <http://news.bbc.co.uk/2/hi/asia-pacific/874086.stm>.

scheme to conceal conflicts of interest which were outlawed under the Constitution. It was found that the assets had been registered in the names of his housekeeper, chauffeur, driver, security guard and business colleagues.[73] The NACC duly conducted its investigation and passed a judgment by an 8:1 margin upholding the allegations. If the decision of the NACC had been allowed to stand unchallenged, the result would have been a 'red card', namely, an automatic suspension from politics for five years operating with immediate effect, thus depriving Thaksin of the premiership. Thaksin refused to accept these findings as part of a legitimate constitutional process. Rather, he maintained that the entire investigation was conducted as a political smear campaign.[74] The decision of the NACC was challenged before the Constitutional Court, where it was argued that the failure to declare these assets was no more than an honest mistake. Although the argument was not accepted, the Constitutional Court voted narrowly in Thaksin's favour.[75] The 8:7 outcome was reached after two votes: the first rejected by a margin of 11:4 Thaksin's argument that he was not required to make an asset declaration; the second rejected by a margin of 7:4 Thaksin's assertion that the concealment of assets had been an honest mistake. Overall, according to the conventions of the Court's unusual voting system, the two votes of four were added together to make eight, which is set against the seven who had voted him guilty on the second ballot. This decision was indeed a surprising outcome on the facts, given that in 17 other similar cases decided previously, the Constitutional Court had always endorsed the decision of the NACC. The failure to act decisively and punish the Prime Minister for this manifest breach of the rules severely undermined the credibility of the combined strength of the constitutional watchdogs. In the face of severe political pressure, and possibly even interference, the Constitutional Court, at the very pinnacle of the Constitution, appeared to cave in. Nevertheless, it should be recognised that quite apart from any illegitimate pressures that may have been placed on them, the judges of the Constitutional Court had an unenviable choice in making their decision.

---

[73] Thaksin's staff were recorded as among the top 10 holders of shares on the Thai stock exchange.

[74] See P Phongpaichit and C Baker, *Thaksin: The Business of Politics in Thailand* (Chiang Mai, Silkworm Books, 2005) at 3.

[75] See D McCargo and U Pathmanand, *The Thaksinization of Thailand* (Copenhagen, NIAS Press, 2005) at 16.

A decision confirming Thaksin's disqualification by the NACC would in effect have invalidated the result of the election, with the prospect of political turmoil, and the ensuing crisis would have placed further strain on the constitutional arrangements with unpredictable effects.

In a later case in 2006, 28 Senators submitted an impeachment petition to the Court against the Prime Minister for conflicts of interest and improprieties in the sell-off of Shin Corp (referred to in the Preface), citing section 209 of the 1997 Constitution which limited the power of ministers to hold shares and partnerships. The Court rejected the petition, a majority of the judges deciding that the petition failed to present sufficient grounds to support the Prime Minister's alleged misconduct. In a case referred by 36 Senators in 2008, the Court ruled that Public Health Minister Chaiya Samsomsap was disqualified from holding office for failing to declare some of his wife's assets, in particular the fact that she held more than 5 per cent of stock in a private company in violation of section 92 of the 2007 Constitution. Senator Prasarn Maruekha-pitak stated that 'the court's ruling demonstrated its role of building trust in the justice system and setting standards for Thai politics'.[76] Nevertheless, the outcome welcomed on this occasion has to be considered against the overall lack of consistency when ruling on high-profile conflict of interest questions.

C. Election cases

Another controversial case concerning Thaksin related to the 2 April 2006 election, called as a snap election, three years ahead of schedule, to counter widespread public opposition to his premiership. This case too has been discussed above (chapter two, Section VI) Although the decision may be applauded on the law, it should be noted that it took a speech by the King to bring about this result. The decisions of the 2007 Court on electoral malpractice and political parties[77] do not indicate that this type of decision can be made without bringing the Court into the realm of political controversy. Given the currently highly polarised nature of Thai politics, this is hardly surprising; but the Court's jurisdiction in this area is one that needs to be carefully scrutinised for the future.

[76] 'Court Bans Chaiya from Office', *The Nation*, 10 July 2008; 'New Blow for Government as Court Finds Chaiya Broke Charter', *Bangkok Post*, 10 July 2008.
[77] See ch 2, Section IV.

Indeed the very credibility of the Constitutional Court was arguably undermined, once again, in November and December of 2010.[78] A series of video clips were leaked to YouTube which not only appeared to show nepotism by Constitutional Court judges in filling vacancies at the Court, but also featured a Democrat Party MP lobbying the Secretary to the President of the Court in relation to the dissolution cases which were pending at the time. These revelations were the prelude to the Court hearing two cases taken by the ECT against the Democrat Party on the application of the Red Shirt opposition. It should be remembered that the outcome here was of the highest importance. Had the verdict in the first case gone against them the Democrat Party faced dissolution and the banning of its executives, including Abhisit Vejjajiva, the current Prime Minister, for five years. The charges in the first case related to allegations of electoral fraud during the April 2005 elections, and in the second concerned an alleged failure to declare, as required by electoral law, donations totalling 258 million baht. The Democrat Party was acquitted respectively by 4-2 and 4-3 majorities. The result in favour of the Democrat Party was not decided on the merits of competing claims, but rather on a technicality, namely, the failure of the ECT to file charges within the required 15-day time limit. These acquittals exposed the Constitutional Court to accusations of double standards. In 2007 the Constitutional Court had accepted, beyond the 15-day deadline, a petition from the ECT against the Thai Rak Thai Party, and had gone on to dissolve the Party and ban its executives. Furthermore, it was difficult to see why the Court had allowed a full hearing of the cases if they were inclined to disqualify on the ground that the time limit had been exceeded.[79]

D. Cases concerning powers of economic regulation

Given the economic situation in South East Asia, and particularly in Thailand obtaining as the 1997 Constitution moved into its implementation phase,[80] it is not surprising that economic regulation featured in many of the Court's early cases. In its very first decision in 1998, the Court ruled on the constitutionality of four emergency execu-

[78] 'Party On', *The Economist*, 29 November 2010.
[79] 'Off the Hook: EC, Judges Slammed Over Verdict' *The Nation*, December 2, 2010.
[80] See ch 1, Section VI.

tive decrees issued by the previous Democrat Government under Prime Minister Chuan Leekpai in response to the economic crisis.[81] The Government had issued the decrees in May 1998, expanding the role of the Financial Restructuring Authority and the Assets Management Corporation, to settle the debts of the Financial Institutions Development Fund through the issue of 500 billion baht (about US$14.2 million) in bonds, and to authorise the Ministry of Finance to seek 200 billion baht (about US$5.7 million) in overseas loans. On the last day of parliamentary debate on these decrees, when it was clear they would be passed and in order to postpone a vote, a minor political party invoked section 219 of the 1997 Constitution relating to emergency powers to question their constitutionality. It was argued that since there was no emergency or necessary urgency as required by section 218(2) of the 1997 Constitution, the Government could not make any emergency decrees. Section 218(1) allowed emergency decrees to be passed on the basis of national economic security, and the Court ruled that it was obvious that the nation was in an economic crisis and that the decrees were in fact designed to deal with national economic security.[82] A similar suit by the same party, impeaching the Prime Minister for signing Letters of Intent with the International Monetary Fund to secure an emergency loan without parliamentary approval under section 224 of the 1997 Constitution, was also rejected on the grounds that the Letters of Intent were not in the nature of treaties falling under section 224, neither were they contractual agreements, as they lacked any enforcement provisions.

The reticence of the Court, faced with a combination of emergency powers and economic regulation, is hardly surprising. In one sense these decisions can be seen as positive. They indicate that the Court will not attempt to second-guess economic policy, but also that the Court might be willing to strike down an emergency decree that was not obviously required by the actual situation in hand.

---

[81] Case 1/1998.

[82] *Ibid.* In a similar case, Case 12/1998, the Court held that statutory immunity of public officials from negligence suits in respect of administrative decisions was not unconstitutional. And in Cases 3–5, 9–35, 38–43 and 50/1999, the Court repeatedly ruled in favour of the validity of economic legislation, including agreements with the IMF, designed to deal with the economic crisis. Clear limits appeared to be drawn in these cases on the Court's willingness to fetter executive action in economic and banking matters: Cases 9–10, 14–15/2001; 33, 35–49/2001; 9, 13, 19–34, 40, 45–47, 49, 57, 61/2002; 4, 8–11, 14, 30, 34–36/2003.

E. Cases concerning appointment processes

One of the most important functions of the Court was to rule on the validity of sometimes extremely complex processes of appointment of State officials and independent agencies, and the qualifications of particular persons to hold office. Many of these cases were politically contentious. As we have seen, this phenomenon commenced during the transitional phase, even before the Court assumed jurisdiction.

A notable example was the case of Auditor-General Jaruvan Maintaka. Jaruvan was one of three nominees for the position of Auditor-General in 2001, but had received fewer votes than one other nominee when the State Audit Commission (SAC) voted on the nominations under the provisions of the State Audit Act 1979. However, all three nominees were forwarded to the Senate, which was constitutionally empowered to advise the King whom to appoint, and the Senate had voted in Jaruvan's favour. It was argued before the Court that the SAC should, under section 135 of the 1997 Constitution, have forwarded only the name of a single nominee, that is the one with the most votes. In July 2004 the Court ruled this selection process unconstitutional, but failed, in an outcome apparently at variance with another similar case concerning the Chairman of the ECT, to hold that Jaruvan should accordingly leave office. Thus the ruling left some uncertainty about her status.[83] In view of considerable public support for her vigorous approach as auditor, she refused to resign without an instruction from the King. The SAC then made another nomination, which was approved by the Senate. Yet again the crisis was resolved by royal intervention. The King refused his assent to the appointment; the Senate rejected a motion to reaffirm Jaruvan's appointment and referred the matter back to the SAC, who voted unanimously in favour of Jaruvan after receiving a memorandum from the King's Principal Private Secretary advising that the situation should be resolved. This episode, although it represented a significant defeat for the Thaksin Government, was hardly a victory for the rule of law. A proper course following the Court's decision, which should have clarified its own consequences, should have resulted in Jaruvan's resignation and a new appointment process following the constitutional provisions.

[83] For a chronology of facts and decisions in the Jaruvan case, see 'Chronology of Events in the Auditor-General's Deadlock', *The Nation*, 30 August 2005.

F. Politically sensitive cases in the 2007 Court

As the final constitutional arbiter on many issues under the 2007 Constitution, the Constitutional Court was soon exposed to intense political controversy. Most notably, it ruled in September 2008 that Prime Minister Samak Sundaravej had violated the conflict of interest provisions[84] by being paid for his appearance on a TV cookery show, and as a result he had to step down from the premiership.[85] Then in December 2008 the Court unanimously decided that his successor, Prime Minister Somchai Wongsawan, and the ruling coalition had been guilty of electoral fraud. Somchai too was forced to step down from office, and the ruling coalition parties were immediately disbanded by order of the Court. The Court's President declared that this 'set a political standard and an example', also observing that 'dishonest political parties undermine Thailand's democratic system'.[86]

These decisions were taken against a background of well-orchestrated anti-government demonstrations by the opposition People's Alliance for Democracy (PAD), culminating in the closure of Bangkok's international airport with far-reaching economic consequences for the entire nation. The judgment of the Constitutional Court, which was in line with the rigorous anti-corruption provisions of the Constitution,[87] had removed an alleged Thaksin nominee as Prime Minister and was therefore hailed as a victory by the demonstrators. At the same time it gave the PAD an excuse to end their action. In the short term the Constitutional Court's decision defused a crisis, but many of the People Power Party government supporters have, perhaps not surprisingly, accused the Court of being partisan and merely doing the bidding of their opponents.[88]

These cases also raise a rather different but related issue, namely, whether the Constitutional Court should be placed in a position sum-

---

[84] TC 2007, s 267.

[85] Case no 12-13/2551 (BE). See also 'PM Disqualified for Violating Charter with Cookery Show', *The Nation*, 10 September 2008.

[86] 'Thailand Prime Minister to Step Down After Court Strips Him of Office', *Guardian*, 2 December 2008.

[87] See eg TC 2007, s 68.

[88] G Wehfritz and J Seaton, 'Thailand Slides Toward Civil War', *Newsweek*, Amsterdam, 15 December 2008.

marily to disqualify an elected Prime Minister and an entire political party for relatively minor abuses.

There were other early indications of a greater willingness by politicians to comply with constitutional norms under the 2007 Constitution. For example, an important ruling of the Constitutional Court in July 2008 prompted the resignation of Thailand's Foreign Minister, Noppadon Pattama, who supported a bid which would have resulted in the Preah Vear Hindu temple on the Thai-Cambodian border being listed as a UNESCO World Heritage Site, despite its ownership being disputed between the two countries. This decision, affecting Thailand's national interest, which was taken without reference to Parliament, was held to be in violation of the Constitution.[89] Ministers are required, before concluding treaties or agreements, to publicise relevant information, make arrangements for public hearings and put the matter before the National Assembly for approval.[90]

X. CONCLUSION

In order to perform its role effectively, any constitutional court requires a cohort of judges who are insulated from direct influence. In the Thai case, the appointment process has been refined further to this end, and it draws upon experienced and independent judges and political scientists. The problem, however, is not only that enormous pressure is implicitly placed on a small judicial panel (sometimes a quorum of five) to decide key constitutional questions with large political implications, but also that the Constitutional Court may become the *main locus* for determining issues that should be regarded as purely political. As a result of this, the Constitutional Court is seen, inevitably, as politically biased, because so many of its decisions have been adverse to the interests of one faction. Even the most worthy and able judges may ultimately be unable to resolve such highly controversial issues in a way that is seen as legitimate.

One view might hold that the solution is to do away with constitutional jurisdiction entirely. On the other hand, where there is a torrid

[89] TC 2007, s 190.
[90] 'Temple Ruling Puts Foreign Ministry Lawyers in a Flap', *The Nation*, 10 July 2008; 'Thailand Foreign Minister Quits', BBC, 10 July 2008; 'Thai Foreign Minister Noppadon Pattama Resigns', *The News and Observer*, Raleigh, NC, 11 July 2008.

constitutional climate, final recourse to a constitutional court has obvious advantages. The court may have the power positively to protect individual and minority rights, and to support other constitutional watchdog bodies; but even where called upon to resolve exposed political questions, a respected court has the potential to provide a more carefully-reflected response, and also to operate as a force for restraint at times of crisis. After 12 years of constitutional jurisdiction, this position still remains a hope rather than an actuality in Thailand, but we have also seen that there are reasons for thinking that this hope might be fulfilled if the dangers and problems outlined can be avoided.

FURTHER READING

T Ginsburg, 'Constitutional Courts in East Asia: Understanding Variation' in A Harding and P Leyland (eds), *Constitutional Courts: A Comparative Study* (London, Wildy, Simmonds and Hill, 2009).

A Harding, 'The Constitutional Court of Thailand 1998–2006: A Turbulent Innovation' in A Harding and P Nicholson (eds), *New Courts in Asia* (London, Routledge, 2009).

—— and P Leyland, 'The Constitutional Courts of Thailand and Indonesia: Two Case Studies from South East Asia' in A Harding and P Leyland (eds), *Constitutional Courts: A Comparative Study* (London, Wildy, Simmonds and Hill, 2009).

J Klein, 'The Battle for the Rule of Law in Thailand: the Constitutional Court of Thailand' in A Raksataya and J Klein (eds), *Constitutional Court of Thailand: the Provisions and Workings of the Court* (Bangkok, Constitution for the People Society, 2001).

V Mahakun, *Kana Khammakan Pongkan Lae Prabpram Kan Tujarit Heang Chat: Adit Pajuban Anakhot* The National Anti-Corruption Commission: Past Present and Future (Bangkok, National Institute on Anti-Corruption, 2009) [in Thai].

S Nitikraipot, *Sarn Rattathammanun Kap Kan Patibat Pantakit Tam Rattathammanun* [The Constitutional Court and its Mission under the Constitution] (Bangkok, Winyuchon, 2003) [in Thai].

W Pakeerut, *Withipijarana Khong Sarn Rattathammanun: Sueksa Priaptiap Korani Khong Sarn Rattathammanun Tangprathet Kap Sarn Rattathammanun Thai* [Procedure of the Constitutional Court: Comparative Study] (Bangkok, Winyuchon, 2003) [in Thai].

6

Administrative Justice

~~~~~~~~~~

Introduction – The Council of State and the Origins of Administrative Justice – The Administrative Courts – The Office of the Thai Ombudsman – Conclusion

I. INTRODUCTION

This chapter reviews the development of administrative justice in Thailand in order to assess the contribution of the administrative courts and the Office of the Thai Ombudsman in establishing an accountable system of government. Thailand's political narrative over the past 80 years has been extremely turbulent, but viewed from a different perspective it is possible to identify a process of institution-building, with the antecedents of the contemporary Thai State originating from the reign of King Chulalongkorn (Rama V) (1868–1910). In particular, the foundations of the modern bureaucracy discussed in chapter two were laid down at national and local level during the late nineteenth century, and the Council of State was introduced for the first time in 1874.

One commentator has defined administrative law as prescribing

> behaviour within administrative organizations; more importantly, [administrative law] delineates the relationships between those inside an administration and those outside it. Outside an administration lie both the statute maker whose laws and regulations administrators owe a duty to faithfully implement and the citizens to whom administrators owe legally correct procedural and substantive action.[1]

---

[1] M Shapiro, 'Administrative Law Unbounded' (2001) 8 *Indiana Journal of Global Legal Studies* 369.

At one level this means that there is an assumption that public bodies will be subordinated to political authority; at another, that the Administration will respect the individual rights and interests of those they regulate and serve. As part of a Continental European legal tradition which came to be influential in Thailand from the last quarter of the 19th century onwards, administrative law was broadly conceived as being the branch of law which deals with the powers and the organisation of the executive organs of the State. To achieve this end administrative law encompasses general principles which apply to the process of administration. Also, in line particularly with the French model, an exclusive administrative law jurisdiction is established, with specialist administrative courts responsible for adjudicating claims against administrative authorities.

In Thailand a national system of Administrative Courts was, after several decades of discussion, finally launched as one of the important innovations of the 1997 Constitution. Indeed, the fact that the Council of State already contained a petition council with a limited jurisdiction to redress grievances, facilitated the introduction of the new courts within four years from the promulgation of the Constitution (1997–2001). This reform should be regarded as part of a continuing modernisation which replicates the institutional characteristics and principles of established Western European and Asian models: there are few, if any, features of Thailand's administrative justice which display obviously autochthonous Thai characteristics relating to traditional law.

It is also worth stressing at the outset that although the English jurist Dicey had a much narrower view of administrative law which rejected a separate jurisdictional basis for administrative justice, his emphasis on the control function exercised by the courts and the general adherence to rule-of-law values resonates strongly in the Thai context. As Harden and Lewis put it when discussing the wider application of the concept:

> The rule of law is a highly connotative, value-laden idea and as such must be sharply differentiated from a rule of law, a specific norm, or guide to action. It speaks to a belief in the kind of polity which seeks to subordinate naked power and elevate civil order and rational progress. It implicitly rejects the idea of immunity from criticism, of being above collective institutions rather than facilitating their operation . . . It is the central legitimating feature of organized public life – the supreme constitutional principle.[2]

---

[2] I Harden and N Lewis, *The Noble Lie: The British Constitution and the Rule of Law* (London, Hutchinson, 1986) 19.

Such a doctrine assumes not only that the State should not have special powers, but also that public servants would be equally subject to the ordinary law. Crucially, this presupposes that there is a separation of powers between the judicial and executive branches, with the rule of law upheld by a system of independent courts. The point is that administrative law rests upon the assumption that there must be a culture of legality which, in turn, becomes a key value that underpins good governance.

This discussion commences by setting out the historical context, with a particular focus on the role of the Council of State. The next section concentrates on the Administrative Courts. The concern is not simply to consider the characteristics of these Courts, but also to assess their performance with reference to both statistical data and important decisions. We then evaluate the role of the Office of the Thai Ombudsman.

II. THE COUNCIL OF STATE AND THE ORIGINS OF ADMINISTRATIVE JUSTICE

As noted in earlier chapters, during the course of the 19th century, under the rule of King Mongkut (Rama IV, 1851–68) and King Chulalongkorn (Rama V, 1868–1910), Thailand was subject to a programme of modernisation and reform which touched many areas of Thai society, including political organisation and law. In particular, we have already seen in chapter four how the foundations of the modern bureaucracy were introduced during the pre-constitutional era at national and local level. The Council of State from which the modern Administrative Courts originated was first introduced in 1874. In fact it was established in its embryonic form as an advisory council.[3] But it came to be closely modelled on the French *Conseil d'État* to assist in exercising control over the King's most prominent ministries.[4] The *Conseil d'État* in France, as it developed through the 19th and early 20th centuries, demonstrated a capacity for judicial independence, and also managed to impose a principle of legality by assuming the role of

[3] See D Wyatt, *Thailand: A Short History*, 2nd edn (New Haven, Conn, Yale University Press) 177ff.

[4] L Brown and J Bell, *French Administrative Law*, 5th edn (Oxford, Oxford University Press, 1998) 6.

overseeing the administrative process. This role was all the more apparent because the ordinary courts were prevented from having jurisdiction
in this area. The *Conseil* originated as a means for petitioning the Crown,
but later acquired a power to issue unenforceable judgments.

> In the second half of the 19th century and in the early 20th century, reform-
> ist politicians, *Conseillers d'État* and doctrinal writers . . . attributed to the state
> administrative qualities of potential irresponsibility and abusiveness that
> rendered legal controls justifiable . . . they perceived a centralized and, there-
> fore, distinct and identifiable administration that could be subject to a dis-
> tinct body of law.[5]

In turn, this led to the emergence of identifiable notions of public
power and public service, supported by an emergent regime of public
law which could serve as a corrective to a potentially irresponsible and
abusive Administration.

The original initiative in Thailand was taken against a background of
factional struggle within the Royal Palace, which saw the King Rama V,
shortly after his accession, having to deal with opposition from the old
guard within the Royal Court.[6] The Council was staffed with a carefully
selected group of loyal and progressive senior officials of *Phraya* rank.
Under King Rama V, the Council of State worked alongside the Privy
Council, which was also formed in 1874, and which had overlapping
personnel and functions. At the same time, the functional reorganisation of ministries and departments based in Bangkok was part of the
reform of the Thai bureaucracy.[7] In particular, King Rama V attempted
to use the law as an instrument with which to oppose the personal influence and corruption which surrounded the court. He was far-sighted
enough to recognise that that this objective could be achieved through
the introduction of a 'principle of legality' comparable to that existing
in France under the *droit administratif*. Such a principle had a role to play
by bringing the performance of every duty under the law. Although the
Council of State had been established by the King early in his reign, it
was often circumvented, with the result that the new body rapidly
became redundant. Chulalongkorn eventually decided to repeal the Act

---

[5] J Allison, *A Continental Distinction in the Common Law* (Oxford, Oxford University Press, 2000) 55.

[6] B Terwiel, *Thailand's Political History: From the Fall of Ayuthhaya to Recent Times* (Bangkok, River Books, 2005) 178ff.

[7] J Girling, *Thailand: Society and Polites* (Ithaca, NY, Cornell University Press, 1981) 52.

on the Council of State in 1893 and to rely instead on the Council of Ministers as a consultative body charged with the drafting of laws.[8]

The point to note is that the Council of State had been conceived as a powerful tool to be placed in the King's own hands, which could be used as a mechanism for the consolidation of centralised power and as an advisory body to help implement royal policy. At the same time, in a different capacity the Council of State accepted petitions from citizens who had a grievance against any administrative organ of the State. It thereby assumed a role in improving the administrative process, and it was this adjudicative function in relation to grievances (in a greatly expanded form) which was more recently given to Thailand's Administrative Courts. However, increasingly during the 20th century the Council of State made a pivotal contribution to the system of law and administration. This was after it emerged as the ministry responsible for drafting legislation. The law-drafting department established under King Rama VI to revise Thailand's legal codes was transferred from the Ministry of Justice to the Council of State following the abolition of the absolute monarchy in 1932. In coordinating the drafting of law the Council of State assisted in the consolidation of centralised power, but it also maintained its petitioning function, which meant that this office was the only body which could play a part in containing the abuse of official power.

In the second quarter of the 20th century the path towards establishing administrative courts was strongly influenced by the politician and scholar Pridi Banomyong, who was, in part at least, responsible for drafting Thailand's first constitution.[9] In his writings Pridi displayed knowledge of the European and Japanese constitutional systems.[10] In addition he was concerned to explain the distinction between constitutional law and administrative law. For him, the former laid down general principles and supreme powers in the country, while the latter codified the regulations and procedures of the executive or administrative powers in detail, and dealt with the use of those powers. Pridi pointed out that there were already many laws which regulated the practices of the Administration, particularly in the areas of policing, social welfare and the economy. In a wider sense, administrative law was thus understood

[8] The Council of Ministers Act 1893.
[9] See ch 1
[10] See S Matsui *The Constitution of Japan: A Contextual Analysis* (Oxford, Hart Publishing, 2011) 7ff.

in terms of the law relating to the Administration or the Government (*kan pokkhrong*). French legal theory had already taught him that the

> legislative power and the judicial power should be separate from the executive power, because if they were combined it may lead to injustice. In other words, those adjudicating are adjudicating on laws which they themselves legislated.[11]

Following the abdication of King Rama VII and the introduction of the first Thai constitution, the Council of State was officially recognised under the Council of State Act of 1933 as falling under the Office of Prime Minister. The Act further proclaimed that the structure and competence of the Council of State was to be equivalent to that of the French *Conseil d'État*.

The introduction of this concept of administrative law meant that if an administrative order was wrong, a process of petitioning to the Council of State became available. In order to perform dual functions the staff of the Council of State were divided into two categories: law councillors, whose primary function was statutory drafting; and petition councillors, who were entrusted to adjudicate administrative cases as prescribed by law.[12] From the 1930s, when this upheaval was taking place, until relatively recently it was much too costly to introduce an administrative court, and therefore the existing system of administrative appeals was expanded into the Petition Council of the Council of State to deal with the administrative cases that arose. In sum, aggrieved citizens were left with a number of options, depending on the nature of the complaint.[13] A petition could be issued against the superior of an administrative official if wrongdoing was suspected, and this would be dealt with by the Petition Council of the Council of State. However, a case might be taken against an administrative official in the ordinary courts. In some instances a statutory right of appeal to a court against the administrative act or order might be available. Finally, it might be possible to petition the King directly.

---

[11] C Baker and P Phongpaichit, *Pridi by Pridi: Selected Writings on Life, Politics and Economy* (Chiang Mai, Silkworm Press, 2000) 43ff.

[12] B Bhalakula, *Pridi and the Administrative Court* (Office of the Administrative Courts, 2001) 13ff.

[13] See the Council of State Act 1933 which introduced petition councillors and the Petition Council Act 1949 which was intended to establish a Petition Commission.

A separate public law jurisdiction on the lines of the *droit administratif* has been justified on the basis that the State should have a monopoly over the exercise of certain types of coercive power, in particular the creation and enforcement of laws relating to the capacity of the State to act as an instrument of social regulation. Without any doubt, it was this strong French influence which contributed to the local conceptualisation of a distinct public law.[14] Such a system is associated with: designing State organisations; ascribing varying degrees of importance to State agencies and State officials in regard to members of the public; and formulating criteria and measures for controlling the discharge of State organs and officials.[15] The Thai Council of State still operates at the very heart of government by continuing to perform the key task of legislative drafting, but the Administrative Courts have now assumed the adjudicative functions which the Petition Council of the Council of State previously exercised.

III. THE ADMINISTRATIVE COURTS

In the intervening period there were several attempts to establish administrative courts,[16] but they were finally introduced under the 1997 Constitution. In addition to the ordinary courts, the Administrative Courts were intended to operate alongside other watchdog bodies to fill a particular gap in the grievance chain by offering full legal redress against official bodies.[17] They were set up by statute in 1999[18] and began operating in 2001, replacing the Petition Council of the Council of State.[19] The

[14]   See P Leyland, 'Droit Administratif Thai Syle: A Comparative Analysis of the Administrative Courts in Thailand' (2006) 8(2) *Australian Journal of Asian Law* 121 at 125ff. The acceptance of a separate public jurisdiction based on the recognition of the distinct objectives of public law has been integral to the French system. See eg J-M Auby and R Ducos-Ader (1966) *Droit Public* 1, cited in B Rudden, *A Sourcebook on French Law*, 3rd edn (Oxford, Oxford University Press, 1991) 14.

[15]   B Bhalakula, 'Administrative Contract in the Thai Legal Context' (Bangkok, Office of the Administrative Courts, 2003) 19.

[16]   Eg, a bill on the establishment of the administrative court was drafted by the Ministry of Justice in 1980 and another bill proposed in 1983.

[17]   See chs 2, 3 and 7; See also P Leyland, 'Thailand's Constitutional Watchdogs: Dobermans, Bloodhounds or Lapdogs' (2007) 2 *Journal of Comparative Law* 151.

[18]   See the Act on the Establishment of Administrative Courts and Administrative Courts Procedure 1999 BE 2542, referred to hereafter as 'the 1999 Act'.

[19]   See TC 1997, s 276 and TC 2007, ss 223–227.

new Courts are based on a two-tier system: the Supreme Administrative Court, and Administrative Courts of First Instance. There are two of the latter: the Central Administrative Court (for Bangkok and provinces local to Bangkok), and the Regional Administrative Courts. However, the characteristics of the Courts and the limits of their jurisdiction can be distinguished from the ordinary courts and from other means of redress that are available. The Supreme Administrative Court, apart from acting as an appellate court, hearing appeals from judgments of the Administrative Court of First Instance, exercises a jurisdiction which is directed at issues relating to the operation of central government. For example, it has competence to try cases concerning the legality of royal decrees or by-laws issued by the Council of Ministers.[20]

A. The independence of the Administrative Courts

An effective separation of powers between the executive and judicial branches depends upon establishing a strong degree of judicial independence, and in this book there is frequent allusion to the difficulties associated with achieving a separation of powers. In a general sense the originators of modern conceptualisations of the separation of powers sought to conceive of a system of checks which would ensure that power vested in governors could not be turned to personal advantage, and that personalised rule by men was replaced by the impersonal rule of rules. To this end, an independent judiciary is required to stand up against the abuse of executive power. In practical terms there are two aspects to this. The first is a set of relatively clear and general rules which can establish an impartial system. The second is the independence to apply the law without fear or favour. In a macro-constitutional sense this independence is most apparent when the judicial branch is seen to be separated from, and thus independent of, the executive branch. Since under constitutional and legal provisions in most countries judicial appointments have to be approved by the executive branch at some point, and members of the judiciary are remunerated from public funds, it is obvious that entirely isolating the judicial branch from political and economic considerations is never straightforward. Furthermore, in an administrative law context judicial independence can have a special significance.

---

[20] See 1999 Act, s 11.

This is because of the potential for the blurring of boundaries between the role of the Executive in implementing the policy of institutions with a claim to democratic legitimacy, and the role of judges called in to adjudicate between organs of the State or when claimants make individual claims that might impact on the collective interest. This issue might arise in cases involving resource allocation in the public domain; for example, in Thailand this could relate to education or health provision.

The Thai Constitution, coupled with the legislation introducing the Administrative Courts, includes elaborate provisions to establish the independence of the Courts' judges.[21] The Court administration is clearly separated from the Executive and made independent from any government department. A Judicial Commission of the Administrative Courts is responsible for disciplinary matters and promotion. Any resolutions for dismissal of a judge or relating to other forms of serious misconduct can only go ahead after the matter has been reported on by a committee, which is itself mainly comprised of by judges of the Supreme Administrative Court.

Important safeguards have been set in place in a number of ways to guarantee that the Administrative Courts are staffed by a cadre of professional judges. Appointments to the Administrative Courts are made by the Judicial Commission of the Administrative Courts, which is itself comprised mainly of judges. Candidates must be legally qualified and must demonstrate relevant experience, for example as law councillors, petition councillors or councillors of State. However, susceptibility to political interference crops up at later stage in the appointments process to the most senior judicial posts, because the appointment of the President of the Supreme Administrative Court requires that a candidate is first nominated by the Commission, after which approval by the Senate is required before the name is submitted by the Prime Minister to the King for final approval.[22] At this stage interference might be possible in the form of opposition to particular candidates from private individuals, or through business interests exerting an influence.

There are other familiar safeguards. For example, judges cannot be taken off a case once they have been assigned to it. Conflicts of interest are prohibited and judges are appointed until the age of retirement at 65.[23]

---

[21] See generally the 1999 Act, ss 12–30.
[22] TC 2007, s 225.
[23] 1999 Act, ss 12–30.

Above all, it is essential that the incumbents are adequately remunerated. Not only are judges' salaries protected, but the generous levels of pay (in Thai terms) are to ensure that judges are unlikely to be tempted into corrupt practices and, at the same time, to attract candidates of sufficiently high calibre. Nevertheless, public sector salaries remain a sensitive subject in Thailand. For example, the practice of self-awarded pay increases by independent watchdog bodies without obtaining parliamentary approval (including the Constitutional Court and the Administrative Courts, and notably the NACC which was forced to resign *en bloc* in May 2005) was subject to far-reaching and continuing controversy, which encouraged scepticism over the constitutional reform programme.[24]

B. Characteristics of the Administrative Courts

It has been stressed from the outset that administrative courts are fundamentally concerned with the accountability of public bodies and the containment of public power (as well as having other responsibilities, for example over administrative contracts and tort claims against public bodies). Given this role, the reach of any public law jurisdiction becomes a question of crucial importance. As we have already noted in the Thai case the system of administrative courts based on the French model has been designed so as to recognise a separate, and at the same time specialised public law jurisdiction which operates alongside the ordinary courts and the Constitutional Court.[25] It is clearly important to see how the Thai administrative courts have interpreted the limits of the public law jurisdiction.[26] The public/private distinction has been made more problematical in Thailand (as in many other countries) by the emergence of a 'contracting State', in which there is expanding private sector involvement in the delivery of public services. This might include the privatisation of formerly State-run industries, and reliance on private companies to construct and manage many publicly-financed enterprises.[27] In fact part of the rationale for the introduction of the Administrative Courts has been as a potent constitutional mechanism designed to regulate the exercise of

---

[24] See, eg, 'Constitutional Court Pay Rise: Give it Back', *The Nation*, 25 October 2004.

[25] See, eg, Auby and Ducos-Ader, cited in Rudden, above n 14.

[26] Bhalakula, above n 15, at 19.

[27] See, eg, the discussion of the EGAT case in section III.D below.

these aspects of public power. It follows that a restricted definition of what constitutes public law matters falling under the ambit of the Administrative Courts would limit the application of public law remedies and exclude judicial supervision over functions, formerly exercised by the State, which are now manifested in private form.

In assessing a claim the Court must decide whether the contested matter has a sufficient public law dimension to fall under its jurisdiction. In cases where this issue is contestable, the judge will consider:

a) whether the body, enterprise or individual is providing a public service;

b) whether a public power is being exercised (the test employed seeks to ascertain if a power has been granted that would not be granted or exercised in the private sector)

From the reported case law it appears that the Administrative Courts have defined 'public' in a broad sense. For example, they have heard cases involving privatised State enterprises which provide a universal service, and have ruled that the Telephone Organisation of Thailand (TOT) remained an administrative agency subject to the jurisdiction of the Administrative Courts.[28] The role of the French *Tribunal des Conflits* in deciding contested matters of jurisdiction is closely replicated by the Thai Jurisdictional Conflict Tribunal, which adjudicates such disputes arising in the Thai legal context. It should be remembered that a major justification for giving the Administrative Courts jurisdictional exclusivity is the introduction of both a special procedure and specially designed remedies.

The Thai Administrative Courts have a jurisdiction which allows them to oversee the proper functioning of the Administration. An application can be made to the Court over an alleged neglect of duty or unreasonable delay. For example, the Office of Atomic Energy for Peace (OAEP) was found to have been negligent in the storage of spent isotopes around the country, and was it ordered by the Central Administrative Court in 2002 to pay 5.2 million baht to 12 survivors of a radiation leak.[29] Equally, the Court can be required to adjudicate over a 'wrongful act or other liability' associated with the Administration or a State official in the discharge of legal duties. In this sense the

---

[28] Red Cases Nos 1733–1734/2002.
[29] See 'Court Ruling: Long Battle Ends in Bt20 Refund', *The Nation*, 10 August 2004.

Administrative Courts have a jurisdiction which potentially overlaps with that of the Ombudsman (see section IV below). Indeed, the Ombudsman is specifically empowered to refer matters to the Court if, in the course of an investigation, he or she believes that any by-law or act of an administrative agency is unlawful. Moreover, as will be explained below, an official of the Office of the Thai Ombudsman may take up a case on a potential litigant's behalf in the Administrative Courts. In this sense the Administrative Courts may be regarded as bodies which line up alongside the other organs of the State which have been designed to act as watchdog bodies at a number of different levels.[30] Causing unnecessary process or excessive burden to the public is recognised as a ground of review in its own right. Additionally, a matter can be referred to the Court by an administrative agency or State official to force a person or body to do a particular act prescribed by law, or to prevent them from acting contrary to the law.[31]

Turning next to remedies, the provision of effective redress is of central importance to any grievance machinery. For example, in the United Kingdom judicial review was constructed around the remedies that were available. In particular, the courts were equipped with the ancient prerogative orders which allowed unlawful decisions of public bodies to be quashed, prevented bodies from taking decisions which were deemed unlawful, or commanded them to act where they were neglecting to perform a lawful duty. The Thai Administrative Courts are in possession of formidable powers when it comes to granting remedies,[32] and many of the remedies they are able to award are tailored to suit an administrative law context. A Court can issue a decree revoking a by-law or an order,[33] and it can revoke an act in whole or part where it is alleged that an administrative agency or State official has done an unlawful act as defined by s 9(1) of the 1999 Act.[34] Furthermore, the Court can direct

[30]   See chs 2, 3 and 7; and Leyland, above n 17.

[31]   See the 1999 Act, s 9(5); Rule of the General Assembly of Judges of the Supreme Administrative Court on Administrative Court Procedure BE 2543 (2000), cl 28.

[32]   1999 Act, s 72.

[33]   Eg, in March 2003, the Office of Consumer Protection Board issued regulations banning the sale of high-pressure water guns, which, following commercial pressure, were considered to be unlawful by the Administrative Court but remained in operation pending an appeal. See *The Nation*, 13 April 2004.

[34]   This includes unlawful issuing of rules, ultra vires acts, neglecting duties, disputed administrative contracts, etc.

whether any such decree is going to have retrospective or non-retrospective effect. In addition, the Administrative Courts have powers which roughly correspond to the mandatory orders and injunctive relief available to the English courts. They are granted powers to order the performance of a duty, or order a person to act or to refrain from an act in compliance with the law. Further still, the Courts have powers to order the payment of money or the delivery of property.[35]

C. The performance of the Administrative Courts and the wider role of administrative law in Thailand

The performance of the Administrative Courts is considered in this section against a backdrop of political instability and conflict, and, at the same time, the serial abuse of power by the nation's rulers. In a formal sense we have observed that the Administrative Courts have opened up an avenue of contestation which allows ordinary citizens as well as non-governmental organisations (NGOs) and other interest groups to challenge the actions of public bodies. It should be remembered that

> grassroots NGOs have established themselves as the popular voice of conscience in Thai civil society. These organizations can be seen as the core of rural-popular civil society, as they have been at the forefront of popular democratic struggles against authoritarian rule and military politics. They have tried to establish a linkage betweeen 'elite urban' and 'rural popular' elements and to push forward grassroots democracy in Thai civil society.[36]

Such organisations act as proxies for citizen interests.

The central question for us to assess is whether this novel departure in providing Administrative Courts has contributed significantly to the superimposition of legality. The published statistics which are considered below give an indication of the routine work of the Courts in providing a remedy to Thai citizens with a grievance against the State. At an entirely different level, prominent litigation has placed the Courts uncomfortably close to the cauldron of political controversy. A sample of these cases is reviewed below as a test bed to establish the degree to

---

[35] See Leyland, above n 14, at 132ff for a discussion of the procedural characteristics and grounds for challenging decisions.

[36] N Thabchumpon, 'NGOs and Grassroots Participation in the Political Reform Process' in D McCargo (ed), *Reforming Thai Politics* (Copenhagen, NIAS, 2002) 187.

which there is evidence of separation of powers and independence which, in turn, has contributed to a new culture of legality in Thailand.

Although the public sector in Thailand has been subject to a significant dose of privatisation, it will be apparent from the discussion in chapter three that the civil service at central and local government levels plays an important part in public administration, and that statutory regulation is also important in many fields. While the throughput of cases appears to provide a broad statistical indication of the contribution that these Courts make, it should also be pointed out that the mere existence of this new remedy might be having a deterrent effect, the prospect of litigation acting as a spur to better administration. Since they were introduced in 2001 until the latest statistics published in December 2009, the Central Administrative Court has dealt with a total of over 35,000 cases, while the Supreme Administrative Court has dealt with 8,884 cases over the same period. The distribution of cases is very much in line with the profile of government ministries and departments: 13,131 cases had been filed against the Ministry of the Interior, which also has responsibility for local government;[37] the next most prominent ministries were Education (5,220), Office of the Prime Minister (4,493), Transport (4,439), Finance (3,846), Agriculture (3,769), Health (1,229), Justice (845), Industry (586) and Defence (480). The government department falling under these ministries with the largest number of cases filed against it has been the Department of Lands (4,854). The case throughputs of other departments were: Local Administration (3,529), Highways (2,066), Office of Basic Education Commission (1,803), Office of the Permanent Secretary (1,486), Office of the Minister of Transport (1,482), Office of the Higher Education Commission (1,440).[38]

D. Prominent Court decisions

In the first category of high-profile litigation, we shall see that the Administrative Courts have been drawn into complex disputes involv-

---

[37] The role of the Ministry of the Interior in relation to local government is discussed in ch 4.

[38] The statistics quoted in this chapter are the only available statistics, and were supplied directly by the Office of the Administrative Courts in March 2010. Also, it is important to note that the referral rate of cases does not seem to have been affected by the military coup in September 2006.

ing conflicts of interest that have arisen in relation to the ownership and control of the media. Essentially, the problem is that broadcasting and print media, as well as telecommunications, have been regarded by politicians as just more businesses geared for profit,[39] and there was in this area widespread evidence of conflicts of interest and abuse of power for political advantage.[40] The legality and the efficacy of aspects of statutory regulation were called into question before the Administrative Courts.[41] The Court in each case was being required to uphold the rule of law in a most politically sensitive area and to provide accountability in a wider public interest. The most obvious examples concerned the broadcasting channel iTV and the Shin Corp under Thaksin's premiership.[42] We also observe in reviewing this litigation the engagement of the hierarchy of Thai justice, with the involvement of the Arbitration Court, the Central Administrative Court and the Supreme Administrative Court.

The TV channel (iTV) was created in 1995 to provide an independent dimension to Thai broadcasting, with a concession granted until September 2025. Under a contract relating to this concession, which had been negotiated with the Prime Minister's Office (PMO), iTV was required to broadcast 70 per cent news programmes and 30 per cent entertainment programmes. Any failure to fulfil its obligations under this contract allowed the PMO to exact fines and penalties of millions of baht per day. A dispute arose when iTV sought compensation from the PMO, arguing that it had been overcharged by the PMO in respect of the concession fee and that the programming stipulation, restricting the amount of entertainment broadcasting, was

---

[39] For further discussion of broadcasting and media in the Thai context, see ch 7.

[40] In a different context, the civil courts were used by the former Prime Minister to suppress free speech and criticism in the media. For example, a defamation action was issued against Supinya Klangnarong for an article in the *Thai Post* in 2003, which drew attention to the profits being made as a result of improper political influence in regard to media ownership. See P Phongpaichit and C Baker, *Thaksin*, 2nd edn (Chiang Mai, Silkworm Books, 2004) 155.

[41] TC 1997 s 40 resulted in the introduction of the National Telecommunication Commission and the National Broadcasting Authority. See also V Muntarborn, *Mass Media Law and Regulations in Thailand* (Singapore, Asia Media and Communications Centre, 1998).

[42] iTV was intended to be an independent form of news-based television, but it was taken over in 2000 by the Shin Corp. See eg D McCargo and U Pathmanand, *The Thaksinization of Thailand* (Copenhagen, NIAS, 2005) 47ff.

unreasonable. The matter was initially referred to the Arbitration Court, which found clearly in favour of iTV in January 2004.[43] It was prepared to allow iTV to pay a lower fee and to continue with a programme ratio of 50:50, which could be geared more towards entertainment. However, the PMO contested the matter before the Central Administrative Court which, in turn, reversed the decision of the Arbitration Court. Not only did this ruling allow the PMO to demand 76 billion baht in penalties and fees (later increased because of the time that elapsed), but it would also require the programme ratio to revert to a preponderance of news scheduling.[44] Of course the effect of the ruling, if the financial penalties were paid, was bound to have a drastic impact on the financial viability of iTV and, if the company was forced into bankruptcy, on all of its employees. The matter was referred for final determination to the Supreme Administrative Court, which also found in favour of the PMO. As a result, iTV has faced fines amounting to 94 billion baht.[45]

In addition, there was a constitutional dimension to this matter, further illustrating the degree of the conflicts of interest which underlie important governmental functions in Thailand. It was mentioned above that iTV was conceived as an independent broadcaster, but this role was compromised when in 2000 the Shin Corp Plc, a company owned by Thaksin Shaniwatra and his family, became the major shareholder in iTV. During the time that he maintained his investment in Shin Corp plc, including most of his term as Prime Minister (2001–06), apart from evidence of political interference in programme content,[46] it suited Thaksin's personal commercial interest to push for lower charges from the Government and to change the programme content to encourage increased audiences. In contrast, it was noted above that the original concession negotiated in the name of the PMO was designed to serve a wider public interest. In consequence, the Arbitration Court and the

---

[43]   For a discussion of the background to the case, see *ibid*, 47–53 and 61.

[44]   'iTV Ordered to Cough up Bt 77.7bn: OAG Wants Broadcaster to Pay at Once', *The Nation*, 20 June 2006. The judgments of the Administrative Courts are enforced only following the exhaustion of the legal process, and thus depended on the decision of the Supreme Administrative Court.

[45]   'The Supreme Administrative Court Ruled on Wednesday in Favour of PM's Office Over iTV Saga', *The Nation*, 13 December 2006; 'Bankruptcy Looms for Reeling iTV, *The Nation*, 14 December 2006.

[46]   P Phongpaichit and C Baker, *Thaksin*, 2nd edn (Chiang Mai, Silkworm Books, 2009) at 149ff and 260ff.

Administrative Courts were called upon to determine a highly sensitive political issue. The imposition of these penalties by the Administrative Court in June 2006 was a judicially-imposed setback for Thaksin, which occurred after he had offloaded his financial investments in iTV. However, his attempt as Prime Minister to ignore statutory rules was decisively rejected by the Court.

Although iTV's position had not at that point been resolved by the Administrative Courts, the matter took a different turn in January 2006 when Thaksin and his family sold their majority investment in Shin Corp Group to Temasek Holdings (a company which is Singapore's State investment arm). The sale was the subject of enormous controversy in Thailand. It resulted in popular protest, and it was one of the factors behind the military coup of 19 September 2006, with Thaksin's opponents arguing that, for example, the deal compromised Thailand's national security by giving another nation effective control of Thailand's communications (*Shin Sat*), including defence communications. A challenge to the deal was mounted in the Central Administrative Court in March 2006, but the Court held that the claimant lacked the necessary standing as he had no contractual link to the takeover, a decision later overturned by the Supreme Administrative Court.[47] However, in 2007, after the military coup, a further challenge was lodged with the Central Administrative Court against the National Telecommunications Commission (NTC) and the Information and Communications Technology Ministry. It was alleged that the failure of these governmental bodies to safeguard the national interest by permitting the ownership of Shin Corp to fall into foreign hands amounted to negligence.[48]

The EGAT case in November 2005 was another prominent decision in which the Administrative Courts ruled against the Government.[49] The Government was proposing to privatise the Electricity Generating Authority of Thailand, EGAT Plc. However, a combination of 11 civic pressure groups, including the Campaign for Popular Democracy, the Consumer Protection Foundation and the Federation of Consumer Organisations, together with representatives from the EGAT labour unions (and with the support of opposition parties), contested the

---

[47] 'Shin Corp Deal in Jeopardy', *The Nation*, 6 October 2006.

[48] Black case 546/2550. 'Shin Sat Sale Row: Court accepts negligence case', *The Nation*, 1 May 2007. The case did not have a full hearing.

[49] Phongpaichit and Baker, n 46, 245.

Government's privatisation plans. The objectors argued that the proposals were likely to result in greatly increased electricity prices for electricity consumers, while giving disproportionate financial rewards to a small group of investors, including politicians with an interest in the scheme who stood to gain directly from the privatisation. The then Prime Minister, Thaksin Shinawatra, and Energy Minister Viset Choopiban were among the five named defendants. It was alleged that there had been an abuse of power because the Government was proceeding with the privatisation without any form of public consultation, although mandatory hearings were required for such a proposal. Further, it was argued that the sale of EGAT shares violated the Constitution because the Government had illegally used two royal decrees to appoint a panel to oversee electricity generation.[50] It was also argued that there were inadequate safeguards for consumers in regard to pricing levels and standards of service. The Court found in favour of the objectors in November 2005, and it issued an injunction which prevented the privatisation from going ahead before hearings had taken place.

The decision had far-reaching ramifications. The interruption of the schedule for flotation in a market-sensitive area which is dependent on investor confidence called into question the economic viability of the entire scheme. At a political level the anti-privatisation campaign had developed into a personal campaign against the Prime Minister, and the Court's decision was a serious blow to a central plank of government policy. The fact that fundamental principles of legality were upheld by the Court, especially given the extremely sensitive issues at stake in the case, suggests that, in this area at least, the 1997 Constitution had managed to establish a relatively independent oversight body.

The independence of the Administrative Courts in comparison to other watchdog bodies can, in part, be attributed to the Courts being perceived by politicians as having an oblique role in regard to deciding controversial political matters, certainly in comparison to the Constitutional Court, the Election Commission and the NACC. Although they have attracted criticism from politicians from time to time, there have been insufficient opportunities overtly to politicise the Courts. An equally important reason for their relative independence is that the Courts were staffed from the outset with a permanent cohort of professional judges

---

[50] These decrees were quashed by the Supreme Administrative Court in March 2006. See 'Egat Listing Shot Down', *The Nation*, 23 March 2006.

and lawyers appointed on merit. Thailand's higher judiciary has enjoyed a reputation for independence since the time of Rama V.

We turn next to the much-publicised controversies concerning appointments to public bodies. Following the liberalisation of the telecommunications industry, the NTC became the new telecommunications regulator,[51] deciding on sensitive issues such as the conversion of various State concessions granted to private operators into a licensing or tax system and the privatisation of State agencies. In March 2003 the Supreme Administrative Court upheld an earlier ruling by the Central Administrative Court in regard to the selection process for the NTC. It held that the selection committee, as it had been set up under the relevant legislation, was a government agency, and therefore conflicts of interest were expressly prohibited under the ethical code. The decision of the Court resulted in a re-run of the selection process; but despite this earlier ruling, many of the same names, with alleged conflicts of interest, appeared on the revised list.[52] There was an unsatisfactory outcome in this instance, because the politicians and their associates responsible for appointing the selection committee continued to ignore these procedural rules notwithstanding the aforementioned judicial intervention.[53] In a virtual repetition of this scenario, the selection of candidates by the Senate for the National Broadcasting Commission in September 2005 was nullified by an order of the Central Administrative Court. This decision was on the identical grounds that the selection committee set up under the National Broadcasting Act had been partisan and not independent as required under the administrative code. The decision by the Central Administrative Court was later confirmed by the Supreme Administrative Court.[54]

In an environmental context, the Administrative Courts have been prepared to intervene on behalf of local people faced with the prospect of pollution from one of Thailand's most important industrial complexes.

[51] See the Telecommunications Business Act 2001 (BE 2544).

[52] 'Thai Court Orders a New Candidate Selection Process for NTC', *World Dialogue for Regulation for Network Economies*, 10 January 2003; 'NBC Candidate Choices Nullified', *The Nation*, 5 March 2003.

[53] See Phongpaichit and Baker, n 46, 151 and 205ff; 'PM Blamed for Telecom Watchdog Setback', *The Nation*, 11 January 2003; and for a report of the Supreme Administrative Court decision, see 'NBC Candidate Choices Nullified', *The Nation*, 5 March 2003.

[54] See 'Broadcasting Panel: Additional Doubt Over NBC Future', *The Nation*, 29 September 2005; 'Rejection of NBC Appeal Upheld', *The Nation*, 7 June 2006.

The *Map Ta Phut* case was initiated by environmental activists on behalf of local residents who claimed, after a toxic leak, that the operating permits for the petro-chemical plant on an industrial estate in Rayong were in breach of section 67 of the 2007 Constitution for not meeting Euro 4 emission standards.[55] Section 67 specifies that any project or activity which may seriously affect the community in the quality of the environment, natural resources and health shall not be permitted without first undergoing environmental impact assessment (EIA) and health impact assessment (HIA); and, moreover, the community is expressly empowered to sue a State agency under section 67 if such an environmental threat arises. In December 2009, the Supreme Administrative Court upheld an injunction suspending 65 projects. This decision had an immediate impact on a number of large companies, including PTT, the State petroleum corporation, privatised under Thaksin. The former Prime Minister retained a large stake post-privatisation, which suggests that the decision delaying the development of the plant would indirectly have an adverse financial impact upon Thaksin by affecting the profitability of PTT. In an editorial *The Nation* commented:

> Thank the Supreme Administrative Court for standing up to foreign and local investors who care for little or nothing about the health and safety of local residents or the environment . . . This is another step against corruption. If the judicial system is allowed to continue in this manner, it will make Thailand the least corrupt country in Asia.[56]

With this intervention the Administrative Court displayed its independence by intervening decisively to uphold the law and protect a local community under threat from this pollution. The decision itself had far-reaching implications, paralysing a major industrial project and affecting not only the profitability of the businesses concerned, but also the livelihood and personal health of many ordinary employees.

These celebrated decisions demonstrate that during a period when the nation was facing acute constitutional and political problems, the Administrative Courts not only continued to function but their rulings, however controversial, have been scrupulously respected.[57]

---

[55] Case 586/2552; 'Map Ta Phut Court Decision Will Hurt Certain Pockets', *The Nation*, 4 December 2009.

[56] 'Kudos to the Court for Map Ta Phut Decision', *The Nation*, 4 December 2009.

[57] 'Map Ta Phut: Abhisit Orders a Review of NEBS Report', *The Nation*, 9 July 2010.

IV. THE OFFICE OF THE THAI OMBUDSMAN

A. Introduction

In recent years ombudsmen have become ubiquitous, and have been appointed in countries with disparate constitutions and political systems.[58] There are obvious advantages in having grievances against central and local government and other public bodies investigated by an independent adjudicator, rather than relying on political representatives to become investigators or expecting the more cumbersome procedures of court-based justice to handle grievances against administrative organs.

The Office of the Thai Ombudsman (OTO) was introduced as a part of a trend towards a new form of participatory democracy in Thailand. It has been observed that the 1997 Constitution originated from a much more inclusive process than existed previously, with many organisations consulted on a nationwide basis before formal codification was undertaken.[59] Influential commentators have stressed that building good governance is the main mission of the Ombudsman.[60] In common with the Administrative Courts and the other constitutional watchdog bodies, the OTO was introduced as part of this wider quest for good governance. The introduction of a body with formidable investigatory powers would not simply assist in delivering better governance, but would be able to make a contribution to the elimination of the institutionalised corruption associated with officialdom in Thailand. The powers and duties of the OTO require action to be taken concerning the ethics of holders of political positions and State officials.[61] The territory patrolled by the OTO is Thailand's extensive public administration at central and local government levels.[62] There are also more than 600 laws, organic acts and other ministerial rules and regulations which these bodies are

[58] See S Roberts and M Palmer, *Dispute Processes: ADR and the Primary Forms of Decision Making* (Cambridge, Cambridge University Press, 2005) at 346ff.

[59] See ch 1 Section VII.

[60] See Professor Dr Bowornsak Uwanno in a conference paper available on the Thai Ombudsman website at <http://www.ombudsman.go.th/eng_version>.

[61] TC 2007, s 244(2).

[62] Ministries, departments, State enterprises and local administrative organisations fall under the purview of the Ombudsman. See J Ockey, 'State, Bureaucracy and Polity in Modern Thai Politics' (2004) 34(2) *Journal of Contemporary Asia* 143 at 147ff.

required to apply. The OTO has been granted jurisdiction over all governmental bodies and the laws applying to them.[63]

Each Ombudsman is appointed for six years by a multi-stage procedure involving a special selection committee followed by parliamentary approval. To avoid conflicts of interest, serving civil servants are expressly excluded from holding the office, as are any persons engaged in any form of business.[64] The suitability of the Ombudsmen appointed can be called into question. Although some have been legally trained, typically the most senior office-holders have gained experience as senior officers in the military or as high-ranking officials. Rather than selection on merit from emerging talent, it is the senior members of the same elite class who have been favoured for selection.

The OTO is empowered to consider and investigate complaints when an official at any level of government violates the law or exceeds the jurisdiction of his or her authority. The Ombudsman is also empowered to investigate when the action or inaction of a public body or official causes harm, damage or injustice to an individual or to the general public, whether or not this action or inaction by the public body or official is within the body's or official's jurisdiction, and regardless of whether the action is in breach of the law. In addition, as we have seen, the Ombudsman is competent to look into the

> performance of or omission to perform duties . . . which unjustly causes injuries to the complainant or the public [more generally] notwithstanding whether or not the action has been lawful.[65]

In other words, it is apparent that a wide jurisdiction was envisaged and has been granted to the OTO. It encompasses routine complaints associated with maladministration, but it also extends to questions of legality; and it goes beyond legal questions to allow investigation of injustice and unfairness.[66] The OTO is responsible for investigation and fact-finding relating to the grievances filed by the public who have complaints in respect of practices of government officials at all levels which result in injustice or loss. In sum, the OTO has a wide remit to investigate, which extends to complaints associated with any governmental

---

[63] Ombudsman Act 1999, s 16.
[64] *Ibid*, s 12.
[65] *Ibid*, s 16.
[66] TC 2007, s 244.

body, including the civil service, State agencies, State enterprises and local government.[67]

Matters constituting maladministration would be expected to fall squarely within the reach of an ombudsman's remit, but the capacity of the OTO to look into contraventions of the law, and at bodies exceeding jurisdiction, potentially overlaps with the territory policed by the Administrative Courts in performing their judicial review function. This occurred in an environmental case previously reported on the Ombudsman's website. After its refusal to issue a certificate for a food formula, the OTO found that that the Food and Drug Administration had adopted inconsistent rules which were in conflict with the Constitution. The rules therefore required modification. Moreover, the role extends beyond considering narrow questions of legality. The OTO is expected to refer any law, regulation or action with constitutional implications to the Constitutional Court or the Administrative Courts for resolution. Action taken by public authorities or officials may be consistent with the law in a narrow sense and yet constitute bad administration. For example, administrative action or inaction may cause unfair treatment or unreasonable delay. In such circumstances the OTO has the right to intervene; and where the citizen has been treated unfairly, the OTO can recommend that compensation is provided or that the offending law should be amended or repealed.

Under the legislation the OTO is excluded from investigating certain aspects of governmental activity: for example, these include policy matters announced by the Cabinet in Parliament, matters under consideration by a court and complaints relating to personnel management or disciplinary action against a State official.[68] Furthermore, the OTO is given considerable discretion in deciding what to pursue. In particular, a complaint may be refused if it is considered not to be in the public interest, if it concerns corruption or misconduct, or if more than two years have elapsed since the alleged conduct.[69]

---

[67] The diverse cases referred to in the 2009 Annual Report include: police and officials exceeding their legal authority; acts of government officials resulting in loss or damage to a complainant; where an official body has failed to act, eg supply enough teachers, police to investigate a case or arrest a suspect, election commission to report a protest against an election; government officials acting without regard to the code of ethical standards. See Annual Report 2009, available at <http://www.ombudsman.go.th/10/documents/Reports52.pdf>.

[68] Ombudsman Act 1999, s 24.

[69] *Ibid*, s 25. It should be noted, however, that the NACC was created with the express purpose of investigating corruption.

B. Remedial action and the Thai Ombudsmen

A guiding principle for ombudsmen is that their recommended remedy, if carried out in full, should place the complainant in the position he or she would have been in, had the maladministration or other unlawful conduct not occurred. But it is also important to recognise that most ombudsmen, including the OTO, combine elements of fire-fighting and fire-watching. They both deal with grievances and can also take a more direct interest than courts in stimulating administrative improvement. They pursue their goals not only by judgments, but also by less formal negotiations and consultations.[70] Indeed, the OTO has stated that a preventative approach is favoured in order to avoid the repetition of problems causing injustice. In other words, the OTO makes recommendations to secure procedural improvements where there has been a high number of complaints in the same field.[71]

Under the 1997 and 2007 Constitutions the OTO has a special power to refer a matter which raises a question of 'constitutionality' to the Constitutional Court.[72] This referral function has been exercised in relation to controversial matters of the highest constitutional importance. The Government passed a 'State of Emergency' decree, which came into effect on 16 July 2005,[73] as a response to the violence from militants in the south of the country. The decree was arguably in contravention of the provisions of the Constitution. It gave the Prime Minister almost absolute authority, by handing over power to declare a state of emergency in specific areas or in all parts of the country. In addition, it allowed the Government to order the use of force to quell unrest, to impose curfews, to curtail freedom of assembly and to introduce media censorship. Moreover, the decree contained powers to detain suspects

---

[70] C Harlow and R Rawlings, *Law and Administration* (London, Weidenfeld & Nicolson, 1984) 199.

[71] Eg, the relevant areas relate to: title to land, encroachment onto public land, compensation for compulsory purchase, local government procurement procedures. See address by Mr Poonsup Piya-Anant, Thai Ombudsman, 8th Asian Ombudsman Association, 28 April 2004.

[72] TC 1997 s 198 and TC 2007 s 245.

[73] Decree on Government Administration in a State of Emergency, 2005. This decree was issued under s 218 of the 1997 Constitution. It placed restrictions on the rights and freedoms listed in ss 29, 31, 35, 36, 37, 39, 44, 48, 50 and 51 of the Constitution, but this was permissible by law.

deemed a threat to national security without charge for up to 30 days, while granting blanket legal immunity to security personnel for action in the line of duty.[74] The opposition Democrat Party and other groups defending civil liberties submitted a petition to the OTO, seeking an interpretation from the Constitutional Court on the constitutionality of the decree. From the moment it was announced, the government measure was regarded as extremely controversial, and it was condemned by the Thai Human Rights Commission. In response to criticism from the judiciary and supporters of human rights, the Government later partly backed down. It issued an addendum to the decree, requiring security personnel to seek court approval before issuing arrest warrants. Further, the detention period for people not charged with offences was limited to seven days. The combination of the referral to the Court linked to political pressure had a major impact on this policy before any ruling took place. It should be noted that in February 2004 the Constitutional Court held, after an earlier referral by the OTO, that emergency decrees issued by the Government did not violate the Constitution if there were sound grounds for issuing them.[75]

The second constitutional issue was in relation to the escalating political crisis in 2006. In response to the wave of anti-Government demonstrations in February and March 2006, a snap election was called by Prime Minister Thaksin Shinawatra for 2 April 2006. This election was boycotted by the main opposition parties.[76] Although Thai Rak Thai, the Prime Minister's party, won the election, the protest vote was stronger than expected. In consequence, the Government was faced with continuing street demonstrations, and the Prime Minister announced that he intended to resign.[77] In the meantime, complaints had been made to the OTO citing irregularities in the way the ECT had set up the election; and, more importantly, it was argued that the short time-frame of 35 days was unfair because it benefited the ruling party and put the opposition parties at a disadvantage. These objections were duly referred by the OTO to the Constitutional Court for resolution.[78]

---

[74] See ch 3 Section X.

[75] 'Emergency Decrees: Split Vote Clears Government Moves on Terrorism', *The Nation*, 20 February 2004. See chapter 5 section IX.

[76] 'Thai Leader's 'Victory' Fails to Resolve Crisis' *Daily Telegraph*, 4 April, 2006.

[77] 'Timeline: The Fall of Thaksin' *The Times*, 4 April, 2006.

[78] See ch 1; see also M Montesano, 'Political Contests in the Advent of Bangkok's 19 September Putsch' in J Funston (ed), *Divided over Thaksin: Thailand's Coup and*

V. CONCLUSION

This chapter has traced the introduction of administrative justice in Thailand. The 1997 Constitution can be regarded a watershed in the domain of administrative law, as this Constitution established a new institutional basis for administrative justice which has continued to function under the 2007 Constitution.

The OTO was set up to provide an accessible remedy against public authorities, but also to assist in the attempt to eliminate systemic corruption associated with public administration. The OTO has achieved a relatively low profile which is reflected in the published statistics. It should be remembered when reviewing these figures that the remit of the OTO includes all government and public bodies at central and local level. For 2009 the annual referral rate was 2,015 cases, of which 1,918 were actually processed. But these figures represent a dip from a peak referral rate of 2,595 cases in 2003, which was achieved when the institution was still in its infancy.[79] Viewed from a different perspective, it is obviously not possible to calculate to what extent the threat of referral to the OTO has acted to deter corrupt conduct or as a spur to good adminstration.

In stark contrast, the introduction of a two-tier system of Administrative Courts closely resembling the French model has been a conspicuous success. Not only have the Administrative Courts from the moment of their activation taken on a considerable and increasing caseload, but in the troubled political circumstances these courts have managed to establish and retain a formidable reputation for professionalism and impartiality. In a variety of contexts they have produced judgments which have been prepared to assert principles of legality, despite often being faced with powerful vested interests. Even at a time when the political struggle between polarised factions has the appearance of getting out of hand, the Administrative Courts have sought to hold the line in upholding the rule-of-law values set out in these Constitutions and in the organic laws associated with them.

Problematic Transition (Chiang Mai, Silkworm Books, 2009) and 'King Halts Thailand's troubles', *The Observer*, 30 April 2006; 'Thai Court Orders New Poll', *Guardian*, 8 May 2006.

[79] See Annual Report 2009, above n 67.

FURTHER READING

B Bhalakula, *Administrative Contract in the Thai Legal Context* (Bangkok, Office of the Administrative Courts, 2003).

R Hungsiri, *Sarn Pok Khrong Lae Kandumdoenkadi Nai Sarn Pok Khrong* [The Administrative Court and Its Procedure] (Bangkok, Institute of Legal Education, Thai Bar Association, 2009) [in Thai].

P Leyland, 'Droit Administratif Thai Style: A Comparative Analysis of the Administrative Courts in Thailand' (2006) 8(2) *Australian Journal of Asian Law* 121.

—— 'The Ombudsman Principle in Thailand' (2007) 2:1 *Journal of Comparative Law* 137.

J Ockey, 'State, Bureaucracy and Polity in Modern Thai Politics' (2004) 34(2) *Journal of Contemporary Asia* 143.

W Pakeerut, *Khumru Bueang Ton Kiawkap Kodmai Pok Khrong* [Basic Principles of Administrative Law] (Bangkok, Winyuchon, 2006) [in Thai].

7

Human Rights

Introduction – Historical and Cultural Context of Human Rights – Human Rights under the 1997 and 2007 Constitutions – The National Human Rights Commission – Human Rights and the Southern Conflict – The Broadcast Media, Conflict of Interest and Freedom of Speech – The *Lèse-Majesté* Law – Conclusion

I. INTRODUCTION

Human rights have already been discussed in the context of constitutional review, and it should already be apparent that a number of cases in the Constitutional Courts since 1998 have failed to display a revised approach reflecting the constitutional norms present in the 1997 and 2007 Constitutions. It is also clear that the analysis of these cases represents a rather small aspect of human rights in Thailand. The human rights context is in fact extremely varied, with numerous issues arising all over Thailand in respect of civil and political rights, as well as social, economic and cultural rights. In addition the National Human Rights Commission (NHRC) has been active since 2003 in its attempts to create awareness and investigate abuses. Our approach in this chapter is to indicate initially the general context of human rights in Thailand from a constitutional perspective, dealing in particular with the NHRC. We deal with some of the prominent human rights issues without attempting to be comprehensive. We also take as case studies two areas which have involved major issues in constitutional reform in the last few years. The first is freedom of religion, which also concerns the problem of the Muslim south of Thailand discussed in chapter four. The second is freedom of expression, where we discuss in particular the issues of media regulation and the law on *lèse-majesté*.

II. HISTORICAL AND CULTURAL CONTEXT
OF HUMAN RIGHTS

Despite the existence of a constitutional bill of rights since 1932, it is only since 1997 that methods of enforcing human rights have become salient in Thailand.[1] Before this time it is true that the Thai citizen came to be endowed with legal rights under the codes of law inspired by France, referred to by Vitit Muntarbhorn and Charles Taylor as even 'a bastion untoppled by coups';[2] many of these could be called human rights in modern parlance, but they were the rights of citizens and had correlative duties, which have always been and are still found in Thai constitutionalism.[3] There is also, however, the background of a de facto immunity generally enjoyed by the State military and security apparatus over many years, of which some evidence is given in chapter one in the context of military coups and in chapter three in the context of emergency powers. Alleged drug-traffickers and other alleged criminals have in recent years been killed in police action or in police custody during a 'war against drugs', a 'campaign against dark forces' in Thai society initiated by Prime Minister Thaksin in 2003. The deaths of an estimated 2,275 people in this 'war' remain unexplained.[4] Even the urban middle classes and university students have suffered oppression at the hands of brutal military dictatorship in 1973, 1976 and 1992, their rights to freedom of expression and personal security being abused on a wide scale. The perpetrators of human rights abuses during the 'Black May' inci-

---

[1] V Muntarbhorn, 'Human Rights in Thailand' in L Palmier (ed), *State and Law in Eastern Asia* (Aldershot, Dartmouth, 1996) 103.

[2] V Muntarbhorn and C Taylor, *Roads to Democracy: Human Rights and Democratic Development in Thailand* (Montreal, Centre International des Droits de la Personne et du Developpement Democratique, 1994) 11.

[3] 1997 Constitution and 2007 Constitution, ch IV.

[4] According to Human Rights Watch at <http://www.hrw.org/campaigns/aids/2004/thai.htm>: 'Beginning in February 2003, the Thaksin government instructed police and local officials that persons charged with drug offences should be considered "security threats" and dealt with in a "ruthless" and "severe" manner. The result of the initial three-month phase of this campaign was some 2,275 extrajudicial killings, which the government blamed largely on gangs involved in the drug trade; arbitrary inclusion of drug suspects on poorly prepared government "blacklists" or "watchlists"; intimidation of human rights defenders; violence, arbitrary arrest, and other breaches of due process by Thai police; and coerced or mandatory drug treatment.'

dent in 1992[5] still walk the streets of Bangkok unpunished, having benefited from an amnesty. Human rights abuses in the Muslim south in
2003–04 remain uncorrected despite a damning NHRC investigation.[6]
Deaths and injuries in the May 2010 crackdown on the Red Shirt protesters in Bangkok are currently the focus of investigation. All these
issues represent a large deficit in human rights compliance from the perspective of the individual right to life and security, and the due process
of law.

In Thailand human rights concerns have also centred on the particular
problems of certain disadvantaged groups, including: those who have to
work as female and male prostitutes to support their deprived rural
families; women and children who are victims of people-trafficking;
oppressed sexual minorities; drug addicts; those who suffer from AIDS
or are HIV-positive; the disabled; the urban poor; the poor rural farmers;
villagers displaced by dam projects; the Muslims of the southern provinces; the indigenous hill tribes of the northern provinces; and the refugees from across the Burmese border.[7]

The concept of human rights has been slow in being accepted in
Thailand. The Law of the Three Seals of 1805, which was designed to
codify traditional law, was not so much a way of defining the legal rights
of citizens, as a way of defining how officials should deal with subjects.
Even the publication of the Law of the Three Seals itself was initially
prohibited. Legal relations were seen in terms of social structure and
relationships, not as consisting in mutual rights and duties. King
Mongkut (Rama IV), who began the process of modernisation, can be
said to have introduced the notion of rights. He introduced the principle of publishing laws; he began the process of abolishing slavery completed in the following reign (a complex business in a society with so
many levels of social status, each of which carried specific legal consequences); he accepted freedom of religion, and encouraged debate
about the merits of different beliefs and scientific theories; and he supported the idea of a woman being allowed to marry her chosen partner

---

[5] See ch 1, section V.

[6] See ch 4, section VIII.

[7] See, further, Muntarbhorn and Taylor, above n 2; J McLaren, 'Whores, Soiled
Doves, or Working Women? Law, Society and the Sex Trade in Australia, Canada
and Thailand' in D Johnston and G Ferguson (eds), *Asia-Pacific Legal Development*
(Vancouver, UBC Press, 1998) ch 8; F Ferrara, 'Thailand for Sale' in *Thailand
Unhinged: Unravelling the Myth of a Thai-Style Democracy* (Singapore, Equinox, 2010) ch 4.

rather than being forced into marriage, a principle he applied to his own royal wives. His successor King Chulalongkorn (Rama V) went further in abolishing slavery completely, as well as trial by ordeal; and by allowing press freedom.

With the enactment of the Penal Code in 1908 there arrived the notion of the rights of accused persons. A significant change, accomplished in 1935 with the enactment of the final version of the Civil and Commercial Code, was that from a polygamous to a monogamous marriage system, which did much to ensure and recognise progress towards female equality. This was evidenced, for example, in it being accepted from the outset of democracy in 1932 that women had equal voting rights with men. Chulalongkorn himself was the last King to have more than one wife, although polygamy went out in style – he had 36 wives and 77 children.

During the constitutional period from 1932 to date, human rights have been progressively recognised and entrenched in constitutional law, but the reality of actual observance of human rights has pointed rather in the opposite direction. The human rights situation has been constantly the object of adverse international criticism.[8] It is, however, precisely concerns of these kinds that have sparked deep public frustration and hastened the advent of the NHRC and the post-1997 era of reform. Thailand has a flourishing civil society sector. The abuses of human rights run counter to the aspirations of those reformist lawyers, academics and politicians who drafted the 1997 Constitution. Indeed, despite the frequency of human rights abuses, some progress has been made in addressing human rights. Thailand does not, however, have a long human rights tradition, and although there has always been a concept of the just State, it has not been part of Thai culture, at least until recently, to make *legal claims* on the State. Indeed Buddhist concepts run counter to the whole idea of positive law as a means of resolving situations of injustice. David and Jaruvan Engel, in their book on tort injuries and legal consciousness in Chiang Mai,[9] discover that a Thai

---

[8] See, eg, reports of Human Rights Watch at <http://www.hrw.org/asia/thailand>; and the Akha Heritage Foundation at <http://www.akha.org/>. Institutions within Thailand are similarly critical, eg the Centre of Human Rights and Social Development at Mahidol University, at <http://www.humanrights-mu.org/rd/research>.

[9] D Engel and J Engel, *Tort, Custom and Karma: Globalisation and Legal Consciousness in Thailand* (Stanford, Cal, Stanford University Press, 2010).

Buddhist suffering an injury may not see an act of injustice caused by an illegal action to be remedied or restored through a process involving attribution of liability, as in western tort law and human rights discourse. He or she is more likely to see an adverse event which occurs in a context that includes the victim's actions in a previous life, and his or her own fault in this life, as well as the fault of another individual and sheer bad luck, to be corrected by a virtuous action on the part of the victim rather than the tearing even further of the fabric of the universe by antagonistic gestures. Those subjected to deliberate infliction of injury and others forms of abuse may not, however, take the religious or philosophical view indicated by the Engels' study, and there is evidence of growing human rights consciousness amongst the rural poor, for example.[10]

Moreover, mass movements have not normally espoused 'human rights' as a concept until the present age of the civil society and globalisation; indeed the current Thai term for human rights (*sithi-manusyachon*) did not come into usage until after the Universal Declaration of 1948. Prior to this the main relevant term was *seriphap*, usually rendered as 'liberty'. Many abuses of human rights took place as a result of 'Red Drum' paramilitary and army counter-insurgency actions taken supposedly under the Prevention of Communist Activities Act 1952.[11] Authority did not always recognise that organising public opinion was even legitimate: a farmers' movement in northern Thailand in the 1970s collapsed when some of its leaders were assassinated with official connivance.[12] The military inflicted horrible slaughter on the students of Thammasat University on their own campus in 1976. It was only when military rule became intolerably harsh and self-serving that the Thai people stood up and demanded human rights and democracy; and only in the 1990s and 2000s have they achieved a form of democratic government that is not simply an interlude between military coups.

---

[10] P Vandergeest, 'Constructing Thailand: Regulation, Everyday Resistance, and Citizenship' (1993) 35:1 *Comparative Studies in Society and History* 133.

[11] K Wongtrangan, 'Executive Power and Constitutionalism in Thailand' in C Sison and R Jose (eds), *Constitutional and Legal Systems of ASEAN Countries* (Quezon City, Academy of ASEAN Law and Jurisprudence, University of the Philippines, 1990) 304ff.

[12] B Anderson, 'Murder and Progress in Modern Siam' in *The Spectre of Comparisons: Nationalism, Southeast Asia and the World* (London, Verso, 1998) ch 8.

III. HUMAN RIGHTS UNDER THE 1997 AND 2007 CONSTITUTIONS

Interest in dealing with human rights at the constitutional level during the reform period after 1992 was sparked by the Black May incident in 1992, in which protesters against the military government were shot in the streets of Bangkok. How, then, did the reform process deal with human rights?

The subject proved in the event to be probably the most controversial and problematical aspect of the reform process. Debate became intense on the issues how and to what extent human rights could be enforced as a fundamental feature of the Thai polity, and the fixing of an appropriate role for the NHRC. In the event the 1997 Constitution set out an extensive array of fundamental rights, supplemented by provisions dealing with the rights of accused persons in the judicial process, and others providing for investigation of human rights issues by the NHRC.[13] The 2007 Constitution sets out very similar provisions. The fundamental rights were expressed, for the first time, to belong to persons in general, even though Chapter III in both Constitutions is entitled 'Fundamental Rights and Liberties of the Thai People'. All State organs were obliged to observe fundamental rights and liberties in applying and interpreting laws, and an individual was able to enforce his or her rights either actively by bringing a lawsuit, or passively by invoking the Constitution in defending himself or herself in court. Under section 28 of the 2007 Constitution this right is now somewhat enhanced:

> A person may bring a lawsuit against the State directly so as to act in compliance with the provisions in this Chapter. If there is a law enforcing the exercise of any right and liberty as recognised by this Constitution, the exercising of that right and liberty shall be in accordance with such law. A person shall have the right to be enhanced, supported and assisted by the State in exercising of [constitutional rights].

---

[13] The fundamental rights provisions were ss 26–63 of the TC 1997, largely repeated in ss 26–69 of the TC 2007. Rights in the judicial process, set out in TC 1997, ss 236–247, are preserved in TC 2007, ss 39–40. Provisions regarding the NHRC are in the TC 1997, ss 199–200; and now TC 2007, ss 256–257. The rights referred to the text that follows can all be found in the sections referred to here, ie principallly in ch III of both Constitutions.

There was in fact no right of direct fundamental-rights petition to the Constitutional Court, but this has been corrected in the 2007 Constitution.[14] The absence of any right of direct petition and the possibility of delay or eventual circumvention of the decision of the Constitutional Court, not to mention the usual difficulties litigants have in accessing justice at all, made the enforcement of fundamental rights, even after the 1997 Constitution, a somewhat hazardous enterprise. Nonetheless, several attempts, some of them successful, were made to invoke this procedure (see chapter six).

Since the Constitution can be amended by a simple majority in both houses of the National Assembly, the fundamental rights could be exposed to being abridged by a majority in the National Assembly. Fundamental rights are therefore entrenched (by section 29 in both Constitutions) by circumscribing the way in which they can be abridged by ordinary legislation. The Constitution requires here that fundamental rights cannot be restricted except:

a) by a law which is specifically enacted for a purpose allowed by the Constitution;
b) only to the extent that is necessary; and
c) provided that it does not affect the essential substance of fundamental rights.

In addition:

d) such a law must be of general application and not intended to apply to any particular case or person; and
e) the provision of the Constitution authorising its enactment has to be specified.

Space precludes any detailed attention to the very extensive provisions on fundamental rights, but a brief overview will illustrate their general scope and character.

There is no attempt in the bills of rights of 1997 and 2007 to construct a notion of rights based on Asian values; indeed none of the rights would be out of place in a European or North American constitution, and no significant right generally enshrined in such a constitution seems to be missing. The intention appears to be to attempt to recognise the fact of human rights abuses historically by adhering broadly to

---

[14] TC 2007, s 212.

internationally accepted norms, at least as an aspiration. An alternative approach might have been to base fundamental rights on some notion of 'Asian values' in which collective interests might be emphasised as against individual liberty, or else peculiarly Thai or Buddhist notions[15] of social ordering and respect for life might form the basis of human rights understanding. A reading of the 1997 and 2007 Constitutions indicates that it is only in the area of rights of traditional communities that the provisions can be said to speak clearly of local traditions.[16] Most of the constitutional rights are therefore based on familiar concepts, but have also been carefully and broadly drafted. For example, the right to equality before the law in section 30 of the 1997 Constitution prevents discrimination on grounds of difference in origin, race, language, sex, age, physical or health condition, personal status, economic or social standing, religious belief, education or constitutionally political view. This provision did not, however, prevent affirmative action measures 'to eliminate obstacles to or to promote persons' ability to exercise their rights and liberties as other persons'. In the 2007 version of section 30, disability is included in the list of prohibited grounds for discrimination; this corrects the result of two decisions of the Constitutional Court discussed in chapter six, section IX.A.

'Due process' rights accorded to accused persons, already in the main recognised in the law of criminal procedure, are all guaranteed: the right to life and liberty; the right not to be subjected to cruel or inhumane punishment or torture,[17] or to arbitrary arrest, detention or search; the right to counsel and to habeas corpus, to bail and legal aid, and to a speedy, continuous and fair trial in a criminal case; the right against retrospective penalties; and the presumption of innocence. Also included are civil liberties such as family rights, the right to dignity, privacy and reputation, and the rights of peaceful habitation; liberty of travel and choice of residence and property, and competition rights; the

---

[15] The NHRC initially used Buddhism as a means of explaining human rights: A Harding, 'Buddhism, Human Rights and Constitutional Reform' (2007) 2 *Asian Journal of Comparative Law* 1.

[16] Sections 46 and 66, respectively.

[17] The TC 1997, s 31, specifically authorised the death penalty; however, the equivalent 2007 provision, s 32, merely refers, by way of exception to the general principle, to 'punishment under judgments of the Courts or by virtue of the law'. Presumably s 32 leaves it open to the Legislature to abolish the death penalty without constitutional amendment.

liberty of communication, freedom of religion, expression and assembly, association and to form a political party. The Constitution goes to some lengths to ensure that the freedom of expression without censorship is real (this right is discussed in more detail in section VI below), and the media are protected from political interference: closure of presses and television and radio stations is prohibited; independence of journalists is guaranteed; even academic freedom is guaranteed. There are also guarantees against *ad hominem* legislation. Further, there is a number of social and economic rights: a right to education for 12 years at public expense; to medical care and old-age pension; special rights for the disabled.[18] Similarly, children and youth are given new rights to protection from violence and to State care.[19]

Some of the rights are indeed decidedly 'third-generation' in nature.[20] Environmental rights include a right to participation in decision-making, to reasons for decisions affecting the quality of a person's environment and to environmental impact assessment. There is also a right of access to information; a right to present a petition; a right to sue State agencies; a right to data protection (new in the 2007 Constitution); and a right to natural justice in administrative decisions ('the right to participate in the decision-making process . . . in the performance of administrative functions which affect or may affect his or her rights and liberties as provided by law'). A right clearly based on historical experience is the right of peaceful resistance to any act committed for the acquisition of power unconstitutionally.

The rights referred to in the last paragraph are part of the reason for the labelling of the 1997 Constitution as the 'People's Constitution': never before had a constitution paid so much attention to rights to public participation. In this respect the 1997 Constitution did indeed bring about significant change. As one Thai political scientist notes:

[P]eople have more awareness of participatory democracy. This has led to a higher demand for public participation than before. Public hearing activity is

---

[18] TC 2007, s 49, contains entirely new protection for the disabled, quite apart from the issue of discrimination.

[19] TC 2007, ss 52 and 55.

[20] That is, going beyond traditional civil liberties and social and economic rights. See, eg, H Steiner, P Alston and R Goodman, 'Human Rights, Development and Climate Change' in *International Human Rights in Context: Law, Politics, Morals*, 3rd edn (Oxford, Oxford University Press, 2007) ch 16.

believed to be an effective channel for public participation and is being widely employed by many state organisations.[21]

It is hard to fault these provisions as representing a huge advance on the rights previously set out in constitutional law in Thailand. However, the constitution-makers of 1997 and 2007 seem to have understood that providing for all of these rights has considerable implications as to practical implementation. Do they represent an aspiration that is entirely unrealistic? Is it even advisable to provide for such rights if practical enforcement is likely to be problematical? The answer to these questions is provided by the introduction of the NHRC, an instrument designed to bridge the gap between law and implementation.

IV. THE NATIONAL HUMAN RIGHTS COMMISSION

In the reform process, separate debates on the Constitution and on the NHRC (the latter debate having continued throughout the 1990s) became joined during the constitution-drafting process.[22] The transitional provisions of the 1997 Constitution (section 334(1)) required an organic law to be passed within two years to set up the NHRC, and this obligation was fulfilled with the enactment of its organic law in 1999. The law went through no fewer than 17 drafts over seven years (1992–99) since its original conception long before the 1997 Constitution itself was conceived. The drafting process was thus longer than that leading to the Constitution itself, disagreements surfacing over almost every aspect of the NHRC, from its powers and organisation to its composition and its selection process. The main issue was whether the NHRC would or would not be an independent body. The story of how the debate

---

[21] T Bureekul, 'Access to Environmental Justice and Public Participation in Thailand' in A Harding (ed), *Access to Environmental Justice: A Comparative Study* (Leiden, Martinus Nijhoff, 2007) ch 10, at 272. The discussion of the Hin Krud power plant hearing (*ibid.* at 278–82) reveals that although the rights of public participation, information and freedom of assembly and association were observed, the hearing did not in fact satisfactorily resolve the environmental issue involved.

[22] For discussion of the fascinating if tortuous details of this process, see J Klein, 'The Evolution of Thailand's National Human Rights Commission, 1992–2001' in M Nelson (ed), *Thailand's New Politics: KPI Yearbook 2001* (Nonthaburi and Bangkok, KPI and White Lotus Press, 2001).

unfolded is an extraordinary saga of unexpected sudden reversals, false dawns and last-minute compromises.[23]

Suffice it to say that the NHRC became a battleground between those who wanted to see a strong and independent NHRC, which they saw as the very foundation of human rights; and those who saw its role as limited, and who emphasised national security and the efficacy of Thai traditions. Human rights advocates were probably too ambitious in expecting that the NHRC could be a kind of human-rights czar with powers to enforce human rights over the jurisdiction of other bodies. The result was a compromise, but one with which Anand Panyarachun, who was instrumental in laying its foundations during his two terms as Prime Minister (1991–92), might well have felt satisfied.

The NHRC selection process was provided in the National Human Rights Commission Act 1999 (NHRC Act), section 8, and remains unchanged by the 2007 Constitution. It involves the Senate appointing a Selection Committee, in this case comprising 27 members, who choose 22 candidates from whom the 11 Commissioners are chosen by the Senate. The 27 members of this Selection Committee comprise the Presidents of the Supreme Court and the Supreme Administrative Court, the Attorney-General, the Chairman of the Law Society of Thailand, all *ex officio*; and the following members elected by the representatives of the relevant bodies from amongst their own number: 10 from registered human rights NGOs; five from the political parties; five from the academic institutions; and three from the media. In the event, the 11 Commissioners selected in 2003 were a fairly representative collection of highly respectable individuals. There were five women and six men. There were three NGO activists, three academics, three lawyers (one judge, one government lawyer and one private human rights lawyer), one educationalist and one journalist. Their expertise covered human rights, freedom of information, legal aid and family law, economic and political development, women's and children's rights, housing, welfare, public and mental health, environment and management.

The NHRC survived the coup and constitution-drafting process of 2006–07. However, new Commissioners had to be chosen when the first tranche completed their six-year terms in 2009. The selection of

[23] See, eg, V Muntarbhorn, 'Human Rights in the Era of "Thailand Inc"' in R Peerenboom, C Petersen and A Chen (eds), *Human Rights in Asia: A Comparative Legal Study of Twelve Asian Jurisdictions, France and the USA* (Abingdon, Routledge, 2006) 336ff.

new Commissioners was controversial due to the shortened time-span for consideration and the consequent lack of public participation. Also there are now only seven Commissioners, a fact which reduces the range of experience available and their representativeness. There are now two women (one is the President) and five men. Their expertise covers peace and conflict, minority rights, medicine, social development, industry, public law and security. The profiles of the Commissioners give an over-all impression of embodying more administrative experience than human rights experience. One is a former police general. Another has been investigated for violation of constitutional rights in respect of environmental management.

The NHRC has genuinely independent financial status and has charge of the execution of its own enabling Act.[24] Active bureaucrats and poli-ticians are excluded from membership; the Commissioners are full-time and salaried. The functions of the NHRC include promoting respect for human rights, education, research, appraisal and dissemination; examin-ing and reporting violations; making proposals in respect of law, policy and international treaties regarding human rights; and promoting coor-dination among public and private agencies.

The NHRC Act emphasises the role of the NHRC in dealing with allegations of human rights violation. These allegations may be received directly from a member of the public, or via a human rights organisa-tion. The NHRC may investigate the facts relating to such allegations and must allow an opportunity for the relevant agencies to respond. It can mediate and secure compromise solutions; it can report that a viola-tion has occurred, indicating remedial action; it can refer elsewhere mat-ters not within its powers. In the event of an agency refusing to comply with the NHRC's report, it can refer the matter to the Prime Minister to order implementation of the remedial measures within 60 days. It can also publicise the refusal to comply where it considers it in the public interest to do so. It can even set out remedial action where no human rights violation has occurred but there is an unjust practice in respect of which an aggrieved person deserves a remedy. The NHRC also has, since the 2007 Constitution, the power to submit a case together with opinions to the Constitutional Court, in any case where the Commission

---

[24] In Thailand great importance is attached to responsibility for implementation, as the department implementing will be able to a large extent to decide matters of personnel, procedure and budget.

agrees with a complainant that the provisions of any law (or before the Administrative Court in the case of any rule, order or administrative act) are detrimental to human rights and beg the question of the constitutionality; or before the Courts of Justice for the injured person upon his or her request if it deems it appropriate for the resolution of human rights violation problem as a whole.[25]

At the time of writing the NHRC has been active for about eight years. During this time it has made some steady progress in human rights education. It has also reported trenchantly on the situation in the Muslim south. It is important to understand that a Human Rights Commission does not have sole responsibility for rectifying human rights violations. It has a duty to investigate where appropriate, but other bodies, including executive, legislative and judicial organs, have direct responsibility for enforcing and supporting human rights. The gap between constitutional aspirations and the actual delivery of human rights is extremely hard to bridge. Despite the progress indicated, it is not possible to assert that the NHRC has had more than a very superficial impact on human rights compliance.

V. HUMAN RIGHTS AND THE SOUTHERN CONFLICT

The upsurge of violence in Thailand's southern provinces has coincided with the recent constitutional commitment to the general introduction of human rights. Not only has this apparent commitment to the protection of rights been set against the background of an escalating conflict, but many controversial incidents involving human rights violations have occurred which have tested the capacity of the State through the law and watchdog agencies to provide effective redress (see chapter 4 section VIII).

It is important to recognise that the rights abuses set out have taken place against the background of a violent conflict which has already been discussed in some detail from the standpoint of regional governance in chapter four. It is worth reminding ourselves of the salient facts. Early in 2004, 20 schools in Thailand's southern province of Narathiwat were torched by Muslim separatists, and four soldiers were killed in an attack on an army camp. Five Thai Muslims accused of these crimes alleged that they were tortured by the police. Their defence attorney,

---

[25] TC 2007, s 257.

Somchai Neelaphaijit, a well-known Muslim human rights lawyer, subsequently disappeared; several years later Somchai's case still gives rise to public concern and nothing has been resolved. In April 2004, the military stormed the Kru Se mosque where armed Muslims separatists were holed up, and 107 of the latter were killed. These events were interspersed with several assassinations of Thai officials in the four southern Muslim provinces. In October 2004, in an incident known as the Tak Bai riot, 78 Muslim protesters were suffocated to death when they were arrested and herded into army trucks. Altogether 85 persons, including mere bystanders, are reported to have died (see chapter 4, page 142ff). The unrest that had existed prior to these events has continued with intensity, and further incidents have been reported, despite a moving apology to the Muslim population by the Prime Minister Surayud Chulanont in November 2006 and the setting up of a National Peace and Reconciliation Commission (NPRC) under former Prime Minister Anand Panyarachun in 2005.[26] However, it was not within the remit of the NPRC to investigate human rights violations as such; and great damage and mistrust have resulted, which will take many years to repair, even with a more enlightened policy.

Although much effort has been devoted to bringing to justice perpetrators of crimes and human rights abuses on both sides, which effort includes an investigation by a sub-panel of the NHRC, no effective action has been taken in respect of the human rights abuses by the military and the police. The Commissioner appointed to chair the investigation stated that extensive field trips and in-depth interviews showed that the whole process, including treatment of protesters, crowd control, dispersal of protesters, detention of suspects, damage compensation and prosecution of suspects, had failed to meet human rights standards upheld by the Constitution and governed by international conventions. It was also reported that 58 protesters had been charged with offences; the sub-panel recommended that these charges be dropped as they had been made randomly. In addition, the sub-panel recommended other measures, including the award of compensation to the victims. Its report was forwarded to the Prime Minister, but apart from a committee dealing with the matter of compensation, no further action has been taken.[27] The findings of the sub-panel showed that the soldiers dealing

[26] *Bangkok Post*, 11 April 2005.
[27] *Bangkok Post*, 5 April 2005; *The Nation*, 3 November 2006.

with the Tak Bai riot regarded themselves as following not only orders but *normal procedures* in dealing with protesters, which is to treat them as prisoners. The fact that they had such orders and saw no reason to exercise some judgment in the matter is already a cause for some disquiet.

Following the military coup on September 2006, the coup leader, General Sonthi Boonyaratglin, cited the actions of the former government of Thaksin Shinawatra in the south as a major reason for the coup. An attempt was made to establish a ceasefire, exploratory talks were held at an informal level between the Thai government and groups associated with the insurgency, and charges were dropped against 50 protestors being held in custody. Nevertheless, a sharp escalation of violence erupted in the south, with 800 deaths in the nine months following the coup.[28] The security forces responded by raiding premises and insurgency camps, with hundreds of Muslims being arrested and some killed in the course of these raids.[29] Although the initial response appeared to signal a change in government policy that would give more emphasis to human rights and good governance, the security forces have continued to fight an active campaign against Islamic insurgents.

The practice of religious freedom has been profoundly affected by the southern conflict, and the issue has not simply been official concern by the Thai authorities over the spread of radical Islamic sects.[30] Recent policy has flown in the face of any conception of Buddhist tolerance. Jerryson explains how, by stationing troops in *wats*, there has been a deliberate but also covert policy of politicising religion, and that this act has served to undermine an important cross-community relationship which previously existed, as well as subverting the fundamentals of Theravada Buddhism. The constitutional commitment allowing a person the full liberty to profess a religion provided that it was not contrary to civil duties, public order and good morals, is not related to any wider values and has failed to protect the politicisation of belief.[31] The monkhood in the south was a traditional stalwart institution, representing something positive in values and rights. As Jerryson comments:

---

[28] See Z Abuza, *Conspiracy of Silence: the Insurgency in Southern Thailand* (Washington, DC, United States Institute of Peace Press, 2009) 81, 198.

[29] *Ibid*, 92.

[30] See further, M Askew, *Culture and Electoral Politics in Southern Thailand* (Bangkok, KPI, 2006).

[31] TC 2007, s 137.

For many non-specialists in Buddhist studies, the idea of a militarised monk conflicts with basic Buddhist principles. A monk's purpose is to avoid life's vulgarity, to aspire toward enlightenment. A soldier's lifestyle is virtually the opposite – they are committed to a job that requires them to confront the vulgarities of life. Beyond the ideological complications, there is the ecclesiastic interdiction that prohibits soldiers from becoming monks.[32]

The sanctity of the Buddhist religion as something peaceful, meditative, supportive and completely opposed to war has been fundamentally undermined, and with it respect for and the authority of the monkhood as a religious institution. The fact that this more militant and militarised form of Buddhism has been endorsed by or even dictated by the State not only calls into question whether the State should be defining the brand of Buddhism or indeed any other religion, it is also symptomatic of profound religious intolerance.[33] This development is, of course, contrary to the spirit as well as the text of the Constitution.[34]

VI. THE BROADCAST MEDIA, CONFLICT OF INTEREST AND FREEDOM OF SPEECH

We proceed to take the media and freedom of expression as a case study in fundamental rights in Thailand. In this section we look at the media, and in section VII below we look at the law of *lèse-majesté*. These issues have great structural resonance in terms of Thai constitutionalism, and have also been much discussed during the period since 2005. The overwhelming control of the media, especially the broadcast media, has the potential to lead to the corruption of information and, as a consequence, to undermine any system of liberal democracy. In Thailand there is considerable evidence to suggest that the pattern of ownership and control of the mass media has directly threatened freedom of political speech. In particular, it has meant that the influence of the controllers and proprietors of TV and radio channels can systematically undermine the capacity of news coverage, and political journalism more broadly, to act as a check on the wider political process. Some of the

---

[32] M Jerryson, 'Appropriating a Space for Violence: State Buddhism in Southern Thailand' (2009) 40(1) *Journal of Southeast Asian Studies* 33 at 47.

[33] D McCargo, 'Thai Buddhism, Thai Buddhists and the Southern Conflict' (2009) 40(1) *Journal of South East Asian Studies* 1 at 6–8.

[34] TC 2007, s 37.

main new rights introduced in the 2007 Constitution relate to the media, and were apparently designed to address the perceived conflict of interests which arose under Thaksin's premiership discussed in more detail below. For example, it is provided that

> [n]o person holding a political position shall be the owner of, or hold shares in, newspaper, radio or television broadcasting or telecommunication business, irrespective of whether he so commits in his name, or through his proxy or nominee, or by other direct or indirect means which enable him to administer such business as if he is the owner of, or hold shares in, such business.[35]

Given that the most recent Constitutions of 1997 and 2007 contain, as indicated above, a strong commitment to democratic values, in considering fitness for purpose, the effectiveness of any provisions designed to secure the relative independence of broadcasting needs to be considered. Freedom of speech and the regime of constitutional and legal regulation of the media must first be assessed against the highly unusual pattern of media ownership in Thailand. A legacy of the former era of military dictatorship was that the Royal Thai Army and the Government retained ownership of broadcasting, including a near monopoly of free-to-air TV, relied on by most Thais for news and entertainment.[36] To partially offset this anomaly, iTV was established in 1995 as a supposedly independent free-to-air channel, under an obligation to perform a public service broadcasting function.

During his premiership Thaksin (2001–06) was able to achieve a very high degree of control over the broadcasting media. In the domain of military broadcasting, Thaksin arranged for Traffic Corner Holdings, a Thaksin family-owned company, to take over responsibility for the delivery of news bulletins on Channel 5 and Royal Thai Army Radio. In addition, there was a sustained attempt not only to cash in on the financial potential of these outlets through (unrealised but) highly controversial plans to engineer the stock market flotation of military channels, but also to appoint as chief executives those who would ensure that these

---

[35] TC 2007 s 48. Section 45 expressly forbids foreign ownership of newspapers or any media business, and would thus prevent a repetition of anything similar to the Shin Corp deal discussed below.

[36] The Mass Communication Organisation of Thailand (MCOT) operates TV stations (Channels 3 and 9), while the Royal Thai Army owns channels RTA 5 and RTA 7.

army channels would favour Thaksin and his TRT Party.[37] Further manipulation of broadcasting was also achieved by the outright purchase of iTV as part of Thaksin's business empire. The concession which created iTV had stipulated that 70 per cent of its programmes were to be devoted to news and current affairs, and that no individual should be allowed to own more than a 10 per cent stake in the company. Faced with an uncertain financial future, the removal of this 10 per cent rule in 2000 by Thaksin's predecessor as Prime Minister (Chuan Leekpai) opened the door for iTV's takeover by Thaksin's Shin Corp.

Under its new overtly political direction, the station's original mission was eventually neglected. Not only were 21 journalists perceived as hostile to Thaksin dismissed, but equally controversially there was an attempt to change the programme content in favour of entertainment in order to increase profitability. The Shin Corp, including iTV, was subsequently sold to Temasek Holdings of Singapore in 2006. However, shortly afterwards the Administrative Courts quashed the 2004 decision by the Arbitration Court to permit this change to entertainment programming, and imposed heavy fines for breaching the concession.[38] Saddled with huge debts, the station ceased broadcasting in January 2008.[39]

Other tactics adopted by Thaksin to reduce media opposition were to make offers to potentially hostile media players so that they were recruited to the government side, and to threaten withdrawal of advertising budgets to anti-government media outlets.[40] In sum, the deliberate manipulation of the broadcast media enabled Thaksin to be in control of the main channels, allowing him to promote a particular view while at the same time blocking out any coverage which might contest that view. In consequence, during the period 2001–06, opposition parties and others were denied an adequate mouthpiece through which to voice criticism.

---

[37] See D McCargo and U Pathmanand, *The Thaksinization of Thailand* (Copenhagen, NIAS, 2005) at 153ff.

[38] P Leyland, 'The Emergence of Administrative Justice in Thailand Under the 1997 Constitution' in T Ginsburg and H Chen (eds), *Administrative Law and Governance in Asia* (London, Routledge, 2009) 244. See also ch 6.

[39] See S Nance, 'Thailand's iTV takes one on the Shin', *Asia Times*, 14 January 2007.

[40] P Phongpaichit and C Baker, *Thaksin* (Chiang Mai, Silkworm Press, 2009) 152.

As well as the constitutional provisions detailed above,[41] since the 2006 coup there have been attempts to reduce the repetition of the conflicts of interest that were so prevalent under Thaksin. In finding a replacement for iTV a very different approach was taken to public service broadcasting. The Thai Public Service Broadcasting Service (TPBS) has been to some extent modelled on the BBC to provide a protected element of State broadcasting. It was set up under the Public Service Broadcasting Act 2007.[42] Moreover, a substantial proportion of the programme content relates particularly to news and current affairs. In fact, the new channel was designed to be truly independent of government, as it is funded not from a licence fee but from a tax on alcohol. It has been suggested that the TPBS could also serve as a model for National Broadcasting Television (formerly Channel 11).[43] The TPBS requires full protection under the Constitution to ensure it is at arm's length from interference. Broadcasters more generally should have a mandate to report news and current affairs from both government and opposition viewpoints. Further, strict rules governing the coverage of elections must be applied impartially to ensure that all recognised parties receive fair coverage. Looking to the future, it remains crucial that constitutional provisions and statutory rules designed to safeguard the public interest, and at the same time prevent the domination of the broadcasting media by monopoly interests, are enforced decisively. The establishment of the TPBS as an independent State broadcasting organ can be regarded as a significant development.[44]

The 1997 Constitution was the first to contain a constitutionally-guaranteed freedom to communicate in radio and television broadcasting.[45] However, as we have noted earlier in this section the lack of effective

---

[41] See TC 2007, ss 45 and 48.

[42] See <http://thailand.prd.go.th/view_inside.php?id=2936>.

[43] See S Nitsmer, 'Public Service Broadcasting in Thailand', *18th JAMCO Online International Symposium*, 16 January to 28 February 2009, available at <http://www. jamco.or.jp/2009_symposium/en/003/index.html>; SEAPA Report, 'Can new Thai PM achieve genuine media reform?' *Southeast Asian Press Alliance*, 22 January 2009 available at <http://www.cijmalaysia.org/content/view/419/9/>.

[44] See Thai Public Broadcasting of Sound and Pictures Organisation Act 2008; A Sennitt, 'Thai Public Broadcasting Service to Focus on Prime Time News, Education Programmes', *Media Network*, 20 January 2008.

[45] D Youngsamart and G Fisher, 'Governance and Administration in a "New" Democracy: The Case of Formal Control of Free-to-Air Television in Thailand (1997–2007)' (2006) 1(1) *Journal of Administration and Governance* 36 at 40.

regulation meant that the constitutional provisions which stipulated that transmission frequencies for broadcasting must be exercised in the public interest were not enforced.[46] By way of contrast, the 2007 Constitution outlined the requirement for a single independent regulatory agency to be made responsible for distributing frequencies, and for supervising TV and radio and the telecommunications industry.[47] Further, as a response to practice under the 1997 Constitution, the 2007 Constitution expressly prevents mergers and cross-ownership, and it prohibits politicians from owning or holding shares in any newspapers, radio, television or telecommunication business.[48]

Legislation has been passed since the 2006 military coup to modify regulation. Nevertheless, the ownership rights of the Royal Thai Army, the government Public Relations Department and other State agencies continue to be recognised under a new Broadcasting Act of 2008.[49] Serious problems relating to conflicts of interest have yet to be addressed; as mentioned, the Royal Thai Army has maintained its ownership role, and it should be remembered that in Thailand senior figures in the armed forces remain major players in Thai politics, both as active figures and behind the scenes. The new legislation introduces a potentially more open structure with the recognition of three categories of broadcasting – public, commercial and community service – all requiring a licence.[50] The Broadcasting Frequency Allocation Act 2010 is intended to introduce a revised framework of statutory regulation by granting to a public authority wide-ranging licensing powers relating to all forms of radio and television as well as telecommunications.[51] Pending the establishment of a new National Broadcasting and Telecommunications Commission (NBTC), these powers were exercised by the National Telecommunications Commission. It remains to be seen whether this new body will prove to be an effective independent regulator after taking up the reins in 2011.[52] The selection process for the NBTC conducted by the Thai Senate has already proved to be con-

---

[46] TC 1997, s 40.

[47] TC 2007, s 47.

[48] TC 2007, s 48.

[49] The full title is 'Thai Broadcasting Service Act 2008'.

[50] 'SEAPA Report: Can New Thai PM Achieve Genuine Media Reform?', Wednesday, 21 January 2009, cited above.

[51] See <http://thailand.prd.go.th/view_inside.php?id=3284> (last visited 14 August 2009). Radio licences last up to 7 years and TV licences up to 15 years.

[52] 'NBTC Law to Take Effect in Eight Months', *The Nation*, 2 March 2009.

troversial for its failure to provide a sufficiently wide list of names.[53] The experience with selecting other watchdog bodies in Thailand suggests that any failure to appoint credible candidates able to resist government interference is likely to undermine the authority of the new body.[54]

The issue of media and broadcasting regulation arose almost immediately under the current 2007 Constitution. The constitutional rules were rigidly applied when the Constitutional Court ruled in September 2008 that Prime Minister Samak had violated the conflict of interest provisions[55] by being paid for his appearance on a TV cookery show, and that in consequence he had to step down from the premiership.[56] Persistent protest by Yellow Shirt supporters, culminating in the occupation of Bangkok's international airport, prompted a change of Administration.

The threat to freedom of expression remains acute, since it appears that executive powers have been used by the Democrat Government, which took office in December 2008, to silence the main opposition. In response to demonstrations by Red Shirt protestors, an emergency decree was used in April 2009 by the Abhisit Government to shut down the D-Station TV channel[57] and at least three local radio stations in the north and north east of the country. This action was taken on the grounds that they had been used as a mouthpiece for the Red Shirt movement loyal to former Prime Minister Thaksin and to stir up unrest.[58]

VII. THE *LÈSE-MAJESTÉ* LAW

In this section we consider the application of the *lèse-majesté* law in the light of the constitutional commitment to free speech contained in the 1997

[53] 'NTC Hopes to Avoid More Dual-Candidate Snafus', *The Nation*, 21 March 2009.

[54] See P Leyland, 'Thailand's Constitutional Watchdogs: Dobermans, Bloodhounds or Lapdogs?' (2007) 2:2 *Journal of Comparative Law* 169.

[55] TC 2007, s 267.

[56] Constitutional Court case 12-13 of 2008; and see A Harding and P Leyland. 'The Constitutional Court of Thailand and Indonesia: Two Case Studies from South East Asia' (1998) 3:2 *Journal of Comparative Law* 118 at 133; 'PM Disqualified for Violating Charter with Cookery Show', *The Nation*, 10 September 2008.

[57] Emegency Situation Decree of 11/04/52 (11/04/09).

[58] 'Thailand: Government Moves to Suppress Media', S Tunsarawuth, 24 April 2009, HRH, Index on Censorship at <http://humanrightshouse.org/noop/page.php?p=Articles/10677&d=1>; 'New TV Station May Replace D Station', *The Nation*, 1 May 2009.

and 2007 Constitutions, and the national commitment to conform to international human rights norms.[59] Indeed, our discussion of the origins of this law and its deployment in the current environment vividly exemplifies a clash between the monarchy, which might be regarded as the very essence of traditional Thai values associated with an age of obedience and respect, and a fundamental constitutional right to free expression which is increasingly demanded under current conditions of instant communication. Thai citizens have been granted a constitutional right to free speech under Section 45 of the 2007 Constitution. This right is made subject to what would appear to be routine limitations in the public interest.[60] In practice, however, the constitutional commitment to freedom of expression has been undermined not only by the imposition of emergency powers, but also by the blanket enforcement of a law which can be called into question for being incompatible with fundamental human rights. Before reviewing its recent application, it is important to understand how the *lèse-majesté* law has come to be constructed.

For the vast majority of Thais, the monarchy under the present King has not only been regarded as a revered institution but it is also a subject of extreme sensitivity, not to be treated with levity or even any suggestion of disrespect. There is evidence to suggest that a particular cult of monarchy has been deliberately promoted by factional interests associated with the military as something superior to any democratic constitution. In fact it was under the military rule of General Sarit Thanarat (1957–63) that the latent reverence for the office and person of the King was rediscovered.[61] It might be argued that despite the occasional genuflection to constitutionalism, there was never any intention by the conservative elite surrounding the King to allow Western-style democracy to be fully embraced. The monarch could be championed as the main character in history capable of uniting the people, the nation and the State ideology. This narrative could be justified because

[59] See generally P Leyland, 'The Struggle for Freedom of Expression in Thailand: Media Moguls, the King, Citizen Politics and the Law' (2010) 2(1) *The Journal of Media Law* 115.

[60] TC 2007, s 45 provides that any restriction on liberty 'shall not be imposed except by virtue of the provisions of law specifically enacted for the purpose of maintaining the security of the State, safeguarding the rights, liberties, dignity, reputation, family or privacy rights of other persons, maintaining public order or good morals or preventing the deterioration of the mind or health of the public'.

[61] B Terweil, *Thailand's Political History: From the Fall of Ayutthaya to Recent Times* (Bangkok, River Books, 2005), 283.

the Thai version of democracy was a defective model, a distortion of its Western counterpart. It emphasized only the process of democracy without paying much attention to another equally important side of the system, namely the principle of objective democracy: the guarantee of life, liberty and the pursuit of happiness of individuals within the common good.[62]

Connors explains that:

Given the threats to stability emerging from social transformation, it was the king who could – as a symbol of social order, place and identity – act as a focal point of loyalty. As a central institution from which the state's ideological practices could be referenced and embodied, the monarchy in effect functioned as a central institution in political development.[63]

This official version of Thai-ness thus demanded

an all encompassing law on *lèse-majesté* crimes to ensure not only proper respect and decorum be strictly observed but also that the not-so-refined aspects of royalty be kept out of public knowledge. Woe betide those who are unfortunate enough to transgress this unusually high standard towards the royalty.[64]

In previous phases of Thai history, any act against the King was regarded as a form of rebellion.[65] Now for the

defenders of the official state narrative, *lèse-majesté* is tantamount to a kind of cultural treason, a national spiritual betrayal of Thai-ness (Khaam pen thai). It is a particularly damaging charge to bring against someone, for it is the only crime, other than treason (which has hardly been used), that impugns patriotism.[66]

The proximity to the crime of treason is because the King and the State come to be perfectly identified with each other; all offences against the State are capable of being offences against the King and vice versa. The present King's persona has been progressively constructed by a

---

[62] K Suwannathat-Pian, *Kings, Country and Constitutions: Thailand's Political Development 1932–2000* (London, Routledge, 2003) 4.

[63] M Connors, *Democracy and National Identity in Thailand* (Copenhagen, NIAS, 2007) 129.

[64] Suwannathat-Pian, above n 62, at 145.

[65] P Handley, *The King Never Smiles* (New Haven, Conn, Yale University Press, 2006) 134.

[66] D Streckfuss, 'Kings in the Age of Nations: The Paradox of *Lèse-majesté* as Political Crime in Thailand' (1995) 37(3) *Comparative Studies in Society and History* 445 at 449, 463.

sustained campaign, with ubiquitous images and tributes to him throughout the nation.

A *lèse-majesté* crime is committed by 'Whoever defames, insults or threatens the King, Queen or the Heir-apparent . . .'[67] If found guilty, the offender will be punished by a term of imprisonment of between three and 15 years. This criminal offence (not civil wrong) is committed if anyone could hypothetically construe an alleged statement or conduct as being detrimental to the reputation of the monarchy. In a nation which treats its royal family with such great reverence, it is not possible for the prosecution to establish the offence by reference to the actual impact of the alleged conduct. In any charge of *lèse-majesté*,

> the prosecution is faced with the utter impossibility of producing witnesses to substantiate the fact that the words 'would cause people to look down on the monarchy'.[68]

This is because any witness who made an admission supporting the prosecution case would himself be committing the offence of *lèse-majesté*. It would be incriminating for such a witness to state in court that his personal view of the monarchy had been lowered as a result of the alleged statement. An earlier interpretation of 'defame' regarded 'anything that has insulted the king, government', or system of governance that would 'cause the people to be . . . without faithfulness or loyalty to the king'. But, as we shall see with recent cases, this has now shifted from the corporality of the King to any threat to the modern State posed by critics, demonstrators or republicans.

The *Wira Musikaphong* case in 1988 clearly illustrates both that the offence can be committed by innuendo and the way *lèse-majesté* has been used by politicians to muzzle political opponents. The essence of the alleged offence was that Wira, a member of a party opposed to the military, in an election campaign had compared himself to a prince in criticising a political opponent. Part of a political speech included the following remark:

> If I were a prince now, I would not be standing here, speaking, making my throat hoarse and dry . . . I would be drinking some intoxicating liquors to make myself comfortable and happy.[69]

---

[67] Thai Criminal Code, Art 112.
[68] Streckfuss, above n 68, at 458.
[69] *Ibid*, at 449.

It was alleged that this reference (a subversive metaphor) suggested that the King did not suffer the privations of the poor and that royalty was lazy. Wira protested his innocence and affirmed his loyalty to the King. A month later, Phijit, a Senator, raised the matter of the 'insulting' speech in the Senate. An explanation and pledge of loyalty to the King agreed with Phijit appeared to have settled the issue. However, once the matter had been brought to the attention of the wider public, a senior general was able to stir up popular feeling against Wira. In turn, this public focus exerted pressure on the police to prosecute. A number of senior military figures appeared for the prosecution against Wira, stating that:

> Any loss of loyalty to the king would give an opening to the communists who seek to infiltrate and destroy the Thai system of governance that has a king as head of state.[70]

After much semantic argument between prosecution and defence as to what the phrases meant, and whether he was in fact referring to the King, Wira was acquitted by the provincial court, but he was found guilty on appeal and sentenced to six years' imprisonment. The truth or accuracy of the words have become irrelevant to the case. The defendant's intent was determined by constructing a hypothetical effect totally out of context. Such an interpretation of the law allows a court to reach a conclusion which disregards other relevant evidence relating to the accused. In the application of this law a court is therefore likely to contravene the constitutional guarantee of the presumption of innocence.[71]

A. Current application of *lèse-majesté*

What might be defended as an understandable desire to safeguard the reputation of a much respected institution in Thailand, has been turned into a political weapon employed by factional interests. As the *Wira* case demonstrates, the more rigorous enforcement of this law did not originate with the King. Moreover, the King and the Royal Family do not personally file charges under this law. In his 2005 birthday speech, King Bhumipol famously stepped back from any aura of infallibility. In

---

[70] Streckfuss, above n 68, at 195.
[71] TC 2007, s 39.

consequence a distinction can be drawn between the monarchy and some of those that project themselves as its keenest supporters.

The *lèse-majesté* law has been vigorously enforced as part of the emerging conflict (2006–10) between the Red Shirts and the Yellow Shirts. An influential Yellow-Shirt People's Alliance for Democracy (PAD) clique, trading on their loyalty to the monarchy, maintain that aggressive enforcement of the *lèse-majesté* law protects the Thai State from what they regard as subversion.[72] Their Red-Shirt opponents would claim that the PAD perceive themselves as being under threat by the extension of a democratic process which tolerates greater freedom of speech.[73] In any event, an offensive has been mounted by the authorities at the prompting of the PAD on a number of fronts. As we shall shortly observe, there have been attempts to use the Computer Crimes Act to prevent internet references to the monarchy, but more generally any Thai citizens who voice dissent from official policy risk becoming obvious targets. The list is headed by Thaksin Shinawatra, the former Thai Prime Minister, who became a fugitive facing a two-year prison sentence following his conviction in the *Ratchadaphisek Land* case. As a populist leader with a strong following he remains firmly in the sights of the PAD, his main political opponents, and faces investigation for *lèse-majesté* charges should he return, although he has never directly criticised the King.

In a much-publicised recent case, Ms Daranee Charnchoengsilpakul (aka Da Torpedo) was convicted in August 2009 on three charges of insulting the King and Queen. She was sentenced to six years on each count consecutively, totalling 18 years' imprisonment.[74] Her most inflammatory speech was a wide-ranging attack on the 2006 military

---

[72] 'Thailand's King and its Crisis: A Right Royal Mess', *The Economist*, 4 December 2008. As *The Economist* puts it, summing up the PAD: '. . . a motley bunch, united only by fanatical hatred of Mr Thaksin. It includes disgruntled businessmen, aristocratic ladies, members of a militaristic Buddhist outfit, formerly anti-monarchist intellectuals and reactionary army types. Its "new politics", consisting of a partly appointed parliament, sweeping powers for military intervention and, of course, a strong crown, is "Premocracy" redux. The army is a big part of the country's predicament. Its generals believe they have a right to remove any government that incurs its, or the palace's, displeasure . . .'

[73] G Ungpakorn, 'Since the Military Coup, Democratic Rights have Come Under Attack. Now the Fightback is Starting', *Guardian*, 18 February 2009.

[74] Case Black at (letter Or), 2812/2009; 'Da Torpedo's Downfall a Warning to the Like Minded', *The Nation*, 1 September 2009.

coup-makers and their conservative allies, in which she repeated the widely-reported but controversial view that the King was behind the military coup in September 2006 and the other military coups during his reign. The court held that this United Front for Democracy against Dictatorship (UDD) member and supporter of Thaksin had made several remarks deemed to be *lèse-majesté* in speeches on the stage at UDD rallies at Sanam Luang on 18 January, 7 June and 13 June 2008. As a Thai citizen, Daranee would have been well aware that the combination of strong innuendo and very intemperate language directed at the monarchy and its supporters contained in her speeches was liable to land her in trouble. Nevertheless, her treatment under the legal system can still be called into question. Not only was an otherwise law-abiding citizen denied bail for over a year, but when in prison awaiting trial on these charges she appears to have been the victim of abuse.[75] Moreover, the trial was held *in camera* with reporting restrictions imposed,[76] and the consecutive sentence handed out might be regarded as grossly disproportionate punishment.

Although foreigners have fallen foul of *lèse-majesté* in the past, the treatment of the amateur Australian novelist Harry Nicolaides was perceived as being sufficiently harsh to make the headlines in newspapers around the world. Nicolaides had published an obscure novel about Thailand which referred to a royal prince. Fifty copies were printed and a total of seven books were sold. After his arrest, despite expressing remorse, he was charged, denied bail pending trial and was sentenced to a term of three years' imprisonment. He had been incarcerated for several months before being released following a royal pardon. The three-year sentence was announced just when the adverse publicity caused by the forced closure by supporters of the PAD of Bangkok's international airport was beginning to recede. The BBC correspondent in Thailand, Jonathan Head, was placed under investigation for *lèse-majesté* after speculating about the relationship between palace and protest groups in relation to these controversial demonstrations at Bangkok's airports.[77]

Indeed, the reaction of the international media commenting on the King and the application of this arcane law has also become a target for the Thai authorities. After publishing an article which discussed the

---

[75] 'UDD Abandons "Da Torpedo" ', *The Bangkok Post*, 24 February 2009.

[76] 'Thailand: Closed Trial Threatens Justice', *Amnesty International*, 25 June 2009.

[77] 'BBC Reporter Jonathan Head Faces 15 Years in Thai Jail', *Huffington Post*, 26 December 2008.

current role of the Thai monarchy and the governing faction, *The Economist* magazine was temporarily banned in Thailand.[78]

Lastly, we come the use of the Computer Crime Act to curtail freedom of expression.[79] This legislation was enacted under the military junta in 2007, ostensibly to combat online pornography, for which there is a maximum sentence of up to five years' imprisonment, and to prevent other online offences such as using the internet to promote terrorism. However, it is a very wide-ranging law, directed at the estimated 12 million plus regular internet users in Thailand. For example, the Act covers import to a computer system of computer data related to an offence against the Kingdom's security under the Criminal Code, for which there is also a five-year maximum term. This form of words is open to wide interpretation, which has included any implied criticism of the King falling under the *lèse-majesté* law. In addition, the Act under sections 5–13 outlaws the transmission, interception or accessing of any computer data which are defined as illegal. Any person using a computer with illegal material is potentially liable under the Act. The legislation grants officials in the Ministry of Information and Communications Technology (ICT) the right to apply for court orders to seize equipment and to block sites. Publishing companies have been shut down for hosting a server.[80] In order to make it easier for the authorities to trace abuse, the Act also requires internet service providers (ISPs) to keep log files of bandwidth consumption and internet traffic, and records of individual users for 90 days. Even users of internet cafes are required to register so that they can be traced.

The application of the Computer Crime Act, which grants such far-reaching powers to the authorities, must be viewed in the light of section 36 of the 2007 Constitution which guarantees Thai citizens the 'liberty of communication by lawful means'. The Thai authorities have directed considerable resources into policing this law by seizing equipment, shutting down websites and prosecuting alleged perpetrators of this new form of Internet crime. However, there is increasing evidence that this law is being employed as a political weapon.[81] In January 2009,

[78] 'Thailand's King and its Crisis: A Right Royal Mess', *The Economist*, 4 December 2008.

[79] Computer Crime Act 2007.

[80] 'The Police get Tough Net Laws', *The Nation*, 18 July 2007.

[81] Among the many recent cases, individuals have been charged for translating media reports about the health of the King. Further, in January 2009, Suwicha

officials at the Ministry of ICT were claiming that they had blocked or shut down 10,000 websites for containing content defaming the monarchy. A report published by Human Rights Watch states that:

> The government also has used both the *lèse-majesté* statute in the Criminal Code and the new Computer Crimes Act to suppress critics of the monarchy and persecute perceived government enemies.[82]

Considerable energy and resources have been devoted by the Thai Ministry of ICT to shutting down websites declared to be anti-monarchist.

B. Human rights and *lèse-majesté*

From the standpoint of the basic human rights of the defendant, this offence displays alarming features. First, it can be committed entirely without criminal intent. There is no need for the prosecuting authorities to bring any evidence to bear relating to foresight by the defendant in relation to the effect of the statement or conduct. This failure to introduce a subjective element removes the vital link for establishing serious criminality resulting in deprivation of liberty. Faced with a serious criminal charge, a person should be judged on the facts as he or she believed them to be. In *lèse-majesté* cases the alleged perpetrator can be brought before a court because someone else understood the remarks as being damaging to the King. This will be the case even if:

a) this was not the intention of defendant;
b) the defendant was not even aware of the implications of the remarks;
c) the monarchy was not actually expressly mentioned in the offending statement.

The offence has been committed because the complainant reports the matter, or because the statement or other conduct is reported to the authorities who then decide to act because of their perception of

---

Thakor was sentenced to 10 years' imprisonment for posting material on the Internet which was judged to be contrary to *lèse-majesté*. See P Rojanaphruk, 'Is Internet Censorship Going Out of Hand and Hurting Users' Freedom?' *The Nation*, 23 January 2009.

[82] 'Thailand: Serious Backsliding on Human Rights', Human Rights Watch, 20 January 2010, available at <http://www.hrw.org/en/news/2010/01/20/thailand-serious-backsliding-human-rights>.

the alleged remarks. The fact that there is a statement which is brought to their notice may be sufficient to secure a conviction, regardless of its effect. Furthermore, unlike the Thai defamation law, *lèse-majesté* does not recognise the defence of fair comment.

Secondly, the insidiousness of the process is compounded by the lack of any prospect of 'independent' justice in Thailand in relation to this offence. The police, prosecuting authorities and judges not only act in the name of the King, but there is an expectation that their loyalty to the Crown will be reflected in an outcome that confirms the dignity of the King at the expense of the accused. Indeed any prosecutor who fails to vigorously pursue a case might himself be made the subject of a *lèse-majesté* charge.

Thirdly, an equally disturbing feature of this crime is the disproportionality of the punishment, as in the Da Torpedo case in 2009, discussed earlier. If the allegations are sustained and a guilty verdict returned, the perpetrator will face a term of imprisonment normally of no less than three years and often a great deal longer. Defendants nearly always apologise profusely and show remorse, but this has relatively little mitigating effect.

Lastly, there must be clear limits on the capacity of the prosecution to appeal when a defendant is acquitted. For example, in Wira's case discussed above, a rule should be introduced to prevent an appeal by the authorities so that there is a subsequent conviction on the same evidence.

These are grave defects in the law, any one of which constitutes a serious affront to human rights in a democratic constitution. The situation could easily be rectified. It would be quite possible to grant adequate protection to the monarchy with a revised law that requires the proof of intention or recklessness. At the same time, proportionate punishment could be introduced by having different levels of seriousness for the offence, with capped punishment for each level. Lastly, clear rules could be drafted for prosecutors in order to prevent the authorities from taking their cue in bringing prosecutions from politicians, the military or other vested interests.

There has been a limited official response to criticism of the abuse of *lèse-majesté*. In late 2009, an Order from the Office of Prime Minister was drafted to formulate a committee to advise the public prosecutor on how discretion should be exercised to protect the right of suspects in *lèse-majesté* and national security cases. It was noted at the outset that

Thailand has international human rights obligations as a signatory to the Universal Declaration of Human Rights, and as a party to the International Covenant on Civil and Political Rights since 1997. The current application of the *lèse-majesté* law arguably breaches this Covenant in a number of respects, as demonstrated by the analysis of the current law and by the cases discussed earlier.[83]

In sum, the problem from the perspective of constitutional law is that the application of the *lèse-majesté* law conflicts with other constitutional values and with Thailand's international treaty obligations. While there may be no doubt of the enormous respect afforded to the King, the fact is that now the King occupies the role of a constitutional monarch in a modern constitution, which recognises free speech as part of a democratic political system. In Walter Bagehot's parlance, the King as a pivotal symbolic icon is 'the head of the dignified part of the Constitution'.[84] In other words, now that executive power is in the hands of the Prime Minister and an elected government, the role of the King has been redefined. Nevertheless, he still has to intervene at vital moments, eg relating to the formation of governments or the dissolution of Parliament.[85] Given the need to perform such functions, it is crucial that he should not belong to, or be perceived as having any direct association with, any political party or faction, and that he should be widely regarded as politically neutral.[86] The invocation of the *lèse-majesté* law by parties or factions within Parliament to cast aspersions on their political opponents also has the effect of fatally undermining the King's constitutional position.[87]

---

[83] Eg, Art 9(3), routine detention in custody of *lèse-majesté* suspects; Arts 14(1) and 14(3)(c), the difficulty in securing a fair public hearing when charged with this offence and in examining witnesses; Art 19, the right to hold opinions without interference subject to respecting the reputation of others.

[84] W Bagehot, *The English Constitution* (London, Fontana, 1963) 66. For Bagehot, the dignified parts were 'very complicated and somewhat imposing, very old and rather venerable . . .'.

[85] See TC 2007, s 171 and s 108. The King has also frequently intervened at times of national crisis.

[86] S Bungkongkarn, 'Politicial Institutions in Thailand' in S Xuto (ed), *Government and Politics in Thailand* (Oxford, Oxford University Press, 1987) 59.

[87] There have been attempts to defend the current law in a Thai context, see eg B Uwanno, ' "*Lèse-majesté*": A Distinctive Character of Thai Democracy amidst the Global Democratic Movement' (Bangkok, KPI, April 2009) (see <http://www.kpi.ac.th/kpien/>).

VIII. CONCLUSION

There are factors related to religion and culture which have been discussed in accounting for Thailand's indifferent record as regards human rights protection. For example, it has been suggested that Asian legal traditions often emphasise social order over individual autonomy and responsibilities over rights:

> Buddhism calls for actions from individuals on the basis of their duties towards others rather than on the basis of an individual's rights. . . . there is a transcendent element which cannot be computed in material terms. The notion of 'karma' – the life-propelling force through one's good and bad deeds – shapes one's well-being through a process whereby the correlation between duties and rights is manifested ultimately in the cycle of reincarnation to which humans are subjected.[88]

In terms of the practical challenges, we have seen in this chapter that the constitutional and legal mechanisms for rights protection have faced rigorous examination at many different levels in recent years, ranging from anti-government demonstrations in Bangkok and the insurgency in the deep south to the treatment of refugees from Burma. Against this backdrop, the achievement of human rights according to the ambitious definition set out in the 1997 and 2007 Constitutions is clearly a task of gigantic proportions. As with several other aspects of constitutional government discussed in this book, a promising start in 1997 and for about five years following the adoption of the 1997 Constitution was quickly clouded by extensive violations of human rights and an almost total lack of accountability for those violations. This latter period coincides with Thaksin's ascendancy and the period of military government. The restoration of elected government under the 2007 Constitution has not brought any significant improvement in the human rights situation. The delivery of real human rights is an aspiration that institutional design is probably not able to achieve by itself given the issues we have discussed. Nevertheless, it is crucial to retain the oversight bodies and related laws which achieve an appropriate balance between the exigencies of the State and the protection of individual rights. To this end it is

---

[88] V Muntarbhorn, 'Rule of Law and Aspects of Human Rights in Thailand: From Conceptualization to Implementation?' in R Peerenboom (ed), *Asian Discourses of Rule of Law* (London, Routledge, 2004) 348.

necessary to have a mechanism that can strike down laws that are contrary to the constitutional provisions (in other words, a constitutional court that is genuinely independent and willing to act in such cases[89]); and another mechanism (in other words, a Human Rights Commission that is genuinely independent, well resourced and authoritative) to bring about the changes necessary in society, education and official training. In this sense the trend of constitutional reform in Thailand has been in our view correctly conceived; but implementation needs to go much further than it has to date.

FURTHER READING

S Chamarik, *Sitthi Manutsayachon Thai Nai KrasæLok* [Thai Human Rights in Globalisation] (Bangkok, Local Development Institute, 2006) [in Thai].

J Ditthaapichai, *Bon Hon Tang Sitthi Manutsayachon* [On the Road of Human Rights] (Bangkok, Institute of Public Policy Studies, 2006) [in Thai].

A Harding, 'Thailand's Reforms: Human Rights and the National Commission' (2006) 1(1) *Journal of Comparative Law* 88.

—— 'Buddhism, Human Rights and Constitutional Reform in Thailand' (2007) 2 *Asian Journal of Comparative Law* 1.

P Leyland, 'The Struggle for Freedom of Expression in Thailand: Media Moguls, The King, Citizen Politics and the Law' (2010) 2(1) *The Journal of Media Law* 115.

C Munger, 'Culture, Power and Law: Thinking about the Anthropology of Rights in Thailand in an Era of Globalisation' (2006-7) 51 *New York Law School Law Review* 840.

V Muntarbhorn, 'Human rights in the Era of "Thailand Inc"' in R Peerenboom, C Petersen and A Chan, *Human Rights in Asia* (London, Routledge, 2006).

—— 'Rule of law and aspects of human rights in Thailand: from conceptualization to implementation?' in R Peerenboom (ed), Asian Discourses of Rule of Law (London, Routledge, 2004).

—— and C Taylor, *Roads to Democracy: Human Rights and Democratic Development in Thailand* (Montreal, International Centre for Human Rights and Democratic Development, 1994).

---

[89] See ch 5 for further discussion of the role of the Constitutional Court.

S Sophonsiri (ed), *Kodmai Lae Sitthi Manutsayachon* [Law and Human Rights] (Bangkok, Foundation for Children, 2001) [in Thai].

D Streckfuss, *Truth on Trial in Thailand: Defamation, Treason and Lèse Majesté* (London, Routledge, 2010).

8

Conclusion: Reflections on the Thai Constitutional Landscape

———◆———

The primary objective of this book has not been to offer a description of Thailand's current Constitution, but rather to consider the broader issue of Thai constitutionalism. For our purposes it might be suggested that

> Constitutions only seek to embed a given set of fundamental principles as part of the prevailing system of government. Constitutionalism, on the other hand, may be said to embody a normative dimension. Here, the constitution not only anchors and enforces certain principles, but also represents a clear set of values ...[1]

The challenge of constitutionalism, then, is not simply to formulate rules at a constitutional level which embody principles of a particular conception of good governance, neither is it simply a matter of designing formal checks and balances; constitutionalism for us requires the achievement of general conformity with such rules by all the main constitutional actors. Why have there been so many Thai constitutions and such an inherent and persistent form of constitutional instability? We would argue that although a particular constitution, such as that of 1997, might greatly contribute to a solution of this problem, many of the problems lie beyond any constitution; we suggest that to understand process of Thai constitution-making it is also necessary to have an understanding of the wider Thai context.

We noted at the outset that Thailand has never been colonised, neither has the nation ever experienced a popular revolution. Viewed from

---

[1] A Harding and P Leyland, 'Comparative Law in Constitutional Contexts' in E Örücü and D Nelken (eds), *Comparative Law: A Handbook* (Oxford, Hart Publishing, 2007) 323.

a historical trajectory, we have seen that the need for Thailand to modernise its institutions, including law and administration, was recognised under King Mongkut and King Chulalongkorn. While the transplantation of European-style legal codes began in a pre-constitutional era – and these have been largely accepted (at least in amended form) – it will be apparent that the subsequent attempts at Thai constitution-making were not part of a grass-roots movement and have not been easily reconciled with pre-existing cultural and religious traditions. In 1932 a small group of just over 100 conspirators led by Pridi Banomyong were successful in engineering a bloodless military coup which brought a permanent end to the pre-existing form of absolute monarchy. However, despite the fact that it resulted in a constitution giving the nation its first Legislature, with the first elections based on universal suffrage held in the following year, this was not a popular revolution. In fact many commentators have viewed it as merely the opening skirmish in an ongoing conflict between progressive and reactionary factions. It came as no more than a prelude to a considerable period of military dictatorship.[2]

Most obviously, although the right to vote was introduced at an early stage, there have been fundamental difficulties in establishing a meaningful form of representative democracy. In the first set of elections held in 1933, before the introduction of universal education, it is estimated that fewer than 10 per cent of those eligible actually cast their vote.[3] One problem is that for the most part Thai politics has been conducted in the absence of political ideology. Political parties have not formed to represent the wider aspirations of voters; rather, Thailand has a politics of personality, which has developed as an extension of the patron-client relationships which permeate many aspects of Thai society. In consequence, the political game has conveniently side-stepped fundamental questions of wealth distribution between the very rich and the remainder of society. The ubiquitous practice of vote-buying has been accepted because there is little else on offer. In other words, the electorate have not had the opportunity to vote to secure the achievement of wider economic or political goals, and so many electors have given their vote for calculated individual gain at election time in the form of cash hand-outs or in exchange for a pledge to deliver a local

[2] See, eg, C Baker and P Phongpaichit, *Pridi Banomyong: Selected Writings on Life, Politics and Economy* (Chiang Mai, Silkworm Books, 2000) 64ff.

[3] D Wyatt, *Thailand: A Short History*, 2nd edn (New Haven, Conn, Yale University Press, 2003) 239–40.

development project. On the other hand, many individuals entering politics have business interests or business connections and regard politics as a means for personal enrichment. In recent years the extensive interface between government and the private sector has led to an enormous potential for conflicts of interest, which in turn has the potential to undermine the integrity of the entire system. As we have seen, this has led to the introduction of many constitutional oversight mechanisms to tackle such abuses of power.

A further impediment to the universal reception of constitutional values based on the stated principles of the 'rule of law' and 'good governance' is the very hierarchical nature of Thai society. From the King downwards, social rank is strictly delineated in terms of wealth, power, birth and status. In one sense the fact that individuals accept their status and defer to those they perceive to be more senior provides stability; but the foundations of such a society depend on not questioning the authority of those further up the hierarchy. This may lead to a strong assumption of deference by prosecutors, judges and officials who are directly responsible for enforcing the law when there has been serious misconduct at the highest level. Furthermore, despite still exercising considerable power and influence, the military and the monarchy have been entirely exempted from any tangible form of constitutional accountability.

In fact, having emphasised the importance of the monarchy and the military, we would argue that a clear and limited role needs to be defined for these powerful institutions for any Thai constitution to function effectively. In particular, the repeated military coups have not just swept aside constitutions, but the threat in the background calls into question constitutionalism itself, and even the idea of having a constitution at all in any meaningful sense. It is therefore essential that other mechanisms are made to work that would obviate the need or perceived need for coups to occur. Without the acceptance of this limitation it is hard to see how the problems discussed in this book can be solved. The same is true of the monarchy; royal intervention should not be regarded as a substitute for constitutional mechanisms, or be required to kick-start those mechanisms into action. The succession will be a test of these institutions to deal with the issues within their remit with finality and authority.

In this book we have presented several aspects of constitutional life – the State in its various levels and roles; political parties, election and the National Assembly; the judiciary and the independent agencies; human rights and their enforcement. While recognising that there will have to be locally-negotiated solutions to all problems which arise, we believe that immediate attention should be given to the revision of certain provisions of the 2007 Constitution and to certain omissions from it. First, the Constitutional Court's power to dissolve a political party was originally included as a drastic solution where the ECT identified malpractice by politicians or officials of a party.[4] Not only is it unjust and disproportionate to punish a national party for the misdeeds of one or more of its members, but the measure is ineffective, since any disbanded party can re-launch itself under a new name and with new office-holders. However, the most unsatisfactory aspect of this provision is its indirect effect. It draws the Constitutional Court into the crucible of political conflict, because the case against any party is nearly always triggered by a rival opposition party. This rule needs to be abolished, or at least restricted in scope, in order to secure adherence to the Constitution by the politicians of 'Red' persuasion, who have been the main victims of party dissolution; and it would in any event be a reasonable reform in view of the rule's abuse and ineffectiveness.

In a different context, we have seen in chapter four that there is a strong regional dimension to the conflict between the 'Reds' and the 'Yellows', and relating to the insurgency in the extreme south. Although the Constitution refers to giving autonomy in accordance with the principles of self-government, there has been limited progress in this direction, and for historical reasons Thailand still has a highly centralised State with power concentrated in Bangkok. The negotiation of some form of regional devolution of power incorporated as part of the Constitution could form the basis for a settlement for the southern provinces, and for a form of devolved regional government to lessen the winner-takes-all effect of General Elections which allows regions to be, in effect, ruled by an alien political party. Moreover, any meaningful discussions between the factions will undoubtedly address a range of other issues mentioned in this book, many of them controversial, including: whether the second chamber should revert to being an elected body; how best to configure the electoral system, and whether it should involve single-member or multi-member constituencies; whether the judiciary should have such an important role in the appointments system; and whether the powers of the Constitutional Court ought to be recalibrated in relation to the other constitutional bodies.

---

[4] TC 2007, s 237.

In order for the cycle of new constitution followed by military coup to be permanently interrupted, there has to be a change of constitutional mindset. This involves accepting the paradox that discussion of any revision of the Constitution should take place within the Constitution itself. In other words, a constitution has to command respect even when it is being amended because it may be defective, simply because it is the constitution. Thai constitutions have largely failed in this respect. Constitutional discussions have frequently taken place in a space outside the constitution, and the constant revocations, redrafts and coups, not to mention persistent unconstitutional behaviour even in 'normal' times, have reduced trust in any current constitutional settlement. Any Thai citizen aged 78 or over will have lived through 18 such settlements. Nonetheless, Thai society does seem to be locked into permanent debate about the proper form of the constitution, and no serious body of opinion appears to advocate doing away with everything that has been put in place since 1997. The notion of an ideal written constitution therefore frames constitutional debates. This is not in itself surprising or counterproductive. But if the outcome is, as it has been, failure to reach anything like agreement on fundamental principles, then debate and political competition become a kind of dysfunctional instability, as the last five years in particular have shown.

This book has amply demonstrated that Thailand has experimented with a very wide range of constitutional positions. In our view the solution is certainly not to draft another new constitution from scratch in search of some constitutional nirvana which might be achieved by a particular form of words. Rather than attempting to introduce a radically new constitution, the factions simply need to agree to work with a particular constitution as the basis for a political settlement. The 2007 Constitution could be regarded as the starting point for negotiation, unless the 'Red Shirts' see this as symbolically tainted with the politics of the 2006 coup. Alternatively, the 1997 Constitution, which is broadly similar, could be adopted or adapted for the purpose. Given the patchy adherence to constitutional rules when they are put in place, it is somewhat ironic to observe the enormous debate that has surrounded quite technical constitutional provisions and devices. The debate becomes a form of political warfare by proxy, an arena where winning may confer only quite small tactical advantages but is nonetheless important in itself. Glancing to the future, it is worth proceeding with any such enterprise only if all the parties involved recognise that they will have to make concessions to each other and that when the negotiations have been completed, all the parties will be required to observe the letter and spirit of any constitution which results from the process. In a climate of acute political confrontation it is difficult to envisage how this might be achieved without the intervention of a peace-broker perceived as being independent.

At the time of writing there is a phase of superficial calm in Thailand after the storm of May 2010. The problem of extreme polarisation and unbridled competition for power exhibited over the preceding five years remains very much in evidence, with confrontational rhetoric from one side and media censorship from the other. The fact that the royal succession now presents itself as an impending and worrying moment in Thai history merely adds to the danger of a return to unstable conditions of government which will no doubt be reflected constitutionally. In our view the Red/Yellow conflict should not be projected as representing an irreconcilable polarisation between proto-Marxists advocating a republican socialist State (although there is a minority faction of this persuasion attached to the Red-Shirt camp), and extreme pro-Monarchists intent on restoring an absolute monarchy and restricting voting rights as advocated by factions associated with the (Yellow-Shirt) PAD. Between these extreme positions there is a great deal of consensus on the need for a democratic constitution which upholds citizens' rights. It is important to remember that Thailand has undergone massive economic and social development in recent years, and now it is a nation with near universal adult literacy and a rapidly expanding educated middle class. However critical the electorate may be about the political system, Thai citizens have been granted the right to vote, and they have an expectation of retaining this right. While there may be a gulf between the nation's economic and social transition and its political and constitutional transition, there is no easy route back to absolute kingship. The lack of competence of the military in government has also been repeatedly demonstrated, most recently in 2006–07. It is not surprising, then, that there is a strong measure of agreement between some elements in Thai society on both sides of the Red/Yellow divide that see constitutional amendment as a way forward towards rapprochement and adherence to a common understanding that constitutional rules should be taken seriously and be adhered to.

The introduction of the 1997 Constitution is regarded by us as perhaps the pivotal constitutional moment to date. It was drafted during a time of economic crisis following a process of genuine consultation. It included a strong commitment to the protection of human rights and the elimination of corruption, but above all, it set in place a sophisticated constitutional framework to achieve these ambitious objectives. Of course, having been tested to destruction, it failed to provide the anchor for a new politics. The military coup in 2006, however disappointing, may not have been a surprise given the intensity of the political crisis which preceded it. Nevertheless, this Constitution went much further than any of its predecessors, and it has in effect set important benchmarks by elucidating a comprehensive catalogue of rights while at the same time equipping the nation with a modified institutional framework of courts and watchdog bodies. Despite the problems extensively canvassed in these pages, some progress has been made in the last 20 years towards a more articulated and effective constitutional order. To progress further it will be essential that military intervention plays no further part and that agreements are reached which reflect compromise rather than complete victory for one side or the other. This, we believe, is a position which is highly congruent with Thai political culture in its most positive aspect.

Glossary*

AMLO: Anti-Money-Laundering Office

BMA: Bangkok Metropolitan Administration

CDA: Constitution Drafting Assembly

CDC: Constitution Drafting Committee

CNS: Council for National Security (the 2006 military junta)

Changwat: province(s)

DDC: Democratic Development Committee

Democrat Party: oldest political party founded in 1946 as a conservative and royalist party currently aligned with the pro-monarchy and pro-military PAD (qv)

Dhamma: the teaching of Buddha which leads to enlightenment

Dhammathat: historical textual tradition of family and customary law

ECT: Election Commission of Thailand

ISOC: Internal Security Operations Command

Imam: Muslim priest

Isan: North Eastern Region of Thailand

Kamnan: village headman

Kan pokkrong: law relating to administration or to the government

Khwaeng: urban sub-district

KPI: King Prajadhipok Institute (a government agency responsible for organizing and training civil servants and promoting good governance)

KRISDIKA: Office of the Council of State (the department responsible for legal drafting and providing the government with legal advice).

Lanna: Northern Kingdom around Chiang Mai

Law of the Three Seals (see Three Seals Law)

---

* The same Thai word appears appears more than once showing alternative English spellings where we are aware of problems of transliteration from Thai to English.

Lèse-Majesté law: strict law which protects the Thai monarchy and royal family from any criticism

Mueang: settlements, districts

Muban/Muban: village

MOI: Ministry of the Interior

NACC: National Anti-Corruption Commission also sometimes referred to as the National Counter Corruption Commission (NCCC)

NBTC: National Broadcasting and Telecommunications Commission

NGO: Non-Governmental Organisation

NHRC: National Human Rights Commission

Office of the Council of State: see KRISDIKA

Or Ror Bor/O Ro Bo: Buddhist local defence volunteers

PAO: Provincial Administrative Organisation (responsible for administering local government at provincial level)

PAD: People's Alliance for Democracy (pressure group loyal to the King which emerged as focus for anti-Thaksin demostrations, support from urban Bangkok based middle class and military)

Patani: refers collectively to all the Muslim southern areas

Pattani: refers to the Southern Thai province that borders Malaysia

PPP: People Power Party (set up to replace the TRT Party; was itself dissolved by the Constitutional Court in 2008)

PTP: Pheua Thai Party (set up in 2008 to replace the PPP)

Rajadharma (also *ratchatham*): the duty of Kings

Rajasat (also *rajathat* or *ratchasat*): law-making by royal decree

Red Shirts: refers to pressure groups forming the UDD (qv) (see also TRT, PPP and PTP)

SBPAC: Southern Border Provinces Administrative Centre

Sangha: Thai monkhood

Seriphap: liberty, independence

Siam: the nation's former name, changed to Thailand in 1938.

Sin nam jai/Sin nam chai: gift(s) of good will

Sitthi manutsyachon: human rights

Sukhaphiban: Sanitary Committee comprises a unit of local government in rural areas

TAO: Tambon administrative organisation

TPBS: Thai Public Broadcasting Service

TRT: Thai Rak Thai ('Thai loves Thai', a populist political party formed by Thaksin Shinawatra and others in 1998; disbanded in 2007 by Constitutional Tribunal)

Tambon: Sub-district administrative organisation (see TAO)

Thammasat: alternative spelling of *Dhammasat* (see above)

Thammayut: Buddhist order set up by King Mongkut (Rama IV)

Theravada Buddhism: the traditional form of Buddhism practised in Thailand.

Thesaban/Thestaban: municipal urban centre

Three Seals Law: compilation of customary and religious law codified in 1805

Tosapitrajadharma/Thosaphitratchatham: the Ten Kingly Virtues

UDD: United Front for Democracy against Dictatorship, political pressure group aligned with PTO and the Red shirts

Ulama: Muslim religious scholar

Wat: Buddhist temple(s)

Yellow Shirts: Political factions loyal to the Monarchy who demonstrate their support by using yellow, the royal colour. See PAD and Democrat Party

Index

29318170R00170

Made in the USA
Columbia, SC
21 October 2018